Islamic Economic Series—1

MUSLIM ECONOMIC THINKING

A Survey of Contemporary Literature

by
Muhammad Nejatullah Siddiqi

International Centre
for Research in Islamic Economics
King Abdul Aziz University, Jeddah
and
The Islamic Foundation, United Kingdom

ISBN 0 86037 082 8 (hard case)
ISBN 0 86037 081 X (paperback)

Views expressed by the author represent his personal views and do not necessarily represent the views of the International Centre for Research in Islamic Economics, King Abdul Aziz University, Jeddah.

Produced by
The Islamic Foundation,
Leicester, United Kingdom.

For

The International Centre for Research in
Islamic Economics,
King Abdul Aziz University
Jeddah

Printed and bound in Great Britain by
Dotesios (Printers) Ltd, Bradford-on-Avon, Wiltshire

بسم الله الرحمن الرحيم

CONTENTS

Foreword — Khurshid Ahmad ... v

Introduction ... 1

Chapter One: ECONOMIC PHILOSOPHY OF ISLAM ... 4

Economic Enterprise; Ownership; Relations of Production; Co-operation; Development and Growth.

Chapter Two: ECONOMIC SYSTEM OF ISLAM ... 11

Goals of the System; The Owner; Share-Cropping; The Consumer; The Entrepreneur, Producer and Trader; Role of the State.

Chapter Three: ECONOMIC SYSTEM OF ISLAM: SOME SPECIFIC ASPECTS ... 21

Public Finance; Zakat; Inheritance; Social Security and Insurance; Money and Banking; Banking without Interest; The Islamic Development Bank; Industrial Relations; Labour and Population Policy; Growth and Development.

Chapter Four: ISLAMIC CRITIQUE OF CONTEMPORARY ECONOMIC THEORIES AND SYSTEMS ... 45

Capitalism; Modern Theories of Interest; Speculation and Forward Transactions; Lottery; Socialism and Communism; Other Systems.

Chapter Five:	DEVELOPMENT OF ECONOMIC ANALYSIS IN THE ISLAMIC FRAMEWORK Consumption; Production; Factors of Production; Exchange and Determination of Prices and Profits; The Role of Zakat; Interest and its Abolition; Nature of Islamic Economics.	54
Chapter Six:	ECONOMIC THOUGHT IN ISLAM Ibn Khaldun; Ibn Taimiya; Abu Yusuf; Nasiruddin Tusi; Shah Waliullah; Other Thinkers.	70
Appendix:	CLASSIFIED BIBLIOGRAPHY	81
Index		126

FOREWORD

Contemporary Islamic resurgence is not simply an exercise in political activism. It is symbolic of more fundamental change in the present-day Muslim world: an effort to move away from the cultural foundations of the Western civilization, which were forcibly grafted on the Muslim society, with callous disregard for their ideological aspirations and historical traditions, and a move towards rediscovering Islam as the basis for the new social system, their future culture and civilisation. This is a creative albeit painful process and embraces almost all aspects of their life, intellectual, social, political, economic, educational, cultural and international. They are engaged in a critical self-appraisal, a re-examination of the cultural developments during the period of West-domination and its continuing influences and the formulation of a new strategy for independent development deriving inspiration from the ideals and the value-system of the Islamic *Ummah*. This is a multi-dimensional effort and is still in its formative phase. Islamic resurgence is an accomplished fact only in the sense that it represents the inauguration of a process. As such it is only a beginning towards a new and challenging future.

Contemporary resilience of Muslim thought is an aspect of this development. There is a new freshness in Muslim thinking: new ideas are being hatched, new approaches being developed. The emergence of the nascent discipline of Islamic economics is just one example of this creative upsurge. It is fair to suggest that the 1970s represent a watershed in the development of Muslim thinking on economics. It has been during this decade that a healthy transition from expositions on 'Islamic economic teachings' to a systematic articulation of 'Islamic Economics' has become recognizable. As such the time has come to pause and take a searching look at the literature produced during the last seventy years on different aspects of Islamic economic thought with a view not only to reviewing the state of the art but also to paving the way for more analytical work by inviting the professional economists to build their system on a set of axioms and values firmly established by discussion delineating the Islamic approach to life and its economic problems.

Professor Nejatullah Siddiqi has done a yeoman's job by painstakingly producing a masterly survey of Muslim economic thinking in the twentieth century. He has based his survey on literature produced up to 1975 in three major languages, Arabic, Urdu and English. This review captures the spirit as well as the substance of Muslim thinking in relation to major issues and themes of economics. The result is a precise but incisive statement of contemporary Muslim economic thought and a challenging document suggesting an agenda for future research. It is an invaluable aid for further research and discussion on Islamic economics. The survey is supplemented by an exhaustive bibliography of Islamic economic literature. This survey was originally produced for the First International Conference on Islamic Economics held in Makka in February, 1976 under the auspices of the King Abdul Aziz University, Jeddah. The paper was revised in the light of discussion at the conference and also took note of the papers presented to the conference. It was included in *Studies in Islamic Economics,* published by the International Centre for Research in Islamic Economics, King Abdul Aziz University, Jeddah and the Islamic Foundation, Leicester. It is being reproduced in book form so as to reach a wider audience. I am sure it is going to help immensely in conveying the message of Islamic economics to the professional economist and the interested layman. It is bound to evoke thought and discussion on different aspects of Islamic economics. This is the purpose for which it is being produced in its present form in the first year of the fifteenth century of the Islamic era.

I take this opportunity to thank Dr. Abdullah Nasif, President, King Abdul Aziz University, Jeddah and Dr. Ghazi Madani, Director, International Centre for Research in Islamic Economics for their moral and material help in producing this book. The Director of the Islamic Foundation, Mr. K.J. Murad, and its Assistant Director, Dr. M.M. Ahsan, also deserve my thanks for seeing the book through the press.

Khurshid Ahmad

The Islamic Foundation
Leicester
Safar 1401
25 December, 1980

Muslim Economic Thinking: A Survey of Contemporary Literature

*Dr. Muhammad Nejatullah Siddiqi**

Introduction

ALTHOUGH Muslim thinkers have discussed the economic principles of Islam earlier, exclusive attention to the subject is a twentieth century phenomenon. It started in the third decade and specialised works appeared in the fourth. Part of the provocation was provided by the worldwide economic crisis during the thirties and forties and the increasing exposure of the Muslim mind to the Socialist doctrines, and the impact of the Russian Revolution. There was a great spurt in these writings during the fifties and the sixties which is related to the emergence of a number of independent Muslim countries, and the rise of a powerful Islamic Movement which raised hopes of serious attention to the application of the Islamic teachings in the practical affairs of the new states. At this stage general discussion on the economic philosophy of Islam is supplemented by efforts at system formulation and discussions on specific issues relevant to modern life. Analytical study of the economic injunctions of Islam and an analytical approach to the criticism of modern institutions from the Islamic viewpoint is comparatively recent in origin, though it is receiving more and more attention.

The modern institutions of banking, insurance, joint stock companies, stock exchange and progressive taxation called for a response from Muslim thinkers and jurists (i.e. ulema specialising in *fiqh*) as they appeared in these Muslim countries and started involving the religious masses. A review of these institutions in the light of the *Sharī'ah*, a search for alternatives in case some of them were found repugnant to Islam, and for arguments for the legitimacy of those which could be accommodated, led to

*Dr. Nejatullah Siddiqi is Professor of Economics and Head of Department of Islamic Studies, Aligarh Muslim University, Aligarh. Dr. Siddiqi is amongst the pioneers of Islamic Economics and has authored over half a dozen works on different aspects of Islamic Economics. Presently he is on sabbatical leave working with the International Centre for Research in Islamic Economics, King Abdul Aziz University, Jeddah.

many works on the subject. By the very nature of this background, the discussions were more juridical than economic.

Most of these writers were ulema or journalists with little knowledge of economics. The system of education the Muslim countries had inherited from Imperial Powers had scrupulously segregated Islamic education from modern education and there were no arrangements for producing a trained economist who had direct access to the Islamic sources. This inhibited professional economists from making any significant contributions to the subject. It also accounts for the fact that the ulema who found themselves constrained to discuss the subject failed to do justice to it. The first works on the subject by professional economists appeared in English in the late forties of this century, but these writers had to rely on secondary sources so far as Islamic injunctions are concerned. Even now when we have quite a number of economists fully equipped to draw upon the original sources of Islam, the subject lacks the most crucial support required for its proper growth – teaching in Universities. Modern economics, as we now understand the term, is largely the handiwork of University teachers in Economics. But Islamic Economics is not a subject being taught at the post-graduate level anywhere in the wide world – with the sole exception of a few universities in Egypt and Pakistan, where both the syllabus and the teaching facilities leave much to be desired.

The institutional framework of a society has a direct bearing on research in Social Sciences, particularly in Economics. The institutions that developed in the Imperialist regimes were alien to the Islamic framework of the society and the economy, and therefore no serious thinking by the professional economist could be directed towards Islamic Economics. The ulema also discussed the economic problems without the actual framework operating on the tenets of Islam. Islamic Economics lacked the live relationship with real life which was a prerequisite to its growth. There was no testing ground for the various hypotheses being formulated and no empirical evidence upon which to draw while making formulations.

In this historical situation it would have made a big difference if a clear commitment to the economic philosophy of Islam had come from some of the new independent Muslim countries. But even this has been lacking till now, and many writers on the subject aimed at soliciting such a commitment from their people and governments, through their writings. They took on themselves the task of convincing their readers of the desirability and viability of the Islamic economic system. They have yet to be called upon to manage the economy and solve its actual problems in the light of Islamic injunctions.

These are some of the important facts to be kept in mind while surveying the literature on Islamic Economics as they explain many of its important features, and the relative emphasis placed on the various issues under discussion. There are indications of some change in the situation described above as evidenced by the increasing attention paid to Islamic economics, both at the popular and the official level. This too is reflected in the recent contributions on such subjects as interest-free banking, *Zakāt* and social security. Analytical study conscious of its relevance to practical affairs is gradually replacing philosophical dissertations on the comparative virtues of the Islamic system, which augurs well for the future growth of the literature.

This survey covers the three principal languages in which the bulk of the literature on our subject has appeared in the last half century – Arabic, Urdu and English. Some contributions were made in the Persian, Turkish, French and Indonesian languages, which are planned to be surveyed separately. Multiplicity of languages coupled with deficient communications has also affected the growth of thinking on the subject. No efficient translation and abstraction services have been available. We do not have a single journal exclusively devoted to our subject. Very few review articles are published on the contributions that are made. There have been no across-the-table discussions at seminars and academic conferences. As a result our writers have had few opportunities of knowing each other's views and of benefiting from scholarly criticism. One finds the same points being made again and again in different languages at different times, while a promising idea suggested by one thinker has to wait for quite a long time before it is taken up by some other writer to develop further. There is controversy but little criticism, there are many opinions but few conclusions arrived at after systematic discussion. The implications of such a state of affairs for the "survey" are obvious.

Constraints of time and space make it necessary to keep this study brief. It has not been possible to go into the details of the subjects discussed in the survey. It was considered specially desirable to avoid details where these details were more juridical in nature than economic. For the sake of brevity we had also to exclude from this survey works on economic history and those relating to the economic problems of the present-day Muslim countries.

A survey of contributions relating to the entire area of economics raises serious methodological problems. One is always left with a feeling that a more suitable scheme could be evolved. It is hoped that in future the different topics covered in this study will be surveyed separately and more critically by some economists.

As a glance at the table of contents would reveal, we begin with a brief consideration of the economic philosophy of Islam, followed by the general outlines of the economic system of Islam. Specific aspects of the economic system which might attract greater attention from economists have been treated separately at some length in the third section. We have tried to focus attention on analytical discussions by dealing with them in two separate sections: Islamic critique of contemporary economic theories and systems, and development of economic analysis in an Islamic framework. The last section notes contributions on the history of economic thought in Islam.

An economist reading the first two sections may feel that undue importance is being attached to views relating to ownership, ends of economic enterprise and the code of conduct for various economic agents. These subjects do not figure very prominently in modern economics as certain views have been accepted long since and nobody feels like questioning them. The concern of Islamic economists with these basic issues is borne of their feeling that the divergence of Islamic economic thinking from the other schools of thought is rooted in this area. They also think that these are the foundation stones for the development of the institutions favourable for the growth of the society and the economy according to Islamic values.

This survey covers books as well as the periodical literature. In the circumstances it is not possible to claim that one knows about each and every contribution to the subject. This is especially true of the papers contributed to the numerous popular journals in the three languages. Yet, I do hope that I have not missed many of them, as a glance at the bibliography will show.

We have generally avoided mention of particular authors when recording a view that is held unanimously. Specific contributions are noted when a subject is controversial or because of their originality.

This survey was completed in December, 1974 for presentation at the First International Conference on Islamic Economics scheduled for March, 1975. The Conference was eventually held in February, 1976 and more than sixty papers were presented on various aspects of Islamic Economics. In revising this survey for publication due notice has been taken of these contributions, along with such other recent works as were available to the writer.

The Bibliography originally appended to this survey has now been replaced by its improved version published separately by the U.K. Islamic Foundation.[1] All numbers appearing in parenthesis in the text of the survey refer to this printed bibliography. The figure following the colon indicates the page number of the reference cited. Other references appear as footnotes. The bibliography is being appended to this survey for ready reference.

I

ECONOMIC PHILOSOPHY OF ISLAM

The key to economic philosophy of Islam lies in man's relationship with God, His universe and His people, i.e. other human beings, and the nature and purpose of man's life on earth. Man–God relationship is defined by *Tawḥīd*. The essence of *Tawḥīd* is a total commitment to the will of Allah, involving both submission and a mission to pattern human life in accordance with His will. The will of Allah constitutes the source of value and becomes the end of human endeavour. Life on earth is a test, and its purpose should be to prove successful in the test by doing Allah's will. The entire Universe with all the natural resources and powers is made amenable to exploitation by man, though it is owned by Allah and Allah alone. Life on earth being a test and all the provisions available to man being in the nature of a trust, man is accountable to Allah and his success in the life hereafter depends on his performance in this life on earth. This adds a new dimension to the valuation of things and deeds in this life.

With every human being sharing the same relationship with God and His Universe, a definite relationship between man and man is also prescribed. This is a relationship of brotherhood and equality. "*Tawḥīd* is a coin with two faces: one implies that Allah is the Creator and the other that men are equal partners or that each man is brother to another man." (7: 35).

While the writers on the subject agree on this basic philosophy, one finds variety of emphasis in their elaboration of the last-mentioned point: the relationship between man and man in sharing the bounties of Allah. It is agreed that for the test life is to be conducted in fair circumstances and no one should go without an adequate share of resources that are needed for survival and a good life. Equality of opportunity and social care of the disabled is the minimum that this calls for. They differ, however, regarding the mode of equal or equitable sharing of these resources by individuals, and the degree of social control necessary – a subject we take up later on.

It is also agreed that Islam rejects asceticism and a good life means, among other things, a materially well provisioned life. Basing his argument on two clear verses of the Qur'ān,[2] another writer declares that sufficiency (*Kifāyāh*) and peace (*amn*) are the two inalienable features of the good life envisaged by Allah (77, 1: 6–9), a point that finds the widest support in the literature on the subject (73: 24).

Economic Enterprise

The above philosophy provides the proper perspective to man's economic activities. No inhibitions attach to economic enterprise. Men are encouraged to avail themselves of the vast opportunities of productive enterprise afforded by the almost limitless bounties of Allah:

> "And if ye would count the bounty of Allah ye can not reckon it."
> (XIV: 34)

Every writer on the subject cites verses from the Qur'ān and traditions from the Prophet to show that agriculture, trade, commerce and industry and the various forms of productive enterprise known in the early days of Islam have been explicitly mentioned in this context. What is crucial, however, is the motivation, the ends of economic activity. Given the right motivation all economic activity assumes the character of worship (*'Ibādah*).

Many writers discuss the proper ends of economic enterprise in detail. These ends may be individual or social. Legitimate individual ends include the fulfilment of personal needs and those of the family. Saving to provide for the future and the desire to leave an inheritance are also recognised as proper ends of productive effort. The minimum necessary for survival is in fact a duty to earn. While no maxima are fixed in quantitative terms, moderation in fulfilment of these needs is emphasised and greed, avarice and the unsatiable yearning for more and more comforts and luxuries is decried.

Moderation is generally defined with reference to the negative concepts of extravagance (*isrāf*) and expenditure on goods and services prohibited by Islam (*tabdhīr*). Indulgence in luxurious living and the desire to show off is condemned (29: 438–453; 120: 68–73). Islam cannot tolerate conspicuous consumption of the leisure class (62: 141–144).

Recent writings on economic enterprise attach great importance to the social ends, which are summed up by the phrase "striving in the cause of Allah". Eradication of hunger and poverty, disease and illiteracy and mobilisation of resources for strengthening the Islamic state and spreading the message of Allah are stated to be the laudible aims of individual economic activities. One who engages in productive activities for these purposes is doing God's will, and is promised adequate rewards here and hereafter (77, 1: 130–138; 24; 619: 25–30; 477). The authors of the *Jamā'at-i-Islāmī* Pakistan Economic Committee Report regard it an end of economic enterprise "to make the Islamic society economically strong so that it develops and is able to compete successfully with other economies the world over" (125: 26).

It is pointed out that in view of the limitless nature of the social ends of enterprise, as against the limited nature of the individual ends, economic enterprise as such is afforded limitless scope and utmost encouragement.

Ownership

The nature and scope of ownership has been one of the most discussed subjects in the literature on Islamic Economics, works exclusively devoted to the subject being available in a number of languages. Every important writer has touched on the subject and all the different approaches to an Islamic reorganisation of the modern economy show themselves in their treatment of property rights in Islam. Below we shall try first to state what is generally agreed upon and then to differentiate between specific contributions.

Real ownership belongs to Allah, man holds property in trust for which he is accountable to Him, in accordance with rules clearly laid down in the *Sharī'ah* and the economic philosophy underlined above. Acquisition of property as well as its uses and disposal are subject to limits set and should be guided by the norms laid down by Allah. Absolute ownership of man is a concept alien to Islam, as it belongs to Allah alone. There are definite obligations towards others attending upon the individual rights of ownership. Besides private property, public ownership is a central concept in Islam. The respective scopes of the two are not rigidly defined but left to be determined in the light of certain principles, depending on the needs and circumstances (3: 8; 62: 111–119, 160–162; 70: 80; 134; 158: 41–90; 171: 150).

Differences centre around three main points:

(a) the central position of private ownership;
(b) the relative scopes of public and private ownership;
(c) the degree of social control on private ownership rights and the circumstances justifying abrogation or abridgement of such rights.

Some writers assert that the Real Owner has bestowed ownership rights to the whole of human society, in the first place and it is wrong to give individual ownership a central position in the Islamic economic system. They stand for social ownership of land and other natural resources, confining private property to articles of consumption, living quarters and the like. Perwez (60) and Nasir A. Sheikh (154: 139–225) in Pakistan and some Arab socialists take that position.

While this extreme socialistic position does not find sizable support in the literature, and is generally rejected as an unsuccessful attempt to mould Islam according to socialism, there are eminent authorities denying a central place to individual ownership rights. The martyr, 'Abd al-Qādir 'Audah deserves quoting at length in this context:

> "The society (*Jamā'ah*) through its functionaries such as rulers and counsellors has the authority to organise the ways and means of utilising wealth. All wealth belongs to Allah but Allah has made it for the good of the society. The rule in Islam is that all rights belonging to Allah are for the good of the society which sits in authority over them, and not the individuals.
>
> "The society, through the rulers representing it, can, when the public interest demands, abrogate the individual ownership of benefits of a property, subject to the condition that a suitable compensation is paid to the owner of the benefits involved.
>
> "Though Islam allows ownership without limit, it authorises society, as the entity for ensuring the rights of God and for organising utilisation of wealth, to subject the individual ownership of par-

> ticular kinds of property to limits, when this is necessitated by public good. This it can do through its representatives. This may apply to ceilings on agricultural holdings or to urban property." (214: 48–49).

This approach gives priority to social good and makes representatives of the society the sole arbiters in determining the demands of social good.

Abdul Hamid Abu Sulaiman recognises the individual's right to own the fruits of his labour, but so far as the natural resources, natural powers, and general circumstances of the society are concerned every individual has an equal share in them. As all individuals do not have equal capacity to put these resources to proper use, the more capable are allowed to use more than their due share. They cannot, however, claim the whole of their produce from this extra use of resources, only the share of labour belongs to them while the part of produce ascribable to natural resources belongs to the society as the representative of those who use less than their due share of these resources (7: 17–19; 8: 69–70). Private ownership of land, capital or other natural powers cannot be allowed to become a means of exploiting other individuals and subjugating them (8: 43). The rationale of allowing inequality in the private ownership of means of production is stated by him in these words:

> "A strict equality in the ownership of natural resources would require very frequent redistribution of those resources among members of society. This would be disruptive to economic activity and social relations. A reasonable alternative is, first, to avoid frequent redistribution and permit private ownership of resources, thus achieving stability; and second, to redistribute equally among members of society that part of income which is due to natural resources, thus achieving equality and justice" (8: 70).

Equal sharing of the "income from natural resources" is basic to Abu Sulaiman's understanding of *ribā* and his views on land rent, share cropping and profit-sharing, subjects which we discuss below at appropriate places. Though he cites specific texts in support of specific views they are basically results of an analytical system rooted in his conception of *Tawḥīd.*

Most of the writers approach the subject in an eclectic manner as their basic source material is the vast *fiqh* literature on the subject. As a position midway between *fiqh*-based eclecticism and a system derived from one basic principle can be mentioned Siddiqi's effort to derive the basic tenets relating to ownership rights from Islam's world view, its social outlook and its philosophy of law (158: 41–90), concluding that "the individual, the state and the society each have claim on property rights in view of the principle that the Islamic State has a jurisdiction over individual rights, being the embodiment of God's vicegerency on earth and representative of the people. This jurisdiction is however, functional, depending upon the values and objectives cherished by Islam" (158: 74). These principles are followed up by a detailed discussion of the circumstances justifying abrogation or abridgement of individual property rights by such measures as nationalisation, ceilings, control on prices, profits and rents and compulsory purchase or borrowing, etc. (221, II: 155–282).

Bāqir al Ṣadr is also critical of the view that in Islam individual ownership is the rule and public ownership the exception. He regards individual ownership, state ownership and communal ownership as three forms existing parallel to one another in Islamic Law (171: 257). Though Tahāwī's eclecticism makes him assign the central position to individual rights of ownership, he puts the state representing the society on an almost equal footing as regards vicegerency of the Real Owner (77: I: 174). This gives the state "the right to intervene in private property by regulating it, putting ceilings or confiscating after due compensation when the owner deviates from the basic role of property – that it should be an instrument of service to the society" (77, I: 217).

The early writings of Mawdūdī lean heavily towards assigning the central place to individual ownership (51: 32). His later views are nearer to the middle position that admits social control whenever social interest calls for it. But he would still like to keep state intervention at the minimum (51: 116). Far from the position taken by Abu Sulaiman, his views on specific issues like land reforms are shaped by this approach, for which he finds support in the *fiqh* literature. A similar position is taken by the martyr Sayyid Quṭb who declares the right of individual ownership basic to the Islamic system. Both of them emphasise, however, the need of ensuring the fulfilment of the basic needs of each and every individual and justify such social action as may be necessary for that purpose (Mawdūdī 51: 404–407; Quṭb 62: 162). This, however, is one of the points on which there is a complete consensus. What distinguishes some of them is their insistence on specific provisions in the *fiqh* literature relating to individual rights that sometimes stand in the way of radical reforms that modern life calls for. One is inclined to agree with Ali Abdul Qadir (224: 11) that the economic philosophy of Islam relating to right of ownership "did not change the ordinary juristic attitude to the practical relations of people and property" which finds expression in *fiqh* literature.

Notwithstanding individual stances, some of the powerful collective movements for Islamic reorientation of modern life have tended towards the approach closer to the "economic philosophy of Islam". Both the *Ikhwān al-Muslimūn* and the *Jamā'at-i-Islāmī* have, on occasions, issued manifestoes recommending ceilings on rural and urban property and other measures of social control (125; 168).

One tends to conclude that the more our thinkers attend to the actual conditions prevailing in their societies the more realistic their approach becomes. Policy recommendations directed at the Islamic transformation of a society moulded over a long period by feudalism and capitalism draw more and more inspiration from the ultimate Goals of the Islamic system rather than being governed by specific legal rulings given in normal circumstances.

Relations of Production: Co-operation

With a positive attitude to economic enterprise and socially-oriented purposive rights of ownership, individuals and groups in the brotherhood of man are enjoined to co-operate with one another in patterning life on earth in accordance with the Will of Allah. Economic relations, especially those in production and exchange of wealth, should be co-operative in nature. "Rivalry and cut-throat competition make no sense in this context" (73: 27). Co-operation is seen as the basic value in Islam's economic philosophy (8: 36; 77, II: 199; 10: 27). Besides being required by human brotherhood and equality, unity of purpose and common ultimate interests, and also besides being explicitly enjoined by the Qur'ān and the *Sunnah* it is the attitude that suits the practical interests of mankind today and can save it from the ravages of capitalistic competition. 'Ali 'Abd al-Rasul calls, in this context, for "constructive competition" aiming at what is best for the society and high quality production, while avoiding all activities injurious to other producers and the consumers.[3]

As regards the institutionalisation of the co-operative attitude, and how far the new institutions will be different from those prevalent in the fields of production, exchange and distribution, detailed studies are still awaited. Siddiqi's study of entrepreneurial behaviour is only a beginning (619: 139–152). Despite the great attention paid to the subject by Kahf (612: Chapter IV) no progress is made along these lines.

The Islamic view of co-operation does not rule out free and fair competition in the market, provided all economic agents adhere to Islamic morality. Competition is emphasised in contrast to monopoly whose elimination is regarded as a prerequisite to ensuring justice and growth (51: 152; 619; 181).

This makes it still more necessary to visualise how the co-operative spirit will translate itself into action where millions of individual units are involved, knowledge is imperfect and communications involve costs.

Development and Growth

Islam's economic philosophy does not stop at teaching men to co-operate after having encouraged them in productive enterprise. It creates a powerful drive for development. A true Muslim looks upon developmental efforts as striving in the cause of Allah (*jihād fī sabīl Allāh*) (595: 128; 477: 36; 484). The Muslim society orients its policies in order to ensure sufficiency and peace for all and any relaxation in this regard is looked upon as rejection of the bounties of Allah (77: I: 6–9). Economic development has become a necessary condition to be fulfilled to enable the Muslim peoples to perform their mission with the humanity that the Qur'ān declares to be their *raison d'etre*. This mission is related to the well-being of all human beings. It cannot be performed while Muslim countries continue to be politically and economically subservient to the powers which stand for alien cultures (158: 130, 484). A narrow nationalistic approach to economic development does not harmonise with the Islamic spirit which calls for a global approach ensuring co-operation between the rich and poor nations to usher in an era of universal prosperity and banish hunger and fear from human society.

As to the Islamic strategy for economic development its chief distinguishing feature is that social justice and growth go together (177: 593). This is ensured by the motivation that Islam provides for economic development (56: 45). Individual profit motive is not the chief propelling force in Islam. Developmental efforts are mainly social and the individuals willingly co-operate in this venture (475: 43, 96–113).

Seen in the context of the Islamic world view, developmental efforts cannot become an end in themselves, nor a rising GNP the only index of "growth" in the Islamic sense. The aim is a good life with all its dimensions, the economic aspect being only one of them. Emphasising this point Ṭaḥāwī (77, II: 229–232) goes on to state how Islam's emphasis on work, on the fullest exploitation of natural resources, and on an active role for the state will ensure growth with justice.

II

ECONOMIC SYSTEM OF ISLAM

While economic philosophy states the overall approach, the economic system comprises ways and means of securing human welfare in general and economic welfare in particular. Economic literature on the subject discusses "alternative methods of determining the bill of goods to be produced, the allocation of resources to produce it, and the distribution of the resulting income".[4] The ownership of means of production and the extent to which the market mechanism or central authority is relied upon for decision making have been the chief criteria for distinguishing one economic system from the other.

Emphasis in Islamic literature on the subject has been somewhat different. The ends of the economic system are discussed, followed by a discussion of those behaviour patterns on the part of economic agents which are expected to go a long way in securing these ends.

The state enters the scene to guide and regulate voluntary actions and ensure the achievement of goals. Allocation of resources, organisation of production and exchange and distribution of the resulting income is effected by the twin forces of morally-oriented free individual action and state regulation. Islam's strategy in organising its economic system rests, therefore, on three main planks: clearly specified goals, well defined moral attitudes and behaviour patterns on the part of economic agents, and specific laws, rules and regulations enforceable by the state.

Goals of the System

Economic well-being is one of the goals emphasised by every writer, though each one of them proceeds to mention a number of other, non-economic, goals too. We shall first consider the contents of this goal, according to various writers, before we pass on to examine their views on non-economic goals.

We have already referred to Ṭaḥāwī's twin goals of sufficiency and peace which can come about by eradicating hunger and fear from society and ensuring the fulfilment of the basic needs of each and every human being. His list of basic needs includes food, clothing and shelter; medical aid for the sick and domestic services for the invalid, education for those who need it, marriage in some cases and "all that is regarded necessary according to the custom of the society" (77, I: 394). This is a point that finds universal support in the literature and the list of basic needs given by Mawdūdī (51: 406), Sayyid Quṭb (62: 240–241), Muṣṭafā Sibā'ī (70: 203) and Siddiqi (221, II: 92) does not differ materially from the above.

Bāqir al Ṣadr emphasises provision of ease and convenience in life, consequent upon growth and development and maximum utilisation of natural resources (171: 595). Kahf makes "maximisation of the rate of utilisation of resources" the first goal of economic policy in Islam (612: 93) along with minimisation of the distribution gap and observance of the Islamic code of conduct by the various economic agents.

In view of the exhaustible nature of the natural resources it would, however, be more appropriate to replace the concept of maximum utilisation by optimisation. The *Jamā'at-i-Islāmī* Pakistan Economic Committee Report comes closer to this view when it states the same principle as "the best utilisation of the maximum amount of natural resources" (126: 25). Abu Aiman (Dr. Said Ramazan) also regards discovering sources of wealth and their exploitation as an obligatory duty (3: 21).

Turning to non-economic goals, it is emphasised that fulfilment of "spiritual needs" must take place besides the fulfilment of material needs (5: 13). Mawdūdī gives priority of place to "safeguarding the freedom of man" followed by his "moral growth" which requires freedom of choice for the individual. Social justice, equality of opportunity and co-operation come next in Mawdūdī's list of basic objectives of Islam's economic system (51: 145). Chapra's list gives priority to "economic well-being" followed by "universal brotherhood and justice, equitable distribution of income and freedom of the individual within the context of social welfare" (115: 5).[5]

Siddiqi discusses the rationale of including these non-economic goals in the ends of economic system and points out the impact their inclusion has on the ways and means adopted for achievement of the ends of economic system in Islam (73: 28). Morally-orientated individual action is expected to ensure the achievement of socially desired results to a large extent. Law and social control are to guide, regulate and supplement individual actions and compensate the deficiencies that still remain. To quote Mawdūdī:

> "For establishing economic justice, Islam does not rely on law alone. Great importance is attached for this purpose to reforming the inner man through faith, prayers, education and moral training, to changing his preferences and ways of thinking and inculcating in him a strong moral sense that keeps him just. If and when these means fail, Muslim society should be strong enough to exert pressure to make individuals adhere to the 'limits'. When even this does not deliver the goods, Islam is for the use of the coercive powers of law to establish justice by force." (51: 145).

Even though recent thinking is far more positive regarding the role of the state in securing the goals mentioned above the emphasis placed by Mawdūdī on morally-oriented voluntary action represents a tendency deeply rooted in the Islamic mind and exemplified by the vast literature on the code of conduct of various economic agents. A distinction is always made in this connection between what is obligatory and what is desirable. The obligatory is legally enforced, the desirable is ensured through education. Any deficiency in the attainment of goals is then made up by the state enforcing the desirable part of the code as well as taking other compensatory and positive measures. It is in this manner that the desired allocation of resources and distribution of incomes is effected. The respective roles of the market mechanism and planned action are determined accordingly. We shall therefore proceed first to study the various codes of conduct for economic agents: the owner, the consumer, the entrepreneur; producer, employer, trader etc. and the labourer. This will be followed by an examination of the role envisaged for the market mechanism and the role visualised for the state.

The Owner

Behavioural norms for the owner have been discussed by a number of writers including Hifẓur Rahman (120: 68–77, 299–302), Mawdūdī (51: 81–96), Sayyid Quṭb (62: 111–112), Siddiqi (221, I: 205–288), Manna' Qattān[6] and A. Mannan (132: 77–85). The owner has no right to destroy useful property. Wasteful use and extravagance is prohibited. He has to avoid using it in a manner injurious to others or detrimental to public interest. Other individuals and the society have a claim on the owner's property. This includes the obligation to support dependents in the nuclear family and other members of the extended family when they are in need (336; 221, I: 252–259).

Besides obligatory *Zakāt* the owner owes help to those in dire need, and should not refuse a loan in cash or kind when a request comes from one who is in real need. Several writers stress the significance of the provision that the presence of a pressing need obliges those with a surplus to surrender such part of their surplus as will fulfil that need (77, II: 214; 221, I: 272–280).

While there is a consensus on illegitimacy of "interest" charged on money loans, the owner's right to income from his property in forms of rent and profit has been a matter of controversy in the literature. The right of the owner to cultivate his own land or employ his own capital in productive enterprise or profitable business is not disputed. In that case he is the owner of the accruing surplus over cost. The legally binding *Zakāt* is of course to be realised from him. Abu Sulaiman advocates a larger share for society in the produce of land where the land holding of the owner is more than his "equal share", as explained above. Controversy centres round giving the land to another person for cultivation on money rent or on the basis of share cropping, or giving capital on a profit sharing basis, i.e. *muḍārabah*.

Abu Sulaiman allows profit sharing but "the share of the capital owner is only to compensate him for probable loss" (8: 59). He is not entitled to a net pure profit. Other writers on the subject endorse the unanimous verdict of all the four principal schools of Islamic law that the two parties to the *muḍārabah* contract are free to agree on any formula of sharing the profits provided these shares are fixed percentage-wise and not in the form of given amounts (176: 30). Abu Sulaiman's opinion is derived from his basic stand relating to the equal sharing of gifts of God (other than the fruits of personal ingenuity and labour). But he fails to counter the obvious argument that an entrepreneurial decision is involved in selecting the right party in *muḍārabah* (221, I: 167–171). He does not support his view by any precedents from the *Sunnah* and gives no argument against the unanimous verdict of *fiqh*. Contemporary writers on Islamic banking, who make *muḍārabah* the basis of its operations, do not stipulate any ceilings on the percentage share of capital in profits.

In discussing money rent on cultivable land a distinction must be made between plain land in its natural form in which the owner has not invested any labour or capital to effect improvements, and improved land. There is no dispute that money rent is valid in the case of the latter variety in lieu of "depreciation".

As regards the first-mentioned variety Abu Sulaiman regards charging money rent by the owner as illegal (8: 30–31 and 41–42). This is the position that can be inferred from Mawdūdī's statement on the subject (232: 60). Abu Sa'ūd also equates such rent to interest charged on money capital (5: 93).

There is no denying the fact that money rent (on agricultural land) usually stands at a level higher than depreciation. A question is raised regarding the legitimacy of such (higher) rent. One asks what would be the rationale behind the capital, time and effort invested in the improvement on land if money rent is allowed only to the extent of depreciation.

The question can be answered after a close look at the nature of the return to these improvements in terms of value. These are uncertain as they involve the uncertain market price of the produce. Should the investor in land improvements himself cultivate the land, the returns shall legitimately accrue to him. Share cropping should also be allowed as it is the physical product that is shared and the share of the investor-owner remains uncertain. To allow him to charge a certain fixed sum, in lieu of investments in improvements, as part of its rent would be tantamount to *ribā* whose essence is charging a certain fixed sum against uncertain value returns.

Ṭāhāwī finds that there are authentic traditions from the Prophet both allowing and prohibiting money rent on land. He thinks the two verdicts relate to two different situations. Money rent on land is to be declared illegal if there is undue attention of people towards agriculture at the cost of industry and trade (77, I: 268–269). He also notes that the jurists who have allowed money rent do so on the basis of "necessity", otherwise they agree that it is against the principles of analogy (77, I: 271). Whatever one's judgment on Taḥāwi's historical account, he fails to provide an economic rationale for his solution.

Nasir A. Sheikh (154: 181) opposes both land rent and share cropping, laying down that "a person can possess only that much land which he can himself cultivate. The surplus he has to surrender to the state". A. Mannan also disfavours leasing of land on rent or on the basis of share cropping (132: 106–108).

Such a dogmatic position is hardly tenable, economically speaking, as Akram points out (613: 34–36). A. Mannan also refutes, like Akram, the view that rent should be prohibited as it is similar to interest (132: 135–154).

S. M. Yusuf discerns "in early Islam a definite tendency to ordain the future development of agriculture in such a way that there is no charge for the use of what Ricardo in his own definition of rent called original and indestructible powers of land". Quoting Iqbal's *Bāl-e-jibrīl* he ascribes the same view to him (242: 34).

Share Cropping

Share cropping is considered valid by most of the contemporary writers such as Mawdūdī (232: 60), Bāqir al Ṣadr (171: 531), Hifzur Raḥmān (120:

236), Ḥāmid (229), Ṭaḥāwī (77, I: 271), Siddiqi (221, I: 184–192) and Taqī Amīnī (226).

Those who regard it as illegal include: S. M. Yusuf (242), Mazharuddin Siddiqi (72: 70), Abu Sulaiman (8: 43–44) and Ḥyder Zamān Ṣiddīqī (244). We shall not enter the controversy in so far as it is based on the various traditions involved and their legal interpretation. As regards the points of economic philosophy involved, we have clarified Abu Sulaiman's position above. Those who allow share cropping compare it to profit sharing and argue that all owners do not have the capacity to cultivate their land directly, and it should therefore be open to them to benefit from it in co-operation with others, as in the case of profit sharing. The crucial question therefore is: in so far as the owner of a piece of land is entitled to the whole net produce of his land when he is the cultivator, his claim is established both on the part of the net produce that is due to his labour, and the part that is due to land. Shall he be allowed to give it to another person and *share* with him the part of the net product that is due to land? It is this question that Abu Sulaiman answers in the negative and others answer in the affirmative. It is clear that a negative answer amounts to the negation of ownership *per se*. If the owner of cultivable land is allowed to hire labourers to get his land cultivated and appropriate the net produce why should he be disallowed from entering into a "partnership" with the same labourer and share the whole of the produce with him? Abu Sulaiman might say that the "owner" is entitled to this much of land – as his proportionate share in the free natural resource that is land – and no more. This provides a case for a ceiling on ownership of agricultural land and not a case against share cropping. So far as the question of supplying the seeds etc., is concerned different schools of Islamic law lay down different formulas and one is free to recommend one that is just to both the parties, but to disallow share cropping as such is not understandable. The share cropping labourer is likely to do his job with greater interest than the hired labourers and may well end up with a higher reward. Those who disallow share cropping seem to disregard both its needs and advantages in their urge to ensure justice for which alternative means may be available.

The Consumer

The list of articles whose consumption is prohibited in Islam is well known and non-controversial. There is no limit to what one might consume to lead a good life, so increasing efficiency and playing the role Islam envisages for a true Muslim in the service of society. But indulgence in luxurious living is undesirable. Some writers recommend a ban on certain luxury items or subjecting them to heavy taxes in order to discourage their consumption, especially when the economic conditions of the society do not permit expenditure of scarce resources on their production (221, II: 172–173, 219).

Bāqir al Ṣadr suggests that resources should not be allowed to be diverted to the production of luxuries until the production of necessaries is ensured in sufficient quantities (171: 611). The consumer must abstain from extravagance defined as expenditure in excess of what is necessary to fulfil a need. Extravagance is related to the average standards of consumption obtaining in a society, the idea being that big departures from these standards should not be permissible. Several writers have discussed the concept of extravagance, including Naiem Siddiqi (74).

The Entrepreneur: Producer and Trader

The code of conduct for a Muslim entrepreneur has been discussed in detail by Mawdūdi (51: 83–89), Siddiqi (619: 35–64), Chapra (115: 27–33) Ali Abdur Rasul[7] and Kahf (612: 15–20), among others. Dishonesty, fraud and deception, coercive practices, and gamblesome or usurious dealings are prohibited. He should not do anything injurious to others. This rules out hoarding, speculation and collusion among producers and traders against the interests of the consumers. Monopoly is also regarded as injurious to the interests of society. He is charged with justice and truthfulness in all his dealings. On the positive side he should serve the interests of the society. Social good should guide him in his decisions, besides his own profit. As to the question how a care for the good of the society would influence entrepreneurial decisions, no deep study is available besides Siddiqi's preliminary discussion in *Economic Enterprise in Islam*. This question raises basic issues such as the role of information in the translation of good intentions into socially desirable concrete results, and the way individual good intentions can be organised and institutionalised. No serious attention has been paid to these sociological aspects of the behaviour of the producer and trader in Islamic society. Some writers have paid special attention to the obligation of the employer towards his employees (425; 426; 438; 444; 165). These discussions also suffer from the limitations indicated above, in so far as they fail to translate the cherished norms into operational programmes of action. A notable exception, however, is Abdul Majeed Qureshi (439; 440; 441) whose views we discuss below, under labour and industrial relations.

This leads us to the question of evaluating the market system. Everyone will agree with Chapra that "although the market system has been recognised by Islam because of the freedom it offers to individuals, it is not to be considered sacred and inalterable. It is the goals of the Muslim society which are more important. . . ."

The market system must therefore be modified as necessary to make it conform to the ideals of Islam as much as possible (115: 23–24). Examine however the following statement by the same author: "In Islam the allocation of resources is optimum if it is first in conformity with the norms of Islam and then in accordance with consumers' preferences. In a truly Islamic society there is no likelihood of any divergence between the two" (115: 82). The meaning of the second sentence is not entirely clear. Does it mean that if all economic agents behave in accordance with the Islamic code of conduct and the distribution of income and wealth is according to the Islamic ideals, the functioning of the market system would result in optimum allocation of resources, in the Islamic sense? An affirmative answer raises questions relating to knowledge, wisdom, power and organisation which have not been discussed so far.

Kahf's discussion on the market structure (612: 29–45) focuses its attention on co-operation and emphasises the role of the government in the market. Both the supervisory and control functions of the government and its social insurance role are seen as permanent features of the market in Islam. He neither poses nor answers the question raised above.

The market system as a means of distributing incomes in society is rated very low by our writers. There is a greater need of modification, through state action, of the market solution in this case than in the case of allocation of resources. As the basic reason calling for such a modification is advanced the argument that in Islam there are two grounds for entitlement to income: work and need. The market may reward work but it cannot possibly provide for need. The final distribution of income must conform to the Islamic ideals of social justice which involves fulfilment of the basic needs of every individual as well as a levelling of the glaring disparities.

Bāqir al Ṣadr regards work to be the chief basis of distribution (171: 309–312). But this results in one class of people earning more than they need and another class earning less than they need. This solution has to be modified by transferring some income from the former class to the latter (171: 313).

Property, which is based in Islam primarily on work, becomes a secondary basis for distribution next to work and need (171: 321). Ṭahāwī also endorses the same theory (77, II: 227–28).

Commenting on distribution, Abu Sulaiman puts great reliance on properly functioning markets. Intervention by public administration is, however, likely to become necessary (8: 71).

Role of the State

Without prejudice to the emphasis on freedom of the individual, the state's role in economic life has come to be emphasised more and more in the literature. This role mainly comprises four types of action.

(1) Ensuring compliance with the Islamic code of conduct by individuals through education and, whenever necessary, through coercion.
(2) Maintaining healthy conditions in the market to ensure its proper functioning.
(3) Modifying the allocation of resources and distribution of income

effected by the market mechanism by guiding and regulating it as well as by direct intervention and participation in the process.

(4) Taking positive steps in the field of production and capital formation to accelerate growth and ensure social justice.

It is agreed that the state enjoys the widest powers for performing these functions, subject to the constraint that it functions in a democratic manner and decisions are taken after due consultation, by true representatives of the people.

Bāqir al Ṣadr has discussed the role of the state in Islam's economic system at some length. Besides enforcing the relevant laws the state guarantees social security, ensuring fulfilment of needs to each individual, and maintains a balance in the standards of living in the society (171: 615–636). The state's direct responsibility as regards social security is based on the general claim of the entire society on natural resources, and on the fact that those individuals of the society who do not have the capacity to work also have this claim (171: 621). Bāqir then proceeds to show how the creation of a "public sector" is the means to discharge this responsibility. As regards maintaining the Social Balance he stresses the point that it refers not to the levels of income but to the standards of living (171: 626). The balance does admit, however, of moderate differences. Besides enforcing the *Sharī'ah* laws, guaranteeing fulfilment of needs and maintaining the social balance, the state has the important function of undertaking fresh legislation to regulate and guide the economic life in affairs left unregulated by the *Sharī'ah*. This "sphere open to fresh legislation" mainly related to relations between man and the world of nature as distinct from the relations between man and man. These relations change with changing knowledge, discovery of new resources, powers of production, etc. They have to be properly regulated in order to ensure justice and protect the interests of the society. Such regulations could not be a part of the permanent law, the *Sharī'ah*, as their need arises *denovo* due to changed conditions of life. Islam authorises the properly constituted government to fill this gap. The government can prohibit something hitherto regarded as "permissible", or make some "permissible" act an obligatory one: "When the Ruler prohibits something by nature permissible it becomes *ḥarām*, when he orders that it be done, it becomes *wājib*" (171: 643). (This power does not extend to what is already prohibited or obligatory in law.) This discussion (171: 637–643) is the clearest one gets in the literature, when read in the light of what the writer has written on the same subject in the earlier part of the book. While the state cannot legalise what is explicitly illegal in *Sharī'ah* or absolve individuals of duties *Sharī'ah* has explicitly charged them with, it can always issue a fresh list of dos and don'ts, to regulate the economy and guide it towards the cherished goals (171: 612).

In his discussions on the role of the state in the economy Muhammad al Mubārak declares the state to be one of the three pillars of the Islamic economic system, along with faith and commitment to moral values and certain principles of organisation. Its function is to establish justice and ensure fulfilment of needs by organising the public utilities and the social security system (134: 106–127).

In his doctoral dissertation on the "Political Economy of the Islamic State", Awsaf Ali (114) concludes that the social philosophy of Islam envisions an economic society based on a wide-ranging state direction of, and participation in, the economic, commercial and financial spheres.

Fazlur Rahman (27: 5) says that "in the basic interest of socio-economic justice, the state shall interfere with private wealth to the extent that socio-economic justice demands". He thinks that "if it is found that the condition of the society is economically irremediable in the visible future without the state taking over direct management of industry, Islam would not only not forbid this but would obviously enjoin this upon the state as a most imperative duty".

Chapra also regards an active economic role by the state to be an inalienable feature of the Islamic economic system (115: 41–42); providing physical and social overhead capital and arranging social security are listed among the necessary functions of a modern Islamic state (115: 40). In a more recent paper on the subject, this list includes maintaining stability in the value of money and harmonising international economic relations, besides the eradication of poverty and the creation of conditions favourable for full employment and a high rate of growth.[8] As a general principle, its sphere of activity is determined by the goals of the Islamic system (115: 50). But he also insists that "the procedure it should adopt is education and not coercion . . ." (115: 50), which indicates a strong influence of Mawdūdī's views on the subject. Nobody will deny the principle that where education serves coercion should be eschewed. But we must be very clear on the point that the goals of the Islamic system have got to be achieved and coercion is allowed where education fails (221, II: 156–165). Among such measures of coercion permitted in certain circumstances have been listed restrictions on individual freedom of action, regulation of business activities, fixation of prices, wages, rents and rates of profit, taxation, taxing away the entire surplus wealth, use of coercion in purchase or hire, nationalisation, ceilings on property, economic planning and financial penalties (221, II: 166–283).

Among close associates of Mawdūdī, Naiem Siddiqi has also spelled out many positive actions by the state which are called for in the circumstances prevailing in some of the Muslim countries (584: 514–522). Chapra is more positive in his recent paper when he lays down that "For a realisation of this objective it would be incumbent upon the Islamic State not to leave the essential function of allocation of resources, particularly scarce resources, or the determination of aggregate demand to the unhindered operation of blind market forces. It should itself play a positive role and consciously contribute towards the attainment of desired goals through (i) rational planning, and (ii) building the necessary physical and social infrastructure".[9]

A very active role for the state is envisaged in the report of the economic committee of *Jamā'at-i-Islāmī* Pakistan, written by Khurshid Ahmad and Naiem Siddiqi (126: 40–52). A trend which is fully reflected in the *Jamā'at* manifesto for the 1970 elections (125: 22–32). Having these very conditions in mind Kalim Siddiqi (494) makes a plea for a very active role by the state, which is to "exercise, on behalf of God, proprietary rights over surplus value or capital and manage and direct further investment" (494: 28).

We have already mentioned Mawdūdī's cautious approach regarding the intervention of the state in economic life. There are several writers who regard the expanding economic role of the state in modern times as unhealthy and want the Islamic system to check this tendency, e.g. Mahmud Abū Saūd (5: 70–71). The increasing emphasis on a more positive role for the state in the Islamic economy, as exemplified by the writers mentioned above, seems to indicate an irreversible trend reflecting the changing conditions of modern economic life which is becoming more complex and interdependent.

III

ECONOMIC SYSTEM OF ISLAM: SOME SPECIFIC ASPECTS

Within the basic framework outlined above our writers have discussed such specific aspects of the system as public finance, money and banking, social security and insurance, industrial relations and development and growth.

Public Finance

A vast literature is available on public finance in Islam in view of the explicit provisions in the *Sharī'ah* in this regard and the historical material available on the subject. Besides Aghnides' *Mohammedan Theories of Finance* a number of specialised works are available, though mostly historical and descriptive in nature (333; 293; 298)[10].

This is also true of the chapters on public finance found in almost every work on the economic system of Islam. Our interest lies in the way the operation of Islamic institutions like *Zakāt* and the application of general principles of policy derived from public finance in early Islamic history is visualised in modern circumstances.

Zakāt

The centre piece of Islamic Public Finance being *Zakāt*, its coverage, rates, beneficiaries and administration have been discussed in detail. The most comprehensive work in Qarḍāwī's *Fiqh al Zakāt* (313). In English "The Law and Philosophy of *Zakāt*" is less original yet comprehensive on points of law (319). Among economists A. Mannan's book (132) has a good chapter on Public Finance and Fiscal Policy, and some of the younger economists have offered analytical pieces on the subject (623; 624; 615).[11]

(a) Coverage

It is generally agreed that the coverage of *Zakāt* has to be extended to forms of wealth not known in the early days of Islam. Shares and securities, savings in the form of insurance premia and provident funds, rented buildings and vehicles on hire, machinery and other capital goods. Qarḍāwī (313, I: 139, 466–486, 581–573), Abu Zahra (300: 181–186) and Mawdūdī (51: 339–342, 351–363) discuss the application of *Zakāt* to these assets and the rates applicable to them.

Many issues continue to be controversial, one of them being the *Zakāt* on machinery and capital goods. Mawdūdī regards only the marketable produce of industrial units to be subject to 2.5% annual tax, like all other merchandise (51: 339) exempting capital goods and machinery installed in these units from *Zakāt*. Akram finds this view to be inconsistent with Mawdūdī's opinion on *Zakāt* of shares in industrial concerns (613: 102). Abū Zahra advocates a 10 per cent tax on the net income (profits) of these concerns (300: 184). Qarḍāwī endorses his view subject to two important modifications. Firstly, he categorises rented buildings and vehicles on hire and also such enterprises as poultry farms and dairy farms along with industrial units. Secondly, in all these cases he advocates a 10 per cent levy on profits *net of depreciation costs* (313, I: 476–482). A. Mannan also stresses the need of making due allowance for depreciation and adds that "the question of the rate of *Zakāt* is linked up with productivity which varies from industry to industry". He pleads for a flexible rate "so that the element of progression may be introduced in fixing the rate of *Zakāt*" (132: 291).

Similar controversies surround some of the other forms of wealth mentioned above. The number of opinions, arguments and counter arguments in each case being too many to be recorded here. Our interest lies in the economic aspect of the discussion rather than in the points of law involved and their interpretations. Analogical reasoning is often supplemented by a reference to the public interest, equity and incidence, etc. The entire issue awaits a thorough re-examination in which the new taxes are seen as part of the whole structure of *Zakāt* taxes, paying careful attention to their functions in the economy.

(b) Rates

The ulema are unanimous in regarding the rates of *Zakāt* as permanently fixed by Islamic law, but a number of recent writers, mostly economists, argue in favour of making these rates amenable to modification by the state. Afazuddin (621: 10), Izadi (613: 14), Husaini (121: 200–205), Salih Tug[12] and Mahmud Ahmad take this stand. Mahmud Ahmad (168: 133) quotes Maulana Abul Kalam Azad's letter to him in support of his view. The economic arguments in favour of flexible rates are met, however, by the ulema when they point out that the state is empowered to levy additional taxes, over and above the prescribed *Zakāt*. It is, therefore, in case of the "new forms of wealth", for which no explicit provisions are found in the *Sharī'ah* that the arguments in favour of flexible rates have practical significance.

The arguments in favour of valuation of the *niṣāb*, i.e. the exemption limits prescribed by the *Sharī'ah* are, however, more formidable, economically speaking. Akram refers to the anomalies existing in the present structure of *niṣāb* (613: 103) and a change in *niṣāb* has been advocated by Rafiullah (314), Zayas (321: 74–76), Uthman (79) and Fanjari.[13] Hasanuzzaman also pleads for rethinking on the subject with a view to having a uniform *niṣāb*.[14]

Waqar Husaini takes the position that "the exact types and rates of taxes used by the Prophet Muḥammad need not be applied in contemporary times" (121: 204). The main economic reason is stated as follows:

> "Logically and practically it is impossible to treat as watertight compartments the three branches of fiscal planning: resource allocation, economic stabilization and income and wealth distribution. . . . In a smoothly running Islamic economic system, the 'redistribution' function through progressive taxation would wither away, leaving it the task of merely maintaining the egalitarian economic system with proportional taxation. To achieve and maintain such an egalitarian system, except for minor direct transfer payments mainly to those mentally and physically deprived of the capacity to earn, the main heads of expenditure of *Zakāt*/*Ṣadaqah*/*Infaq* tax revenues would be in the resource allocation and stabilisation branches. This would be consistent with the multiple goals of the Islamic economic system, spending on all the beneficiaries enumerated in the Qur'ān by maintaining full employment and enabling everybody to acquire earned income and wealth in a manner that preserves human dignity".[15]

Husaini's stand is contrary to the consensus on the juristic principle involved. There has been unanimity as to the sanctity of the rates explicitly fixed by the Prophet. This permanence has been regarded as a virtue as it rules out tampering with the law of *Zakāt* by the rulers with a view to reducing the share of the have-nots in the wealth of the haves. As regards the need for increasing this share, the state is allowed to levy additional taxes. This coupled with the flexibility in disbursement of *Zakāt* funds, introduces sufficient flexibility in the system to enable it to meet the changing requirements of fiscal planning. One of the major roles of progressive taxation in a modern economy is an equitable sharing of the burden of raising income for the state. Progressive taxation ensures equitable sharing of this burden. As the need for such income is likely to go on increasing, there is no possibility of doing away with progressive taxation.

(c) Disbursement of *Zakāt* Revenue

Among other issues on which there is a difference of opinion is the way *Zakāt* benefits should flow to the various groups of the beneficiaries listed in the Qur'ān. Some ulema insist on direct transfer payments to the beneficiaries. These include Mufti Muhammad Shafi of Pakistan (317: 59–62). Most writers, however, permit the *Zakāt* benefits to flow to the beneficiaries indirectly through institutions providing needed services. These include Mawdūdī (51: 350), Amin Ahsan Islāhī (309) and Ya'qūb Shah (318: 48). According to Qarḍāwī the beneficiaries fall into two groups. To the first, which includes the needy, the officers in *Zakāt* administration and "those whose hearts are to be won over" the *Zakāt* revenue must be transferred directly. The rest can receive the benefits indirectly (313, II: 612–614, 633). But Islāhī argues that the insistence on direct transfer to certain beneficiaries has no basis in the text of the law (309).

Some writers tend to interpret the category "in the cause of Allah" too broadly to include all social services, but Qarḍāwī's thorough discussion on the subject limiting it to the promotion of the cause of Islam in general, in all its possible forms, appears to be balanced and decisive (313, II: 635–669). Most of the specific suggestions made by Muhammad bin Jamāl (625) can be accommodated in the broad framework provided by those who do not insist on *tamlīk* in every case. Such is the stance taken by the *Jamā'at-i-Islāmī* Pakistan Economic Committee Report (126: 93–96).

Akram sees a useful instrument of fiscal policy in the discretionary use of the principle of *tamlīk* by the Islamic State (613: 107).

(d) *Zakāt* on Agricultural Produce and Mineral Wealth

The *Zakāt* levy covers the agricultural produce in the form of '*Ushr* and its half depending on whether the land is irrigated by Nature or by man. This levy applies to every Muslim. But some lands are subject to *Kharāj*, or land tax (i.e. rent payable to the state), irrespective of who owns them. According to majority opinion a Muslim owner-cultivator of such lands will pay *Kharāj* as well as '*Ushr* (or its half), as Qarḍāwī has explained (313, I: 415).

The majority opinion levies '*Ushr* (or its half) on the gross produce of land, but Qarḍāwī has convincingly argued the desirability of making an allowance for the costs incurred on fertilizers, seed, etc. (313, I: 394–397). The same view is taken by ‘Abd al-Salam.[16]

On mineral wealth contemporary opinion tends to gravitate towards making the state own all such resources and assuming the responsibility of exploring and exploiting them (Syed Quṭb (62: 121) and Siddiqi (221, II: 19–22)). Individuals who discover any mines may be awarded prizes or given concessional contracts for their exploration.

Several writers, including Qarḍāwī discuss the principles underlying Islamic taxation which are shown to be in conformity with the criteria laid down for just and efficient policies by the modern economists (313, II: 1038–1052). Atif al-Sayyid[17] explains how *Zakāt* surpasses all civic taxes in having three virtues: the *Zakāt* payer has a deep sense of duty towards the Law-Giver, he has a genuine dedication to the aims and objects of this levy and he is aware of his ability to pay it. Mabid Mahmood finds in *Zakāt* a powerful means of redistributing political power which he regards to be a function of wealth (624: 43). Several writers discuss the economics of *Zakāt* in relation to savings and investment to which we shall turn later in the chapter on economic analysis.

Inheritance

The Islamic laws of inheritance are invariably mentioned by our writers along with *Zakāt* in view of their redistributive function, and their role in removing concentrations of wealth is highlighted by almost every writer. Whereas *Zakāt* redistributes wealth in the present generation, the Islamic laws of inheritance do so between the outgoing generation and the present one, so that the wealth accumulated at one point, despite *Zakāt*, is further dispersed.

Social Security and Insurance

Social security is generally discussed in the context of *Zakāt*. Historical material on how the early Islamic State arranged social security is presented by almost every writer on the subject. It is affirmed that new institutional arrangements can always be devised and the various institutions in modern welfare states are referred to approvingly. The principles involved have been discussed, among others, by Bāqir al Ṣadr (171: 615–623). The subject has also been discussed at the International Islamic Conference at Cairo, Kuala Lumpur and other places and practical suggestions mooted (300; 405).

Besides *Zakāt* which provides the Islamic State with funds to finance social security measures, Islam lays great stress on voluntary assistance to the needy. An elaborate concept of mutual responsibility has been presented by Sayyid Quṭb (62), among others. Kashif[18] conceives of a social security scheme in which the state collects *Zakāt* from the haves and transfers it to the have-nots; the employers contribute towards the pensions and Provident Funds of their workers; and the individual with a capacity to pay, contributes in the form of insurance premia. While *Zakāt* caters to the poor and the needy, insurance takes care of the risks to which life and property are exposed.

Insurance

Insurance continues to be one of the most controversial subjects in the literature. Opinion is sharply divided both on the principle of insurance and the forms of its organisation.

Several writers see nothing wrong in insurance, in so far as the basic principles underlying insurance are concerned. It is free from gambling, can be freed from interest which is involved in its present practice, and the ignorance (*jahl*) and uncertainty (*gharar*) involved are not of a degree large enough to call for its prohibition. These writers include Zarqa (380)[19], Yousuf Moosa (256: 101, 181), Ali al Khafeef (361), Mohammad al Bahy (351), Sanousi (373), Roohani (372), Ṭaḥāwī (77, I: 441–470), Taqi Amini (556: 231–232), Sheikh Mahmud Ahmad (168: 201–203), A. Mannan (132: 353–360), Siddiqi (374), Shaheedi and Awad.[20]

Some writers agree with this view so far as general insurance is concerned, but they find life insurance unacceptable as it involves gambling and uncertainty and militates against the Islamic conception of *taqdīr*. Abu Zahra (376; 365), Ahmad Ibrahim (357) and Shaukat Ali Khan[21] take this stand.

There are some *ulema* (Scholars of Islamic Law), who find an element of gambling in all kinds of insurance as a matter of principle. They also find some other objectionable features, such as *ribā* and uncertainty (*gharar*) inalienably associated with insurance. Some of them, finding that it does not conform to any one of the various contracts validated by Islamic jurisprudence, regard it to be an unnecessary innovation. Sheikh Bakheet (355: 72), Abdullah al Qalqeeli (365), Mustafa Zaid (597; 376), Mufti Mohammad Shafi (531), Jalal Mustafa al Sayyad[22] and Shaukat Ali Kahn[23] take this stand.

Those who find insurance acceptable in principle generally prefer mutual insurance which is organised on a co-operative basis and does not lead to exploitation. The same is true if insurance is organised by the state. But commercial insurance involves exploitation and certain other objectionable features, and is therefore ultravires of Islam. Abu Zuhra (355; 376; 365), Issa Abdouh (350), Muslehuddin (369), Dasooqi (355) and Ahmad Fahmi Abu Sunnah[24] who otherwise find the principle of insurance acceptable, have offered this opinion. Aṭṭar[25] refutes the view that insurance is gambling but he finds it unacceptable as most of its present forms involve a high degree of uncertainty and the possibility of fraud. He allows mutual insurance schemes but prescribes a number of measures directed at purging commercial insurance of its undesirable features (pp. 41–42). He envisages a system of insurance which is based on *Zakāt*.

Several writers, including Sheikh Ali al Khafeef, Zarqā[26] (380), Siddiqi (374) and Ṭaḥāwī (77, I: 441–470) argue, however, that the same principle underlies all forms of organised insurance. It is possible to regulate commercial insurance in such a manner that it functions without exploitation.

Mawdūdī has opined that insurance, which presently involves interest, gambling and a violation of Islamic laws of inheritance can be reorganised free of these evils (51: 408–411). But he has not spelled out the details. The same is true of Yūsufuddīn (165, II: 452–454).

Insurance has been discussed at a number of Islamic conferences but a favourable verdict on commercial insurance has been withheld in view of the objections of the above-mentioned eminent scholars. This is brought out by the resolutions passed at the 1965 Islamic Research Congress at Cairo (211) and those adopted in 1969 at Kuala Lumpur (405: 202). As recently as 1976 the First International Conference on Islamic Economics held at Makka resolved that: "The Conference feels that commercial insurance as presently practised does not realise the *Sharī'ah* aims of co-operation and solidarity because it does not satisfy the Islamic conditions for it to become acceptable.

"The Conference recommends the establishment of a committee consisting of specialists in *Sharī'ah* and Economics to recommend a system of insurance which is free from *ribā* and speculation, promotes co-operation in accordance with the *Sharī'ah*, and helps replace the current form of commercial insurance."[27] Most of the *ulema* in India and Pakistan responding to a questionnaire issued by *Majlis Tahqīqāt Sharī'ah*, Lucknow (366) also regarded insurance as legitimate in principle.

The most important issue in the controversy is whether insurance involves gambling. Those who insist that it does quote the relevant definitions given by early jurists. But several writers including Zarqa (380), Ali al Khafeef (361), Aṭṭar, Awad[28] and Ṭaḥāwī (55, I: 451) have pointed out the difference between insurance and gambling. Siddiqi has shown the difference between the risk taken by the gambler, which he creates for himself, and those involved in the ordinary business of life that the insurers try to meet, utilising the law of large numbers, at a cost (374). He has also discussed the economic roles of gambling and insurance. Gambling upsets the normal system based on work and reward and is inimical to equitable distribution of income and wealth, whereas insurance protects the disruption of the system by accidents and events beyond human control. Sayyad[29] has failed to take these points into consideration and dismisses some other dissimilarities between gambling and insurance on insufficient reason.

Next to gambling the commercial organisation of insurance has been the target of attack. The recent trend has been in favour of nationalisation of insurance. Most writers make a plea for a comprehensive system comprising *Zakāt*-based social security and insurance administered by the state. Mutual insurance should be allowed in matters not covered by the state system. As regards commercial insurance it may be allowed to function in certain areas where great importance is attached to innovation and initiative (374).

Most of the contributors on the subject have been *ulema* who have little knowledge of Economics. As a result there is little economic analysis in most of the works on the subject. Very few have referred to the law of large numbers which lies at the basis of insurance and little effort has been made to assess the economic significance of insurance in modern life. Some writers seem to be under the misconception that a comprehensive social security system will do away with the need for insurance. They fail to distinguish between the fulfilment of needs and arrangements designed to increase efficiency and ensure the smooth functioning of large-scale business and industry.

They ignore the obvious point that individuals should be encouraged to provide for themselves, as far as they can, and protect themselves against insurable risks. The state should be called in for helping only those who do not have the capacity to do so, or fail to do so.

As ably argued by Fanjari in a recent paper,[30] there are separate roles for *Zakāt*-based social security and insurance organised on the basis of contributions made by the individuals involved (pp. 7–8). This point is increasingly being appreciated and one tends to agree with Fanjari that the area of consensus is widening and that of controversy shrinking in respect of commercial insurance also (p. 35).

Money and Banking

It is the privilege of the state to issue money and control its supply, that much is above controversy. The introduction of paper currency raised some new issues for the jurists but it was soon agreed that it made no difference.

Bāqir al Ṣadr (171: 325–331), Mahmud Abu Saud (5), Mahmud Ahmad[31] and Kahf (612: 65–68) have paid special attention to money and its role. Bāqir and Saud conclude that the use of money as a store of value is a source of many troubles. While Bāqir regards *Zakāt*, which discourages idle cash balances, and abolition of interest, which frustrates the desire to earn guaranteed profits by using such money, as sufficient remedies for the troubles in the Islamic system, Abu Saud does not stop at that. "It is necessary to issue a new kind of money and subject it to a tax other than *Zakāt* to check hoarding and ensure its continuous circulation and stop all usurious earnings arising from it" (5: 47). As a practical measure he favours the idea of stamped money,[32] suggested by Gessel and briefly tried in the municipality of Woergl, Switzerland in 1922 (5: 40–45). The idea has failed, so far, to find support in the literature.[33] One tends to agree with Kahf when he says that "Abū Saud's proposal discriminates between money assets and non-money assets" and "involves injustice by not taking into account the change of hands during the period and leaving the whole burden of the stamp on the last holder" (612: 67). Kahf thinks that, generally speaking, Islamic writers have overlooked the inter-temperal use of money, i.e. its function as a store of value, which is a boon and not a bane.

Of special interest in the context of money in an Islamic economy is the contribution of Mabid al Jarhi[34] who pleads for the creation of a "fiat means of exchange" by the state and their supply free of cost (i.e. interest) to the public. This method, adopted along with abolition of interest will raise real income.

Akram has discussed money in the international context. An "Islamic solution" to the present international monetary crisis lies in prohibiting interest, speculation, hoarding of gold and suspension of the foreign exchange market, the central banks becoming the only dealers of foreign exchange. Private use of gold may be banned and all the gold mined should flow directly to the monetary authorities (558). Such sweeping reforms cannot be considered, much less accepted, unless they are supplemented by a detailed discussion on the pros and cons, which Akram fails to provide.

Banking

The Islamic evaluation of modern banking centred around the evils of the institution of interest. Very soon it developed into an exploration which bears great promise of giving modern man a new and just institution, of banking without interest.

In discussing modern banking some writers attack the institution of credit and its creation by commercial banks. Mawdūdī's otherwise brilliant study is a case in point (521: 117–133). Issa Abdouh also thinks that credit creation by banks is prejudicial to the interest of people with small incomes (382). Muhammad Uzair blames wide fluctuations in money supply and credit creation for trade cycles (422). This trend culminates in the suggestion made by the Economic Committee of *Jamā'at-i-Islāmī* Pakistan that the power to create credit be taken away from Commercial Banks (126: 80–82). Kahf also deprives private sector banking of the power to create credit, which should be the privilege of the state, the sole creator of money (612: 65–68). Naseer A. Sheikh also regards the power of banks to create money or to extend credit to be the cause of money ills (154: 78), and so do Assal and Fathi.[35]

A: Banking Without Interest

The earliest references to the reorganisation of banking on the basis of profit sharing rather than interest are found in Qureshi (526), Naiem Siddiqi (419) and Mahmud Ahmad (168) in the late forties, followed by a more elaborate exposition by Mawdūdī in 1950 (521). We are not aware of any work on the subject in Arabic during the forties. Three early works on Islam's economic system in Urdu by Hifzur Rahman (120), Gilani (28) and Yousufuddin (165) do not mention the subject.

Qureshi's reference to the subject is brief (526: 156–160) and it is based on a wrong notion of *muḍārabah*. Naiem Siddiqi is more elaborate, having separately discussed the depositor-bank and bank-businessman relations. He suggests a larger share of profit on long-term deposits, as compared to that on short term ones. Despite originality, his scheme also suffers from a misconception about *muḍārarbah* (419). Mahmud Ahmad bases his scheme on partnership. It is not entirely clear whether he distinguishes *muḍārabah* from *Shirkah* (168: 190–224). In Mawdūdī's scheme deposits will be accepted from the public on the basis of partnership, profits being distributed on these "shares". Deposits will also be accepted as "loans" repayable on demand and "*amānāt*" repayable on demand. The "loan" deposit funds will be utilised by the bank for making advances to businessmen on the basis of *muḍārabah*, a facility against which they will be obliged to give short-term interest-free loans from out of the same funds.

Mawdūdī has expressed himself against collection and disbursement of *Zakāt* funds by Islamic banks (133: 304–305).

Though a small booklet of 21 pages, Muhammad Uzair's "An Outline of Interestless Banking" has the distinction of being the first published work exclusively devoted to the subject by a professional economist (422). It contains the core of all the future proposals on the subject, basing depositor-banker and banker-businessmen relations on *muḍārabah*, which is defined correctly. It does not discuss central banking and takes the unrealistic stand that there should be no credit creation. It contains a good, though brief, discussion on international financial relations. In a later study (423) Uzair suggests centralised management of all foreign transactions in the banks of the state.

Ahmad Irshad's work (400) is also devoted exclusively to the subject and contains useful suggestions on the creation of reserve funds to absorb losses. It discusses Industrial Development banks, building corporations and consumption loans. The scheme suffers from a wrong notion about *muḍārabah* as sharing of both profits and losses by the business partners.

Abdul Hadi Ghanameh's 1968 paper on the subject (392) takes a line different from the one along which further thinking on the subject has developed. He relies on issue of common stock for long-term financing and the use of mutual funds for short-term financing. "A mutual fund is an investment company that buys the common stock of other industrial or commercial companies" (392: 96). Unfortunately, the comprehensive book which Ghanameh promises in this paper is not available to us to enable a detailed comparison between his scheme and the one that seems to have now found general acceptance.

Muslehuddin's[36] rejection of *muḍārabah* as the basis of interest-free banking is largely a product of his narrow legalistic approach to *muḍārabah* and of his failure to realise that the very concept of banking is bound to undergo a change once it is organised on a basis other than interest – a point ably argued by Tawfiq Shawi.[37] One such change is a sharp decline in the banks' lending activity and an increase in investment proper.[38] As a matter of fact, an interest-free bank cannot function as a purely commercial bank.

Muslehuddin's contention that the "Islamic bank will not be able to make advances to the concerns which have already invested capital of their own . . . for it will be quite against the principle of *muḍārabah*,[39] has no basis in Islamic jurisprudence and ignores the evidence cited in favour of the contrary from all the four schools of Islamic Law" (176: 72–85).

Another argument against the feasibility of *muḍārabah* is fear of fraudulent practices by banks' business partners who may understate their profits. This view has been controverted by pointing out the possibility of financial and management audit taking care of such practices. It has also been argued that firms failing to report good profits will lose the chances of getting more bank advances and this would serve as a deterrent to such practices.[40]

As regards the supply of short-term credit in an interest-free system it is recognised by almost every writer on the subject that *muḍārabah* can be a basis of such credit only to a limited extent. This does not, however, preclude other solutions as discussed below.

Having rejected *muḍārabah*, Muslehuddin fails to provide an alternative basis for interest-free banking. As banking for him means commercial banking, he ends up with a plea for allowing the banks to realise "service charges" on loans.[41] The main issue of intermediation between savers and investors on a basis other than fixed-interest payment remains unresolved.

The view that *muḍārabah* cannot provide an alternative to interest in the reorganisation of banking has also been expressed by Dr Mahmud Abu Saud on a different ground.[42] He thinks such a reorganisation will lead to the emergence of a "black market" in which interest will reappear.[43] Should the authorities succeed in enforcing the legal prohibition of interest successfully, savers will prefer the stock market and buy shares rather than deposit in *muḍārabah* banks.[44] Hoarding will increase and the monetary authority will be constrained to create more and more cash.[45] This, coupled with the increased demand for interest-free loans and the possibility of the sudden release of the hoarded cash on the stock exchange will pose a constant threat of inflation to the system.[46]

His own solution to these dangers lies in *Zakāt* which can be best applied by taxing money in circulation in a way similar to that suggested by Silvio Gessel.[47] We have already examined this suggestion above. It is obvious that Abu Saud has not cared to examine in detail the recent elaborations of the *muḍārabah*-based model of banking, briefly discussed below. His reference to this model as the "Mawdūdī-Qureshi School"[48] and his failure to take notice of the more systemic works appearing in the sixties and seventies bears this out.

A mature and comprehensive model of interest-free banking has resulted from works appearing in the late sixties by the late Dr. Abdullah al Araby (384), Siddiqi (417), Bāqir al Ṣadr (387) and Najjār (411). Followed by the Egyptian study in 1972 and the deliberation at the Karachi Conference of the Finance Ministers of the Islamic Countries in 1970, they lead us to the adoption of the charter of the Islamic Development Bank in 1974, which is the first major institution of its kind in history. In between we have the "Kuwaiti Investment House" project (405) and some periodical literature contributed by Shalbi (415), Mahmud Ahmad (628), Huda (397), Mannan (407), Muhammad Uzair (420; 421) and Ibrahim Dasooqi Abaza (381).

A. Mannan's textbook on Islamic Economics (132) has a separate chapter on the subject and Dr. Issa Abdouh has also written on the subject (382; 505).

More contributions have been made during the early seventies, including fairly comprehensive studies by Gharib al-Gammal (391), Mustafa Abdullah al-Hamshari (396) and Sami Hamūd,[49] besides the papers presented at the Makka Conference on Islamic Economics.

With the exception of Najjār's scheme, the first mentioned works conceive the bank mainly as a financial intermediary mobilising savings from the public on the basis of profit-sharing (*muḍārabah*) and making advances to entrepreneurs on the same basis. Profits of enterprise are shared by the bank according to a mutually agreed percentage. The bank shares these profits with depositors in the *muḍārabah* accounts according to a percentage announced by the bank in advance. Liability to loss in capital in the bank-entrepreneur deal attaches to the bank, though the bank is not likely to incur losses on the totality of its advances due to diversification of investments. Depositors in *muḍārabah* accounts can be absolved of the risk of loss, attaching to them in principle, by a number of practical devices. A different position is taken by Bāqir which is noted below. The banks shall also accept deposits in current accounts with the promise to pay on demand. No profits are to be paid to such depositors from whom a service charge may or may not be collected. The bank shall be obliged to grant short-term interest-free loans on a limited scale.

This being the essential core of the model, individual contributions have special features to which we turn now.

Najjār's banks are institutions designed to promote savings and effect their useful employment in the rural sector. They would be actively involved in developmental projects resorting to partnership, instead of *muḍārabah*. They have a "Social Service Fund" attracting *Zakāt* donations from the public and organising social services in the locality. They are a decentralised chain of institutions sharing the features of a local bank, a co-operative society and a social service organisation. Najjār does not discuss the other issues involved in commercial banking and central banking. He regards the reorganisation of banks without interest as part of the larger issue of restructuring the backward economies of the Islamic countries so that stagnation is ended, dynamism introduced and the process of development started, utilising Islamic values and traditions. The model of interest-free banking he presents is incidental to this larger theme.

Bāqir's work is a response to a questionnaire by a group of people in Kuwait who wanted to know how they could launch a banking company without interest. He presumed that he had to take as given the actual reality obtaining in Kuwait and elsewhere, that the rest of the system continues on un-Islamic lines, and the other banks and financial institutions with which the proposed bank would have to interact and compete continue to function on the basis of interest (387: 57). Accordingly his work does not answer the theoretical but larger question: how banks would function in an interest-free Islamic society. His frame of reference also excluded any discussion on credit control, consumer finance and finance for the government. Credit creation and financial papers are discussed in the very limited context of the operation of a single interest-free bank surrounded by a sea of interest-based institutions.

Unlike Najjār's banks, Bāqir's bank is a financial intermediary not directly participating in productive enterprise. Another significant feature of his bank is that depositors are absolved of the liability to loss, even in principle (387: 72, 187). He is mostly concerned, however, with the juristic justification of this guarantee and does not go into its economic rationale. This preoccupation with the legality rather than economics of the various provisions he has suggested has a deep impact on his entire work. For example, he discusses the various "valid" ways of the bank charging a fee (*Ji'āla*), which appear to be devious methods of ensuring a reasonable income to the bank itself – something to which a straightforward approach is also possible. He has even suggested that the bank make a deposit with some other (interest-based) bank in order to earn interest to meet a particular need (387: 104). Such a suggestion may not be morally repugnant to some people, but what is important for this study is its irrelevance for Islamic economics where what matters are viable alternatives to the present arrangements that have universal validity.

As exemplified by Bāqir's Appendices three and five, his keenness to absolve the depositors of even the theoretical liability to losses has given rise to serious difficulties relating to the legal status of the bank and justification of its share in profits. It is no longer the working partner (*'Āmil*) in relation to the depositors and the capitalist partner in relation to the businessmen, in *muḍārabah* contracts – a position it enjoys in the models suggested by Siddiqi and Abdullah al-Araby. He seeks to resolve this difficulty by relying on particular juristic opinions whose general acceptability is very doubtful. Kahf rightly notes "the suggested application of the principle of the prize, *Ji'āla* as called in Islamic jurisprudence, as percentage of the time deposit bears only a formal difference from interest and I could not find any difference between them as far as content is concerned", and that "to have a workable set up in the long run being built on legal tricks as part of its structure does not seem to me logically sound" (612: 91–92).

Though the major part of Abdullah al-Araby's paper deals with the evils of contemporary banking, his brief discussion on interest-free banking contains the essential core of the model stated above. Besides, he has also discussed international banking, agricultural banks, industrial banks and savings banks.

Siddiqi is mainly concerned with the economics of interest-free banking, having disposed of the juristic issues in a separate work (249). He has full length discussion on the creation and control of credit, consumer finance and finance for the government and, provision of short-term interest-free loans to business. He introduces certain financial papers to replace bonds and securities. His main contribution lies in a number of novel suggestions relating to central banking.

> "The central bank will offer refinance facilities against interest-free loans made by the commercial banks, in case these banks need additional cash to maintain their liquidity. The extent of accommodation provided by the central bank will be fixed as a ratio to loans made by commercial banks" (158: 105).

It is pointed out that the "refinance ratio" would serve as a means for contracting credit in inflationary situations and as an instrument of selective credit control, as different refinance ratios could be fixed with respect to loans given to different sectors of the economy (158: 105).

Siddiqi suggests the use of "shares" issued by the government for financing public sector enterprises as a means of open market operations by the central banks (417: 123–129). Loan Certificates of various denominations and different maturities, to be issued by the government, are suggested as a means of providing short-term finance for it. He suggests tax concessions as an incentive to the "buyer" of these certificates (417: 149–182). He has also suggested how incentives could be built into the system in order to make the banks provide short-term interest-free loans for business (417: 44–60). The problem how to ensure an equilibrium between the demand for interest-free loans and their supply has been discussed by Siddiqi in his recent paper.[50] Much of the demand for call money and very short-term loans emanates from within the financial sector itself and is likely to be eliminated as that sector shrinks in consequence of the abolition of interest. In the production sector, the total demand for short-term credit depends on the volume of long-term investment and the extent of trade credit (credit by one firm to another). Credit needs for the week or the month can be estimated at the macro-level. This could be done by the central bank – which would then ensure a supply commensurate with the demand by manipulating the "refinance ratio" and the "lending ratio". The task of allocating these loanable funds at the micro-level would then be performed by individual banks on the following criteria:

(1) Specific credit needs of a firm.
(2) Social priority attaching to the enterprise.
(3) Nature of the security offered against the loan.
(4) Whether the credit seeker has also obtained long-term advances from the bank for the same enterprise.
(5) Annual, monthly or weekly average of the applicants balance in current account with the bank.

It is within the competence of the Central Bank to exercise direct and indirect influence on banks' decisions on the second ground. Discriminatory use of the refinance ratio is a case in point. Banks are expected to prefer good securities over the not so good and patronise client firms over enterprises in which they have no stakes. A credit seeker's average balances in the current account may provide a basis for overdraft facilities – one form in which short-term credit is granted.

"The Egyptian Study on the Establishment of the Islamic Banking System" envisages a *Zakāt* Fund and a "local and public Islamic Fund", besides organising the normal banking functions on the basis of *muḍārabah*. While the essential core of the model remains the same as stated above, the proposed scheme has a number of distinguishing features.

Depositors in the current accounts are offered, besides being free from service charges, "a part of the profits due to the bank as its contribution" (390: 20). They are given priority in banking services such as "accepting bills of exchange" without interest. Depositors in "savings accounts" are offered overdraft facility, without interest, as well as other services such as letters of credit and acceptance of their bills of exchange, besides their due share in profits on the basis of *muḍārabah* (390: 21).

As regards interest-free loans to the public, they may be given out of *Zakāt* funds. Regarding bills of exchange two ways are suggested. The bank may give cash to the creditor and become a sharer in the profits of the buyer, on the basis of *muḍārabah*. Alternatively, it may cash the bill (which amounts to an interest-free loan to the buyer) provided the parties concerned have a current account with the banks with an average annual balance amounting to a certain percentage of the value of the bill (390: 25). The second method is recommended only in case the first is not feasible. It might be noted that Mawdūdī (521) and Siddiqi (419) had suggested the same.

Ali Abdur Rasul allows discount on bills of trade.[51] The legal principle involved in "leaving a part of a loan to (be appropriated by) the one who gets that loan repaid (by the borrower) as a reward of this service of securing the repayment".[52] It follows that if a loan is not actually repaid no reward can be paid.[53] This view does not find support in the literature for the obvious reason that it amounts to charging interest on the advance made against a bill of exchange. While Ali Abdur Rasul's reference to Maliki jurists deserves consideration by experts on Islamic law, a look at the economic implications of his suggestions is more appropriate for us in this study. It would not be objectionable if a reasonable service charge was allowed to the bank which makes an interest-free loan against a bill of exchange, subject to the condition that the borrower will repay the loan if the bill is not honoured by the drawee on maturity. The intent and impact of a discount is different, being similar to interest on the sum lent, irrespective of profit or loss in the business which is financed. Ali Abdur Rasul says nothing as to the rate of this discount, maybe its determination is left to the market, as is the rate of interest. Some writers have rightly pointed out that a profit arrangement should be possible in case of most of the bills of exchange.

Uzair thinks the annual rate of return in an enterprise can be applied for calculating the returns on advances made for a period of one to three months.[54] Alternatively we can try to determine the specific rate of return on the funds advanced. But it may not be possible to do so in many cases. For short-term loans for less than a month, Uzair suggests "service charges" on a per transaction basis.[55] The bank would not get any reward for lending as service charges will have to correspond to the actual costs of servicing these loans. Uzair has rejected the idea of arranging the supply of short-term credit as a free service on the ground that "the solution for a business problem has to be found on business lines rather than as a goodwill gesture".[56] One wonders how lending could be a business proposition once interest is abolished. Defining business as an activity directed at profits, a "business loan" is a contradiction in terms as a "loan" cannot carry a profit under Islamic law. The need to "modify the conceptual framework of economics to suit the requirements of Islamic economics"[57] is not confined to the concept of capital alone. The concept of "loan" also qualifies for this purpose.[58]

The problem of bad debts is solved by means of "Co-operative Insurance" to which "borrowers contribute a certain sum of money to cover the possible risk" (390: 43). *Zakāt* funds provide the other source out of which bad debts can be recovered.

Local banks may carry out direct investment besides advancing capital on the basis of *muḍārabah.*

The Egyptian study also spells out the salient features of central banking and international banking. The International bank would serve as a link between the national banking, commercial, developmental and *Zakāt*-based institutions in Muslim countries. It would finance commercial and developmental institutions in these countries. It would also organise commercial exchange between Muslim and non-Muslim countries, besides functioning as a clearing house for intra-Islamic transactions. The study also envisages the setting-up of an investment and development body of Islamic countries.

The "Kuwaiti Investment House" project which antedates the Egyptian study, and also the works of al-Araby and Siddiqi, was much limited in scope (405). It was to be a joint stock banking institution making diversified investments on the basis of *muḍārabah*. An outstanding feature of that project was its elaborate scheme of precautionary reserves and profit distribution designed to protect the interests of the depositors and share-holders. It envisaged collection and disbursement of *Zakāt* funds and the supply of interest-free loans on a limited scale. Recently a number of banks have been established which are committed to eschew interest and promote Islamic ideals, the foremost being the Islamic Development Bank at Jeddah.

B: The Islamic Development Bank

The purpose of the bank is "to foster economic development and social progress of member countries and Muslim Communities individually as well as jointly in accordance with the principles of the *Sharī'ah*" (389: Article 1). It will "participate in equity capital of productive projects and enterprises in member countries", "invest in economic and social infra-structure projects in member countries by way of participation or other financial arrangements", "make loans to the private and public sectors for the financing of productive projects, enterprises and programmes" and "establish and operate special funds for specific purposes including a Fund for assistance to Muslim communities in non-member countries" (Article 2, i–vii). It will also operate Trust Funds, accept deposits and raise funds in any other manner. It will provide technical assistance to member countries and assist in promotion of foreign trade, especially in capital goods, among member countries (Article 2: vii, ix). It intends "to co-operate . . . with all bodies, institutions and organisations having similar purposes, in pur-suance of international economic co-operation" (Article 2, xii). An important function of the bank shall be "to undertake research for enabling the economic, financial and banking activities in Muslim countries to conform to *Sharī'ah*" (Article 2: xi).

"The authorised capital stock of the Bank will be two thousand million (2,000,000,000) Islamic Dinars . . ." (Article 4, 6), one Islamic Dinar having the value of one special Drawing Right of the IMF (Article 4a).

As to financing "the Bank shall seek to maintain a suitable ratio between equity investment made in, and loans granted to, member countries" (Article 16, 4). "The Bank shall retain the option to sell its equity participation" (Article 17, 4). Normally it will not provide loans to an enterprise in whose equity it has participated (Article 17, 6). It shall "seek to maintain reasonable diversification in its equity investment" (Article 17, 8).

"The bank shall levy a service fee to cover its administrative expenses" (Article 20, 3).

Regarding the distribution of profits it has been provided that "no part of the net income or surplus of the Bank shall be distributed to members by way of profit until the General Reserve of the Bank shall have attained the level of twenty five per cent of the subscribed capital" (Article 42, 1). This distribution "shall be made in proportion to the number of shares held by each member" (389: Article 42, 4).

Discussing the distinctive features of the Islamic Development Bank in the light of its Articles of Association and the highlights of the Islamic economic and banking systems, Shawi[59] points out that the crucial decision not to operate on the basis of interest has led the IDB to devise unique methods not traditionally adopted by development banks, such as participation in development projects at all levels – supply of capital, management and sharing of profits and losses.

The decision to attract deposits from the public (e.g. through issue of investment certificates) is another unconventional step the IDB has taken in view of the fact that it cannot go to the money market to obtain funds.

Shawi also points out the important place given to social progress side by side with economic development. This again is unique as conventional banks are financial institutions interested in profits or in the case of development banks, in "economic" development. The IDB is an expression of the solidarity of the Islamic peoples. The concept of the Islamic Dinar is a pointer towards a currency union of the Islamic countries.[60] Its adoption as the unit of account will protect the bank from the consequences of price fluctuations in the countries with which it is dealing. The provision that the value of the Islamic Dinar equals the value of one SDR is transitional. It suits the member countries under the present circumstances, but they can specify its value otherwise if and when they find it advisable to do so.

The evil consequences of interest have been well known to the economists as well as the laymen, but they had no alternative before them in banking and finance. Attempts at escaping from these evils through co-operative institutions of various types had failed because they catered only to the interests of particular groups of people and had to work as a part of the all-pervading interest-based system. The significance of the Islamic Development Bank lies in being the heralder of a viable and just alternative.

With the huge amount of investible funds available out of the oil revenues of some of the members of the Islamic Development Bank, and the vast opportunities of development waiting for investment in Asia and Africa, the stated objectives of the Bank charge it with great responsibilities and justifiably raise many expectations. Only the future can reveal how far these potentialities could be actualised. It seems however advisable to work for a network of similar institutions throughout the individual countries and communities involved in the process. Many writers mentioned above advocate this step. It is hoped that the subject will increasingly attract expert attention, now that an impetus has been provided by the establishment of the IDB.

The IDB has already gone into operation and a report on the first year of its working is available.[61] Large unused resources are understandably causing a problem as Islamic avenues for the profitable utilisation are not immediately available. Yet the Bank has successfully participated in a few projects in Algeria and elsewhere.

The establishment of the IDB has been followed by a few more Islamic Banks at Dubai (386), Cairo and Khartoum. The Dubai Islamic Bank established in 1975 has successfully completed the first year of its operation. It has mostly gone into real estate business and construction projects. No reports are available on the one established at Cairo in 1976 and its counterpart at Khartoum. The Philippines Amanah Bank has also been working without interest as a subsidiary of the Central Bank of the Philippines which, as the custodian of its reserves, earmarks the interest due for a special fund for Muslim welfare.

Industrial Relations, Labour and Population Policy

Those who have paid special attention to labour and industrial relations emphasise dignity of labour in Islam, the religious significance of good, honest work, and the labour's right to a decent wage commensurate with the average standards of living in the society. There is great emphasis on co-operation between labour and enterprise and on mutual consultation as a mode of decision making. Hameedullah (433), Yusufuddin (165: 365–388), Gamaluddin (425; 426), Chapra (115), Ṭaḥāwī (77), Ali Abdur Rasul,[62] Abdul Hadi[63] and Assal[64] are some of the writers sharing this emphasis. Abdul Majeed Qureshi, the *Jamā'at-i-Islāmī* labour expert in Pakistan, makes a strong plea for just wages for the labour and that the privileged position of capital be taken away from it and be restored back to labour. " 'Depreciation' of labour must be paid for: just as the expenses for maintenance, repair and reconditioning of buildings and machinery are accounted for in the expenditure of the business, similarly maintenance of health and medical aid should be fully accounted for in regular expenditure" (341: 27). Qureshi reserves half of the total profits of a concern for labour and would also like to see labour own 60 per cent shares in the concern at which they are working (441: 26–28). His notion of just wages are, however, regarded as undefinable by Faridi (431: 64) who thinks

Qureshi had adopted the Marxian approach. Shafi Malik too regards Qureshi to be vague and confused (435: 90). But the *Jamā'at-i-Islāmī* Pakistan Economic Committee report (126) echoes some of Qureshi's ideas. The just wages are defined by the report as a need-based minimum plus a differential according to nature of work, technical competence, course of work, productivity and profitability of the industry. These wages must be supplemented by a number of other facilities: residential, medical, educational, recreational, etc. Labour is also entitled to a bonus or profits and to the produce of the industry at commercial rates, if not free. He should be given financial aid or interest-free loans (repayable subject to capacity to pay) in case of emergency. The idea of making labourers shareholders in the concerns in which they are working also finds strong support in the report (126: 28–32). Mawdūdī has also endorsed this view "so that they (labourers) become interested in the growth of the industry in which they are employed" (51: 405). The suggestion finds a place in the *Jamā'at-i-Islāmī* Pakistan Manifesto for the 1970 elections (125: 29).

Examining the notion of "just wages" as elaborated in the above-mentioned report, Muhammad Akram finds its economic rationale dubious and suggests another model in which the wage rate is linked with the profits of the firm (613: 43–44). Distinguishing between need-based minimum wages and ideal wages which would "bridge the gulf between the living conditions of the employers and the employees" Chapra leaves the actual wages to be determined between these two limits "by the interaction of supply and demand, the extent of economic growth, the level of moral consciousness in the Muslim society and the extent to which the state plays its legitimate role" (115: 12–13).

Population Policy

Population control through family planning has been one of the most controversial subjects in the literature. The permission or otherwise of birth control by individuals in certain circumstances, in the light of the Qur'ān and the *Sunnah*, though relevant for this controversy, is not the matter that concerns us here. From the viewpoint of Islamic Economics we are interested mainly in two points. Does there exist an economic case for population control? And if it does, is family planning permitted by Islam, as a means to this end? It is only on these points that we will record the various opinions below.

Writing in the late thirties Mawlana Mawdūdī strongly opposed family planning. There is no economic case for population control. The argument based on scarcity of resources is dismissed as unrealistic and amounting to a loss of faith in God (458: 104–130). Population control has no place in Islamic culture (458: 67–80). God is the real planner of the human population (458: 150–153). Birth control leads to many physiological, moral and social ills (458: 81–98). Economically too, it is harmful. It will decrease aggregate demand, reduce employment and cause depression (458: 99–100). As to the argument that family planning enables better nourishment and education of children, Mawdūdī refers to the beneficial effects of adversity and wants on human character (458: 132).

According to him the only solution Islam presents for the problem of increasing world population is "augmentation and full utilisation of the resources of His bounty that God has created and a perpetual effort at discovering hidden resources" (457).

Endorsing Mawdūdī's views, Khurshid Ahmad (454), notes that the Malthusian prognosis on population growth has been belied by history (454: 168–172). There was never an economic case for birth control. This movement is a tool of Western imperialism to check the population of poor nations from rising and posing a threat to Western domination (454: 176–180). "Increase in population is generally beneficial economically" (454: 189). He has little faith in population projections. "If the organisational structure of the economy is developed in accordance with population there is no question of the population problem arising economically". . . . There is abundance of natural resources . . . if only the whole of the world was treated as one unit. "The real cause of economic decadence in the world is the selfishness of the Western man" (454: 191). "The real solution lies in improving economic and cultural resources and increasing production" (454: 201).

Similar views have been expressed by Sheikh Abū Zahra who opposed population control through family planning on religious grounds (448; 449). He, along with Sheikh Khidr Husain, and most of those participating in a symposium held at Cairo in the early fifties (459) took this stand while allowing birth control for individuals in certain circumstances. The same is true of the deliberations at the international Islamic Congress at Cairo in 1965 (211). This is also the dominant view in India and Pakistan.

The International Planned Parenthood Federation organised a conference on this issue in December 1971 at Rabāṭ, of which the complete proceedings are now available in two volumes covering 1000 pages (452). Most of the participants considered population control through family planning as lawful in Islam and many regarded it as having become a necessity under the present circumstances. These scholars have discussed in detail the relevant issues of jurisprudence and the points of law involved. An appendix quotes a number of *fatwā* by eminent authorities on Islamic law such as Sheikh Abdul Majeed Saleem (which, however, touches only the individual aspect of the matter), Sheikh Mahmud Shaltūt (which goes only a little further), Sheikh Hasan Mamoon (which permits family planning but warns against coercion) and Sheikh Abdullah al Qalqīlī (which allows population control through family planning) (452: 541–566). Those who participated in the conference and supported family planning and population control include Ahmad al-Sharbasi (468) and Salam Madkoor (456). Another eminent scholar supporting population control through family planning is al Bahi al Khauli who declares that it is open to the rulers to appeal to the community to adopt this method, and to provide facilities for the same, when they find the social, economic, political and external circumstances of the community calling for such a policy (455: 192).

From among Islamic Economists who have discussed this issue, A. Mannan (132: 117–126, 138–147) admits that the issue is controversial, but he recommends population control through family planning, under the present circumstances and advances social, physiological and eugenic reasons in support

Growth and Development

That one of the main objectives of modern Islamic states will be to achieve rapid economic development (221, II: 123–141) is a point stressed by all recent writings on the subject. Economic backwardness of the present-day Muslim countries and communities is seen as a hindrance to the fulfilment of their Islamic role in the world and a blot on their Islamic identity. What, then, is the strategy of economic development in the Economic system of Islam?

Some writers, including Akram (483) and Fanjari (477; 478) lay the main emphasis on the transformation of man, and the ethos of an Islamic society.

Abāẓa (473) like Fanjari (477) sees a great role for Islam in economic development as it regards developmental efforts to be *jihād*. Once that idea catches on we can expect big results. Ṭaḥāwī also thinks that invoking the Islamic injunctions in the context of developmental efforts will prove to be the most effective way of generating a powerful movement for economic development among the Muslim masses (77, II: 32).

According to Abāẓa (473: 1127) the *Sharī'ah* calls for interaction and co-ordination between production and distribution in the framework of comprehensive economic planning, but conditions prevailing in the Muslim countries at present necessitate that priority be given to directing maximum efforts towards increasing production. Distribution can take priority when the fruits of these efforts are available. It is not the distribution of a static quantity but that of a dynamic and growing one that is visualised by Islam.

Malik ben Nabi (484: 51) questions the thesis that the key to economic dynamism is capital investment. The source of dynamism lies in man and in the collective will of the society. Islamic strategy for economic development should not blindly accept the supremacy of capital lest it is frustrated because of capital shortage in Muslim countries. It should rely on awakening the man in the land of Islam and should generate a will for the performance of the Islamic mission for which economic development has become a necessary prerequisite. "The crucial issue in the world of Islam is not that of availability of capital, but that of harnessing the social forces: man, land and time, in a project propelled by a cultural will undeterred by any difficulties" (484: 84).

Malik ben Nabi regrets to note that countries in the Third World focus their attention on capital in planning for economic development. As they do not have enough capital they must borrow from others and depend on foreign expertise which has no intimate knowledge of the local situation. This strategy has failed to deliver the goods. He cites the experience of point Four programme to prove his point (484: 89–90).

As a recent example of economic regeneration based on the cultural will of the people and a strategy tailored for the local conditions Malik ben Nabi refers to China (484: 85, 90).

Malik ben Nabi is highly appreciated by Austervy who has some important points to make in an essay devoted to Islam and Economic Development (475). He finds the Islamic temperament uncongenial for the dynamic entrepreneurial role of Schumpeter's egotistic and highly individualistic innovators. The unsatiable urge for profits, the propensity to take risk and the will to dominate which lay at the root of the economic revolution in the West are conspicuous by their absence from the Islamic personality (475: 38–43). The motive force for economic development must, therefore, emerge from religion itself. Nourished by a desire to recapture the past glory of Islam, its mode has to be collective rather than individualistic, in consonance with the nature of the desire and the temperament of the Muslim *Ummah*. Economic development in an Islamic society has to be a co-operative affair (475: 96–113). He envisages a significant role for planning in economic development in Islam.

Faridi refutes the view that Islamic values are inimical to economic progress and points out that "the present acquiescence in established institutions and practices has been borne of internal political organisations, colonialism and other vested interests. Islam has little to do with it" (479: 53).

Kalim Siddiqi's Islamic development plan regards the "socialisation of surplus value" as the crucial issue and declares that "only Islam can motivate voluntary sacrifice of it by the peasant and labourer" (494: 26–27). It is for the Islamic State to ensure correct motivation. He concludes on the need for a new Islamic model of industrialisation, finding the contemporary approach inept and unproductive.

While the afore-mentioned writers envisage a process of economic development that will be distinctively Islamic in view of the incentives, the collective mode and the way distributive justice is inalienably associated with the process of growth, there are others who regard development dependent on certain economic processes, of savings, investment and technological advancement and proceed to declare that all these shall find sufficient encouragement in the Islamic society to ensure growth. Listing the principal causes of growth as the effort to economise, knowledge of production and increasing amount of resources per head, Marghoob Qureshi cites the Qur'ān and the *Sunnah* to emphasise that Islam ensures all of them (492).

Zubair[65] finds Islam conducive to all the essential prerequisites of growth: it encourages accumulation of capital as well as human capital formation which leads to expansion in productive capacity. The resulting rise in income leads to increase in consumption as well as investment as Islam discourages idle cash balances.

Economic development in an Islamic framework has recently attracted several writers including Namiq[66], Khurshid[67] and Siddiqi.[68] Khurshid Ahmad notes the "crisis and revaluation" through which Development Economics is presently passing. Admitting the importance of technological relationship in any plan for development he stresses the point that technological decisions are made in the context of value relations. Man is the active agent of change, and change in the hearts of men is no less important than change in the environment.

He includes development of human personality as well as continuous sustained increase in national product with the correct product mix in goals of development policy in Islam. In this context he emphasises production of necessaries, defence goods and capital goods. Improvement in the quality of life involving distributive justice and employment come next. Balanced development, evolution of indigenous technology and "re-education of national dependency on the outside world and greater integration within the Muslim world" are the other goals listed.[69] Siddiqi regards increase in production, distributive justice, environmental balance and improvement in the quality of life in the cultural sense as the four necessary dimensions of development in an Islamic framework. Discussing the process of development in some detail and focussing on Africa and South and South East Asia, he concludes by enumerating the "main steps required for initiating and accelerating all-sided development" as under:

(1) Transforming the individual through a massive educational drive, aiming at 100 per cent literacy, commitment to social goals and inculcation of Islamic values.
(2) Strengthening the Muslim states through a powerful Islamic movement resulting in popular democratic Islamic regimes committed to the Islamic mission.
(3) Creating a popular will to develop, under the leadership of the state supported by the socially-oriented entrepreneurs, involving the

masses in productive work and fuller utilisation of natural and human resources.

(4) Curbing conspicuous consumption, both private and public, and guaranteeing a minimum level of consumption to all, accompanied by fiscal discipline ensuring the channelisation of the additional incomes generated to capital formation.

(5) Regional planning to ensure economic co-ordination of the countries in North Africa and South and South East Asia to effect a balanced development of the entire region making it self sufficient in food and agricultural products and most of the manufactured goods.

(6) Decreasing the dependence of the region on the developed countries by providing aid to the oil-poor countries out of the surpluses of the oil-rich countries and promoting trade between the countries of the region.

(7) Reorganising the financial institutions to free them from instruments of exploitation and the means through which the few centres of high finance exercise control on the economics and societies of the poor countries.

(8) National planning within the framework of the regional plan to ensure growth with justice, environmental balance and improvement of the cultural life.

(9) Increasing co-operation with all the developing countries of the world through trade, aid and other suitable means with a view to decreasing inequalities between nations.

(10) Vigorous participation in the efforts to secure a new world order ensuring peace, progress and social justice.

IV

ISLAMIC CRITIQUE OF CONTEMPORARY ECONOMIC THEORIES AND SYSTEMS

Criticism of Capitalism and Communism dates back quite early in the literature on Islamic Economics. It started during the twenties and the thirties and it was largely the challenge of these alien economic philosophies which provided the impetus for the first works on the subject that appeared during the fourth decade of this century.

Both *laissez faire* capitalism and Marxian socialism have been subjected to severe criticism. This criticism is generally based on the end products of these systems, in terms of injustice, human suffering and loss of individual freedom. But the philosophical and theoretical bases of the two systems have also been examined and refuted. The philosophy of Natural Law,

Individualism, Utilitarianism and the view that pursuit of self-interest by individuals results in ensuring the social good, have all been rejected as baseless. Similarly the Labour Theory of Value, the view that forces of production determine relations of production which determine "the superstructure of values" and the Marxian Theory of state have also been criticised and rejected. The two systems have been characterised as two extreme and unbalanced approaches to solving man's economic problems and Islam has been projected as the Middle Way assimilating the good points in both the systems and free from the imbalances from which they suffer. The great poet of Islam Muhammad Iqbal[70] (d. 1938) had already popularised this approach long before scholars and journalists took up the subject.

Capitalism

Mawdūdī (607: 26–51) mentions private property, freedom of enterprise, profit motive as the sole incentive, competition, discrimination between the rights of the employees and those of the employer, reliance on natural forces for growth and the principle of non-intervention by the state as the basic tenets of modern capitalism. He recognises an element of truth in these principles but finds them carried to extreme by capitalism. Undue emphasis on rights of individual ownership and freedom of enterprise played havoc during the industrial revolution causing widespread suffering and privation. The legalisation of usury added to the anti-social character of capitalistic enterprise leading to concentration of wealth and pauperisation of the masses. Undue emphasis on self-interest and the profit motive produced a society devoid of humane character, brotherhood, sympathy and co-operation. He reviews the reforms introduced in capitalistic countries allowing an active role for the state and a better deal for labour. Despite these changes, large-scale unemployment and the existence of unsatisfied needs when production resources lie unutilised, the occurrence of trade cycles and the domination of society by usurious financiers continue today (607: 100–106).

Mahmud Ahmad rejects capitalism's claim of being a self-adjusting process leading to maximum satisfaction of human wants, by pointing out the chaos it has led to. Economic crises are sufficient to refute such a claim (168: 4–17). Quoting Halm, A. Mannan (132: 37–38) criticises capitalism due to its failure in maintaining full employment and ensuring free competition.

The main weakness of capitalism according to Bāqir is its failure on the distribution front. Its emphasis on more and more production is misplaced as more production does not ensure greater welfare (171: 240–241). Mabid Mahmud (624) and Chawdhri (620) make the additional point that it is through equitable distribution of the social product that welfare and satisfaction can be ensured and the size of the cake is not always relevant in this context. Every increase in the size of the cake in the capitalist system decreases human welfare and satisfaction as it increases the gap between the rich and the poor.

A strong condemnation of capitalism comes from Syed Qutb (500) who finds it to be thoroughly inhuman and un-Islamic.

Modern Theories of Interest

While the main targets of attack have been the absolute conception of individual ownership rights and the unrestrained nature of freedom of enterprise in capitalism and the cut-throat competition, the inevitable rise of monopoly capitalism, exploitation of labour and emergence of imperialism, the most criticised institution is interest which is regarded as the source of many evils in the system. While we summarise the Islamic economists' views on the institution as such in the next chapter, here we note their criticism and rejection of the various theories which seek to explain and justify interest.

Mawdūdī (521) and Anwar Iqbal Qureshi (526) are the earliest contributors in this field in which Mahmud Ahmad (168), Issa Abdouh (504; 505), Mahmud Abu Saud[71] and Nasser A. Sheikh (154: 71–75) have also contributed.

Abstinence and waiting cannot entitle the capitalist to a reward unless it is proved that the use of borrowed capital necessarily results in profits. In the same manner merely taking a risk does not ensure augmentation of the capital risked. Productivity theory is without any proof as value-productivity of capital is subject to the uncertain conditions of demand and supply. Mawdūdī finds Time Preference and Liquidity theories as partly valid in so far as an *explanation* of interest in the modern economy is concerned. But an explanation does not amount to a *justification*. An institution can be justified only with reference to its role in society and its usefulness for mankind. Mawdūdī examines this role and finds interest to be the cause of many ills in society; economic and political as well as moral and spiritual.

Qureshi (526: 10–43) notes that there is no agreed theory of interest – a point emphasised by several writers on the subject. He criticises the classical theory of interest along familiar lines. Rejecting the Productivity Theory as circular in its reasoning and the Time Preference Theory as based on false psychological assumptions he finds the Monetary Theories of Interest in their neo-classical and Keynesian versions as less concerned with causes of existence of interest than with how its rate is determined. He quotes Keynes to establish the possibility and desirability of a zero rate of interest. Mahmud Ahmad (168) and Farid (514) cite Harrod to establish the same point. Siddiqi (158: 113–114) quotes Shackle to belittle the role of interest and underline its "paradoxical nature".

In his brilliant essay on "Semantics of the Theory of Interest" Mahmud

Ahmad (628)[72] notes the confusion that is found in economic literature between the terms profit and interest. He gives numerous excerpts from Smith, Ricardo, Say, Malthus, Sismondi, Marshall, Fisher and even Bhom Bawerk in this context. He distinguishes between the entirely different economic roles played by loan capital and risk capital. Defining capital as "that part of wealth which is used to create further wealth" he notes that "risk capital is that variety of capital which agrees to relate its reward for its service of participation in the productive process to the measure of value that its participation creates" (628: 179) but "loan capital dictates its price of participation in the shape of a fixed rate of interest. Its charge i.e. interest, is the first charge to be met out of the value of our product . . ." (628: 176). "Loan capital for this reason imparts a peculiar rigidity to the entire range of economic consideration, risk capital, on the other hand, projects a peculiar flexibility to the enterprises concerned. Loan capital by virtue of its interest, sets a limit to the marginal efficiency of productive effort, risk capital imposes no such limit and leaves it free to exploit all natural resources and employ all available manpower" (628: 176). He regards interest to be the "primary cause, with certain secondary causes which are themselves, reflex projections of this primary cause, which virtually perpetuates underemployment equilibrium". Interest raises prices, profits and rents (628: 182–187). Mahmud Ahmad examines the arguments in justification of interest by analogy with rent and hire and finds them faulty. As to rent he notes that land is essentially productive whereas money capital is not: "Money without labour will not produce anything at all. . . . Land even without labour will produce something, it may be only grass to graze cattle on or bushes to provide fuel" (628: 185).

In case of hire: "When there is loss by mischance or miscalculation, in the case of a hired item, it is the *lender* who suffers the loss; whereas in the case of money loan, every loss, whether by mischance, miscalculation or any other reason has to be borne by the *borrower*". He castigates Marshall for having invoked this false analogy between hire price and interest.

He concludes that interest is neither of the nature of profit nor of the nature of rent and hire. Mahmud Ahmad discusses the nature and purpose of savings and finds the claim that advancing savings as loan is equivalent to foregoing a need or that it involves a sacrifice, to be a false claim with no basis in reality (628: 191–192).

Uzair also notes that the origin of capital and the accompanying justification of its remuneration are derived from the concept of physical capital – capital goods – accumulated in the primitive society. When the same justification for reward is applied to money capital it creates confusion.[73] As stressed by several writers the uncertain world in which production takes place does not guarantee a positive value-productivity even to physical capital.[74]

A searching criticism of some recent attempts to justify interest has been made by Mahmud Abu Saud[75] who also warns "against the tendency of treating money capital as if it were capital goods or real assets, a tendency that has become quite frequent in modern literature".[76] He examines the views of Samuelson, Patinkin, Joe S. Bain besides those of Schumpeter and Keynes. Samuelson equates the price with the rental of use of money, giving the impression that to use the service of money is exactly as to use the service of a doctor. The obvious objections to treating interest as rent are that money as a medium of exchange is not supposed to depreciate and that you do not rent something that perishes or disappears once you use it.

Patinkin considers interest as one of the forms of income from property. The argument is fallacious as interest is paid not only before the realisation of income but also irrespective of such a realisation. Moreover, Patinkin's justification fails to cover the interest paid on consumption loans. Joe S. Bain equates the loanable funds with capital goods. Abu Saud points out that the owner of money capital is *not* the investor.

Of the two definitions of interest given by Keynes, the money rate and the commodity rate, the former is paramount to his time preference maxim as he considers that interest is the difference between the price of money today and its price at a future date. But what is that price? asks Abu Saud. "The only way to find the price of money is to define its purchasing power . . . this can be done for the present, but how can we find this price of money in the future?"[77]

Keynes implicitly mentioned another definition of interest, a definition more indicative about its *raison d'etre*. In the course of analysing the reasons that make money rates of interest more acceptable than commodity-rates, he mentioned that " . . . the power of disposal over an asset over a period may offer a potential *convenience* or *security*, which is not equal for assets of different kinds, though the assets themselves are of equal value. There is, so to speak, nothing *to show for this at the end of the period in the shape of output*, yet, it is something for which *people are ready to pay something*" (General Theory, p. 225). Is it a fact nowadays that we have more security in future payments in money than in any other asset? Or is it the contrary? It is of course more convenient to be paid in currency, but it is not safer at all, so much so that it would have been more true to say that the interest at present is a premium – not of security, but – of insecurity inherent in future money. Keynes went on describing his liquidity preference, ending by approving a "depreciating or stamped-money". If this is the case, then the whole concept of positive interest becomes void and the liquidity preference attribute would no longer be valid as a justification for interest.[78]

Turning to time preference Abu Saud notes that "the conception of future demand or the preference of present goods over future ones, seems to me more of an arbitrary postulate than a real fact".[79] With reference to Bhoem Bawerk's first two grounds of time preference he asks how come the lender charges a majoration because the *borrower* prefers present to the future? And what is the countervalue of the agio, or what right has the money lender acquired to entitle him to this extra amount?[80] As to the third ground, technical superiority of present over future goods, a reference is made to its refutation by Keynes. Further "it is extremely important to notice that neither Bhoem Bawerk nor Irving Fisher distinguished between *liquid* or *money* capital and *capital goods*,"[81] and in fact Fisher is telling us why there is interest by assuming the existence of interest, as the word "capitalized values" inevitably implies interest.[82] Thus the confusion between money capital and capital goods is the bane of all modern theories of interest.

To emphasise again the importance of discriminating between the two terms, one would simply consider the case of an investor who is in need of tangible assets (capital goods) and who goes into the market for buying them. The "price" is then negotiated on the basis of the conditions prevailing strictly in this specific market of capital goods. In course of settling the price of the purchased goods, the buyer takes into consideration the three Fisherian elements: time preferences, capital productivity and approximations or enterprise risks. On the sellers side there would be the cost of production, the profit, the risk (here represents the price of replacement plus the carrying cost plus obsolescence).

If the buyer has got the money in cash, the deal would be smoothly concluded. If he has no liquid means of exchange he will have to go to a money holder who would charge a price for the money needed. This new deal is completely different and independent from the first. To start with, there are no real goods involved, and if we apply the term "medium of exchange of a good for another" adopted by the neo-Keynesians, and taking for granted that money in this second transaction would be rendering a service to the investor by facilitating his deal, we are now talking of a different transaction of a different nature. Here we have the capital market where savings are mainly decided by incomes and where the final price – if it is a price at all – will be decided on elements other than the simple demand of investors.[83]

For Schumpeter the socially significant kind of interest is the payment made by the entrepreneurs to the capitalist for the use of purchasing power which enables him to earn profit. What if the entrepreneur fails to earn profit? asks Abu Saud. The argument is hardly convincing in periods of depression and cases of loss and failure. As to Schumpeter's argument that "the demand for productive loan funds with interest at zero would always be greater than supply which is always limited", Abu Saud regards it to be the old classical theory, linking saving and investment via interest, which has been refuted by Keynes.

Schumpeter implied that there would be no positive rate of interest unless there is either innovation or some positive demand for capital goods with marked time preference. Abu Saud regards it to be a description of the actual practice rather than a valid explanation or justification of interest. Would there be no innovation at zero rate of interest? he asks. In conclusion he notes that Schumpeter was convinced that interest is a tax on profits and suggests that "its elimination would be an extra stimulation to more developments as long as funds are available".[84]

Speculation and Forward Transactions

Another institution of capitalist economy severely criticised by Islamic economists is speculation. Many writers have briefly referred to this institution and have noted that Islam does not permit it.

Maulana Muhammad Taqī Amīnī, in a detailed juridical discussion on speculation and stock exchange transactions, declared purchase and sale on the stock exchange to be illegal (556: 118–155). Qureshi had also characterised speculation to be unlawful in Islam. He considers trade cycles to be the result of brisk activity of foreign transactions (526: 101–102). Naseer A. Sheikh (154: 128–135) regards speculation to be anti-social. He examines the arguments given in defence of forward trading and finds them to be unconvincing. A great harm done by speculation is that "money that ought to have been invested in industry and commerce finds its way into the speculative market where it is feeding disguised and parasitical workers like brokers and shrewd operators" (154: 132). A. Mannan (132: 195–197) thinks that "in so far as speculation renders social service by helping production and controlling sudden fluctuation of prices it is in conformity with the spirit of Islam". But speculators being interested in private gains create artificial scarcities which result in inflationary pressure on the economy". Such speculative practices, as well as forward transactions, were condemned by Islam.

Kahf notes (612: 75–76) that Islamic economists' disapproval of speculation is based on two reasons. Firstly, it is considered as a kind of gambling, and secondly, it involves a sale of what one does not own. Discussing speculation in the context of international monetary crises Akram notes that it is not generally acknowledged "that until speculation is retired, stability for the world economy would remain an illusion" (558: 15). Efficient arbiterage through time is, however, as much a social need as is the one through space, and the Islamic economists' discussion on speculation has yet to come to grips with this issue.

Lottery

Another modern institution attacked by our scholars is the system of lotteries. While the *ulema* giving their opinion on the subject have unanimously declared it to be unlawful on account of gambling, and have indicated the economic and social evils consequent upon the adoption of this method (560; 561; 562), a thorough analysis by some economist is still awaited.

Socialism and Communism

Islamic criticism finds Socialism in conflict with the basic requirements of the moral and spiritual growth of human personality, chief among them being freedom of choice and action. Private property and freedom of enterprise, within certain limits and subject to public good, are regarded essential for such freedom. Total nationalisation of means of production is considered to be incongruous with democracy which is an essential feature of the political structure of Islam. The methodology of change adopted by communism is bound to lead to a coercive regime. Materialism, class conflict and moral relativism, essential tenets of communism, are inimical to the Islamic way of life. As an economic system socialism is found to be wanting in many respects as it fails to answer important questions relating to organisation of society and strategy of economic development.

Exploitation of man by man cannot be eliminated by changing the hands that control the means of exploitation. The only way to achieve this end is a moral reorientation of the individuals which makes them servants of society and workers for the social good. This is what Islam does by relating man to God and making him live in accordance with His will so that he treats property as a trust and exercises his freedom with restraint. As a trustee of God he looks upon the welfare of fellow human beings as his own responsibility for which he will be accountable to Allah on the Day of Judgment. The extent of this accountability is directly related to the wealth and power possessed by one.

Mawdūdī, examining the various schools of socialism, finds that evolutionary socialism failed to make any headway and it was Communism that actually took roots. It succeeded in appropriating the Social Surplus for the state which could now use it for furthering the social good. Centralised planning succeeded in removing unemployment and decreasing waste. But this was achieved at a great cost in terms of human lives. Communism deprived people of their liberty and denied moral values. Corruption became rife and a totalitarian regime took recourse to more and more repressive measures. A sizeable portion of the social surplus had to be spent on internal security and defence (607: 52–83).

Bāqir regards the Marxian approach to be no less individualistic than that of capitalism, as it appeals to the self-interest of the have-nots to seize power and wealth from the capitalists. Real socialism required a change of attitude and not merely a change of the hands that wield power and wealth (171: 218).

Masud Alam Nadvi (589) regards the undue emphasis on distribution and the move to abolish private property to be mere reactions to the evils of capitalism. Man does not have to opt for such an extreme solution as the

Middle Path shown by Islam is sufficient to ensure the elimination of these evils and secure the legitimate ends of socialism.

Siddiqi examines and rejects the arguments in favour of socialisation of all means of production (221; I: 93–118) and concludes that individual ownership is a necessary condition for democracy and spiritual and moral growth (221, I: 119–124). A balanced approach would accommodate individual ownership under social supervision as well as socialisation whenever necessary.

Mirza Muhammad Husain condemns socialistic doctrines as they ferment class war (580). Dawālībi also finds instigation of the have-nots against the haves and a belief in the inevitability of class war to be the distinguishing features of Revolutionary Socialism (575). Abdul Hameed Siddiqi (181) refutes the Marxian theories and finds that Communism has created more problems than it has solved. Husain Khan (584: 198–284) seeks to establish, on the basis of the historical experience of Socialism, that it is a hindrance in economic development. Mahmud Ahmad (168: 77–78) regards the problem of efficiency as the greatest one faced by Communism which completely disregarded incentives and rewards. A. Mannan (132: 48–52) accuses Communism of having grossly over-emphasised the problem it sought to solve, with the result that the solutions are highly unrealistic and unworkable.

In his comprehensive study, Khurshid Ahmad accepts economic planning as a useful contribution of Socialism which should be assimilated by contemporary Islam without recourse to totalitarianism (584: 138). The bold and forward looking exposition of Islam's Economic System by Mustafa Sibai finds Islam to be far superior as a system ensuring social justice while upholding human dignity and liberty. Yet Muslims can benefit from the Communist experiment, as an economic system seeking to bring about social justice which was denied to mankind by Feudalism and Capitalism (70: 237–238).

Dialectical Materialism, Labour Theory of Value and Surplus Value

Time and space do not permit us to summarise Islamic criticism of the various Marxian theories. They have been examined in detail, among other writers, by Mazheruddin Siddiqi (595), Bāqir (171: 17–212), Taḥāwi (77: II: 111–196), Khurshid Ahmad (584: 15–160), Siddiqi (221, I: 96–112), Mirza Muhammad Husain (580: 18–20), Dawālībi (595) and Abāẓa (598).

Other Systems

Besides Capitalism, Socialism and Communism, Islamic writers have also criticised State Socialism, Fascism and Nazism (607: 84–95; 168: 136–168; 132: 53–60). These systems were reactions to the other systems, and they achieved very little, at great cost to humanity (for sake of brevity we do not go into details).

V

DEVELOPMENT OF ECONOMIC ANALYSIS IN THE ISLAMIC FRAMEWORK

As the number of trained economists taking up our subject increases analytical approach to the issues under discussion gains in strength. The generation represented by Dr. Anwar Iqbal Qureshi and Sheikh Mahmud Ahmad is followed by a number of younger economists like Khurshid Ahmad, Monzer Kahf, Abu Sulaiman, Muhammad Sakr, Anas Zarqā, Faridi, Chapra, Abdul Mannan, Masudul Alam Chawdhri, Uzair, Mohammad Akram and Siddiqi, who go further and deeper into the analysis of abolition of interest, *Zakāt* and *muḍārabah* and analyse the behaviour of economic units under the influence of Islamic teachings. Though most of these attempts are still rudimentary, they indicate uncharted explorations which might lead to new insights and better policy prescriptions. It is the promise and not the performance that persuades us to pay closer attention to the contributions relevant for this section. This we do under the following heads:

(i) Consumption
(ii) Production
(iii) Factors of Production
(iv) Exchange and Determination of Prices and Profits
(v) Profit Sharing (*Muḍārabah* or *Qirāḍ*)
(vi) The Role of *Zakāt*
(vii) Interest and its Abolition
(viii) Nature of Islamic Economics

(i) Consumption

Both Siddiqi (619: 88–90) and Kahf (612: 7–13) discuss economic rationality assumed by modern economics and indicate the various ways in which this concept must be modified and made broader before it is applied to the behaviour of the consumer in an Islamic society. Kahf notes that "the time horizon of an Islamic individual is extended to include the hereafter" which implies that he "should not limit his behaviour to doing things which he can collect the benefits resulting from them in this life, he is so oriented that he will do what is good or useful for its sake" (612: 10). According to Siddiqi the consumer "must, first of all, be satisfied that he is living up to the Islamic standards. To get this satisfaction he can forgo any satisfaction in the economic or utilitarian sense of the term" (619: 89). Despite this modification which introduces non-temporal, non-individualistic elements in the objectives of the consumer, these writers still find the principle of rationality applicable. As Siddiqi puts it Islamic rationality implies "orientation of action towards maximal conformity with the Islamic norms" (619: 90). Kahf proceeds to affirm, on the basis of this point, the validity of the maximisation proposition in the context of consumer behaviour in Islam (612: 13).

Siddiqi's attempt to trace the impact of "Islamic rationality" on the pattern of demand throws up some interesting points. Obviously, prohibited articles of consumption will go out of demand, but that is followed by the observation that "the extent of complementarity" amongst these goods (along with items of luxury whose demand he expects to decrease, relatively speaking) is greater than "in the group that constitutes the necessaries of life". "The abandonment of 'wine, women and gambling' as a way of life, is therefore sure to tell upon a host of other goods and still more upon services attached to this way of life" (619: 93). He also makes a point made earlier by Hameedullah in a different context (433: 229), that "leisure" may be in greater demand in an Islamic society (456: 95). Social wants are also visualised as gaining ascendancy on the ladder of priorities (619: 97–98).

While the above-mentioned points relating to the pattern of demand have several precedents in the literature, Kahf has sought to present a model of household decision assuming an Islamic system with *Zakāt*, replacement of interest by profit sharing (*Qirāḍ*) and of competition by co-operation, where economic units maximise utility or profit (615). He describes the behaviour of the consumer as maximisation of utility subject to two constraints, the size of income and a desire to maintain wealth. Abolition of interest encourages current consumption at the expense of deferred consumption but *Zakāt* urges a higher savings ratio.[85] It also raises the aggregate consumption by redistributing wealth in favour of classes having a higher propensity to consume. The combined effect of *Zakāt* and non-interest is called the "Consumption effect" (615: 22). A resolution of these conflicting "effects" takes place by the direct linkage between savings and earnings (profits) through investment on the basis of *Qirāḍ* (profit sharing) that the abolition of interest ensures in the system. This leads Kahf to the most important conclusion of his brilliant paper: "saving is positively related to investment opportunities and expectations. This relationship implies that at times of declining investment expectations saving will decline and consumption will rise, this in turn increases aggregate demand and raises business expectation" (615: 26). The question arises, however, what might happen to the level of income if the volume of investment decreases "at times of declining investment expectations", and if a fall in the level of income may not *decrease* aggregate demand despite a rise in the *propensity* to consume? Kahf has neither raised this question nor answered it.

Najjar (58: 280–286) questions the validity of the proposition that savings are a function of income. With reference to poor developing countries, availability of suitable channels of investment play a significant role in mobilising voluntary savings, as experienced by Najjar while conducting the experiments of interest-free banks in Egypt in the early sixties. Failure to note this possibility has led to a policy of forced savings and deficit financing with disastrous consequences.

Recently Anas Zarqa had a closer look at the utility function of a Muslim community which "has a new variable in it, namely, the reward or penalty in the hereafter".[86] Using a diagram to explain interaction between consumption and reward, he concludes that "rational Islamic behaviour should lead the individual to settle somewhere between the sufficiency threshold and the prodigality frontier".[87]

(ii) Production

Siddiqi summarises the main aspects of business motivation in Islam as under (619: 103):

(1) "Full compliance with the Islamic idea of justice.
(2) An urge to serve the society which makes the entrepreneur take the welfare of others into consideration, while he makes his entrepreneurial decisions.
(3) Profit maximisation within the limits set by the operation of the above principles."

The last point is seen to imply that:

(1) Producers would not be maximising their profits if, and when, they feel that by lowering their profit margins they can further the good of the society by satisfying unsatisfied needs.
(2) No producer, in any circumstances, shall increase his profits at the cost of explicit injury to the consumers or to his competitors. . . .
(3) Producers will generally be content with satisfactory profits. . . . (619: 136).

He tries to define "satisfactory profits" with reference to an upper limit permitted by the circumstances (without violating the legally-binding part of the Islamic code of conduct) and a lower limit affording the entrepreneur a decent living and a surplus to average out the losses. "Satisfactory profit . . . is any profit, in between the two limits defined above, which satisfies the entrepreneur's sense of goodness as well as his urge to earn money, maintain and develop his enterprise, and keep it in the good books of the customers, the government, and the people in general" (619: 107). This notion of satisfactory profits has, however, been criticised as subjective and vague (616).

Reviewing the subject, Kahf rejects "profit maximisation because it does not fit the Islamic rationale as far as the time horizon and the connotation of 'success' are concerned". He thinks, however, "that profit maximisation can be used as fair approximation if we look at it as constrained not only by cost but also by a minimum level of goodness guaranteed by both ethical values and legislation" (612: 20). The notion of constrained profit maximisation is also upheld by Chapra (115: 20–21) and Taḥāwi (77, I: 227–230).

Whether we regard it as multiplicity of goals (including non-economic goals) or interpret it as constrained profit maximisation, entrepreneurial behaviour ceases to be predictable and uniform once the simple maximisation hypothesis is abandoned. Tracing the unpredictable and potentially varied behaviour of the Islamic entrepreneur is therefore a hazardous task few have attempted. Siddiqi's rudimentary analysis indicates a weakening of the competitive process and its inevitable transformation into a "co-operative" one (619: 137–141).

(iii) Factors of Production

It is interesting to note that Islamic economists have given different answers to the question: what are the factors of production? Mawdūdī endorses the traditional list: land, labour, capital and organisation and finds its justification in the Islamic law relating to profit sharing (*muḍārabah*) (51: 159). It also fits in with his views on the legitimacy of share-cropping (*muḍārabah*).

Abu Saud reduces the list to three: elements of nature, good work and capital (5: 54–55), subsuming labour and organisation under one category. He views capital as resulting from the operation of human labour on elements of nature. Baqīr notes these three factors as they are so characterised by Political Economy but remarks that labour (including organisation) is not material wealth subject to ownership but the human element in production. Capital results from the operations of this factor. Hence nature is the chief source of production (171: 396–397). A. Mannan also proceeds on the basis of this tripartite categorisation of the factors of production, considering capital "not as a fundamental factor of production but as an embodiment of past land and labour" (132: 126).

Taḥāwī (77, I: 277) includes land and capital in "wealth" so that there remain only two factors of production "wealth" and labour, which includes enterprise. As all wealth belongs to God, He is the real owner of the return to this factor, i.e. of the return to land (rent) and capital (interest). He notes, however, that rent is sometimes allowed to be appropriated by the "owner" of land in view of man's needs. The return to labour belongs to the labourer. Najjar would also confine the list to labour and capital, including land in capital and entrepreneurship in labour (58: 106).

Abdul Ḥamīd Abu Sulaiman rejects the idea of characterising "labour" as a factor of production, regarding it as a result of the capitalistic philosophy which views production as an end in itself. He would characterise only land and capital as factors of production, labour – or more exactly man – being the entity for whose benefit these factors are created (7: 16–17). As a corollary to this distinction between capital and land on the one hand and labour or man on the other hand he lays down the rule that the entire produce of land and capital must be distributed among those who work on them. To regard labour itself as a "factor" of production might pave the way for their subjugation by others.

Of special interest is Malik ben Nabi's concept of Capital as stored up surplus labour (484: 81). As a result of the process of accumulation capital became a "prison house" for labour, denying to labour every right except that of serving its (capital's) interest. Our thinking on economic development is also clouded by the newly assumed importance of capital as we tend to forget its real nature and the fundamental importance of labour and enterprise. This, he regards to be a curse for the Third World. Man, land and time, are the only factors crucial for the destiny of the backward nations, a fact recently demonstrated by China. These factors guided by a "cultural will" and not capital is the condition for economic development of the under-developed countries. For him the prime value rests in Man (484: 79–94).

It is clear from this brief resume that the divergent approaches to the apparently innocuous issue of what are the factors of production are not without a deeper significance. They have important bearings on the authors' views on distribution and growth. Further development of thought in this area might produce some thesis of greater significance.

An important point has been made by some writers relating to the definition of capital. Wealth granted as loan or borrowed does not become capital, says Alavi (10: 30–31) and Mahmud Ahmad clarifies that it is only risk capital that actually participates in production and can be characterised as productive. "Loan capital" does not do so (628).

Stressing the "need to modify the conceptual framework of economics to suit the requirements of Islamic economics" Uzair[88] says that "a beginning will have to be made by redefining the factors of production. . . . Capital as a separate factor of production does not exist but it is a part of another factor of production, namely enterprise".[89] In his opinion "the separation of enterprise and capital has created not only conceptual problems but has also caused practical problems in the operation of the economy".[90]

(iv) Exchange and Determination of Prices and Profits

While the analysis of the functioning of a "co-operative" market guided by Islamic norms has yet to yield any formal results, attempts have been made to analyse exchange and discover the root cause of the malaise in the free economy. Bāqir's analysis (171: 326–328) lays the blame on the use of money as a store of value which makes exchange a means to the accumulation of wealth. This distorts the equilibrium between supply and demand. The Islamic remedy lies in *Zakāt* and the abolition of interest which will confine money to its basic role of mediating between production and consumption.

Freed of monopoly, hoarding, speculation and other un-Islamic practices the free working of the competitive forces is expected to result in prices which may be regarded as normal. This seems to be the assumption underlying the following definition of just profits given by Khurshid Ahmad and Naiem Siddiqi (126: 33).

> "That which is determined in average and normal conditions according to the law of demand and supply in a free market – provided that the laws of the state, its plans and policies, or any other controls are not interfering with the system of sales and purchase, production and supply of commodities and with free competition. Monopoly should not be allowed to influence the market and there should be no emergencies and accidents affecting the market."

In the same vein Kahf declares, after defining the framework within which the market would function in an Islamic society, that:

> "All prices, whether of the factors of production or of products, stem out of this mechanism, these prices are looked at as just or fair prices in this respect" (612: 44).

In the context of "just price" Kahf disagrees with Siddiqi's reference to cost of production (612: 88) and refers to Ibn Taimīya's "price of the equivalent". This concept originated in juridical literature to serve as a guide to the judges in the courtroom. According to Kahf, Ibn Taimīya's norm was a price determined in a market free of imperfections (663: 23).

In view of what has been noted above about the role of government in the market, it can be safely concluded that Islamic analysts are not quite sure if the working of the market will ever result in prices, rates of profit and wages that satisfy the Islamic norms. The concept of just or fair prices and profits oscillates between what the modern economists regard as "normal" and what the Islamic economists will find satisfying to their norms. Najjar (58: 123–124) has some new points to add in this connection.

There is some disagreement among our economists regarding the nature of profit. According to Bāqir, Islam does not consider "risk" to be a factor of production (171: 558) and profit is not the reward of risk bearing. It devolves on present work or past labour congealed in the form of property. He disagrees with the view that the share of the supplier of capital in *muḍārabah* contract can be regarded as a reward of uncertainty bearing (171: 559). This is in sharp contrast to Siddiqi's point of view (221, I: 157–171). Bāqir explains rents also with reference to labour that originally resulted in ownership of property.

(v) Profit Sharing (*Muḍārabah*) or *Qirāḍ*

Profit-share, defined as the percentage share of the supplier of capital in the profits of the entrepreneur, or the working partner, in the *muḍārabah* contract is compared and contrasted with the rate of interest in its function and role in the economy. The rate of profit-sharing is also being explored as a tool of analysis and a possible instrument of policy.

Kahf defines *Qirāḍ* (*muḍārabah*) as "the act of transforming money assets into factors of production as a result of a joint action between the two parties". Two crucial differences between profit-share and interest are stated. Firstly, "the profit-sharer has direct interest and real concern in the activity of the firm"; second, "profit-share is a long run phenomenon in which the preference for liquid assets is almost neglected, whereas interest is a dual phenomenon, short and long run, for which the economic thought could not provide any serious theory to provide the term structure. . . . In profit-share the short run changes do not interfere in the finance of investment unless through their effect on the rate of return expectations only, so that one source of long run fluctuations is eliminated, namely variation in short run interest rate" (612: 62–63).

He proceeds to discuss the equilibrium rate of profit-share which should be equal to the return on partnership, i.e. on share capital in joint stock companies (612: 85–86).

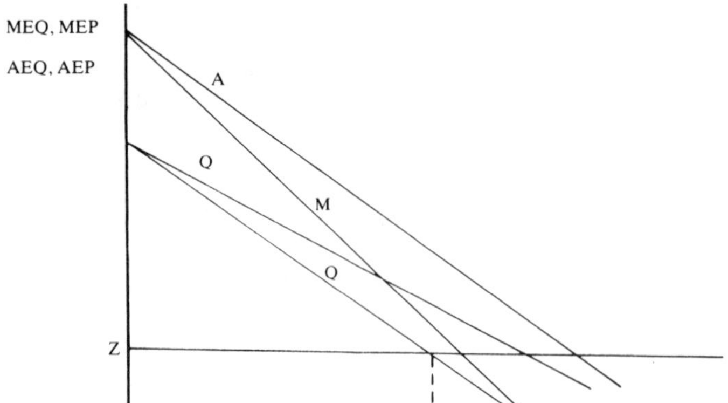

In a novel integration of *Zakāt* analysis with the analysis of profit-share Kahf finds that "the critical situation where the expected dividend (considered in percentage terms) . . . is below az-*Zakāt* line can be distinguished from the situation where the expected dividend is at or above az-*Zakāt* line" (drawn at a height of 2.5 per cent above X axis in the diagram reproduced above), "the difference between M and Q is the remuneration of the entrepreneur" which he calls profit (612: 81–82). Then he proceeds to analyse the behaviour of investment, depending on the elasticity of Q curve and the determination of profit. Traditional economic theory fails to determine profits (612: 82, fn. 84) whereas his own theory is able to do so. Turning then to the capital market he notes that "in the traditional theory this market determines the rate of interest but not the entrepreneurial profit, whereas by having prices to be sought in percentage terms both profit-share and profit are determined simultaneously" (612: 85–86). "It is noted that the demand and supply functions in this (capital) market are really more likely to offer curves known in international trade theory than ordinary demand and supply curves. The other difference lies in the slope of the demand for finance which is positive in this market; this, in fact, reflects that, as the ratio of capital/entrepreneur rises, the profit-share offered by entrepreneur increases in order to attract more capital" (612: 86).

Kahf's analysis goes further than the earlier attempts by Muhammad Akram and Siddiqi. Akram's attempt is vitiated by his misconception about liability to losses in the *muḍārabah* contract and some of his assumptions relating to supply of savings in an Islamic society (404). Siddiqi pointed out the elasticity of the savings curve in relation to profit-share (417: 24).

A recent contribution to the subject is a paper by Chowdhury (620) in which he shows that the only value which comes nearer to a suitable capitalisation rate or acts as a reasonable substitute for the interest rate, is the rate of profit actually realised by the firm or the economy or the individual at any time during the period and process of capital formation.

(vi) The Role of *Zakāt*

Zakāt, one of the main pillars of Islam's economic system, has attracted the attention of almost every writer on the subject, who emphasise its redistributive function, besides emphasising its educative role in giving the individual the right approach towards society and its needs. Since it is difficult to record these contributions with names we confine ourselves to a statement of the points made, mentioning only some recent contributors distinguished by their analytical insight.

1. *Zakāt* transfers part of the wealth of the haves to the have-nots, lessening the inequality in the distribution of income and wealth, and counteracting any tendency towards concentration of wealth.

In a recent contribution (624) Mabid Mahmud correlates the distribution of political power and the distribution of wealth. He finds that:

(1) "The degree of association between the distribution of wealth and that of power increases with the size of the political unit measured in terms of the number of voters.
(2) That degree of association increases with the degree of monopoly in information media" (624: 41–42).

He concludes that "the association between the distribution of wealth and that of political power can be broken by a redistributive scheme. This scheme must operate on wealth, not income. . . . It should be designed to check accumulation on an asset by asset basis, taxing more remunerative assets more heavily, for they provide a greater prospect for power accumulation . . . the conditions of such a redistributive scheme are all fulfilled in az-*Zakāt*" (624: 43).

2. As a result of this transfer there is an upward shift in the aggregate demand function because the marginal propensity to consume of those who receive the transfer payments is comparatively higher.

As noted above, Kahf finds the "consumption effect" of *Zakāt* re-enforced by abolition of interest (615: 22).

3. *Zakāt*'s distributive role involves an allocative role, too, as the *Zakāt* funds are mostly used on essential goods and services. Factors of production are thus diverted to the production of necessaries from that of luxuries on which the taxed persons might have spent these amounts. Hasanuzzaman argues that *Zakāt* will also lead to "a fall in the rich man's demand for imported luxury items"[91] thus resulting in foreign exchange savings.

4. *Zakāt* discourages hoarding and accumulation of idle wealth. It tries to put the waiting resources back into economic activity as increased capacity, through the investment of such wealth, or as increased demand for consumption. "It helps in pushing every bit of wealth into productive activity by increasing the cost of waiting" (612: 51). This point has been made by several writers including Mahmud Ahmad (168: 124), Nasir A. Sheikh (154: 90) and Hasanuzzaman.[92]

Afazuddin (621: 9) points out that "the incidence of *Zakāt* falls on liquidity preference and negates its influence on the rate of interest". The latter part of this statement means that *Zakāt* would encourage the cash holder to employ it in a profitable manner so that *Zakāt* is paid out of the profits and no depletion is caused in the assets. This would cause an addition to the supply of cash while liquidity preference works the other way round. But Afazuddin has apparently ignored the fact that cash is very often held in expectation of better investment prospects in the future and in that situation *Zakāt* would fail to negate "liquidity preference".

5. Kahf ascribes a "savings effect" to *Zakāt* assuming a desire on the part of the household to maintain its level of wealth intact and a similar urge on the part of the firm to maintain non-decreasing capital (615: 21; 612: 51). . . . If the rate of return on wealth is 10 per cent, one needs to save 27.5 per cent of one's income in order to keep one's wealth constant.[93] What is significant is that "it makes every individual merge . . . the decision of income allocation with that of savings utilisation". Obviously, Kahf's "savings effect" assumes a positive return to its utilisation through investment.

Qarḍāwī's comprehensive work on *Zakāt* compares it with modern taxation and explains the virtues of *Zakāt* as a tax on capital (313, II: 1027–30). *Zakāt* on agricultural produce, mineral wealth and salaries and rents can, however, be treated as a tax on income (313, II: 1033–1034). After making a comparative study of *Zakāt* and other taxes in the light of universally acclaimed principles of taxation (313, II: 1038–1052) he proceeds to explain why there is no progression in the rate of *Zakāt*, and dispels the misconception about there being a negative progression in the rates of *Zakāt* on livestock (313, II: 1054).

Mawdūdī has pointed out that the burden of *Zakāt* on merchandise cannot be shifted to the consumers (51: 362–363), but the reasoning is weak and unconvincing.

(vii) Interest and its Abolition

Islamic economists have analysed the role of interest in the economy and have traced the consequences of its abolition. They also compare interest and "profit-share" as means of mobilising savings and channelising them into the productive process. A discussion of these points necessitates a restatement of the causes why Islam has abolished interest.

A: Rationale of Prohibition

The main reason why Islam abolishes interest is that it is oppression (*Zulm*) involving exploitation. In the case of consumption loans it violates the basic function for which God has created wealth, which envisages that the needy be supported by those who have surplus wealth. In the case of productive loans, guaranteed return to capital is unjust in view of the uncertainty surrounding entrepreneurial profits.

The second reason why interest has been abolished is that it transfers wealth from the poor to the rich, increasing the inequality in the distribution of wealth. This is against social interest and contrary to the will (*marḍī*) of God, Who would like an equitable distribution of income and wealth. Islam stands for co-operation and brotherhood. Interest negates this attitude and symbolises an entirely different way of life.

A third reason why interest is abolished is that it creates an idle class of people who receive their income from accumulated wealth. The society is deprived of the labour and enterprise of these people. Such a way of life is also harmful for their personalities.

Mawdūdī has pointed out that a basic imbalance is caused between production and consumption by the phenomenon of interest. This happens in two ways. Firstly, interest on consumption loans transfers part of the purchasing power from a group of people with high propensity to consume to a group with low propensity to consume. This latter group mostly reinvests its income from interest which means that the decrease in consumption demand is accompanied by an increase in production.

Secondly, interest on productive loans raises the cost of production, hence the prices of consumption goods. Once again the amount taxed away from the people, in the form of higher prices falls in the hands of a class with a lower than average propensity to consume.

This imbalance is seen as the source of many evils such as stagnation and depression, monopoly and ultimately imperialism (521: 85–87).

Supply of interest-free loans to needy consumers and denial of a guaranteed return to capital removed this basic imbalance. The incomes generated by the process of production in the form of wages, profits and profit-share are more equitably distributed. *Zakāt*-based transfer of wealth from the rich (profit earners) to the poor (wage earners) removed the remaining imbalance.

Hameedullah (433) pointed out that the institution of interest introduces an essential duality of interest between the capitalist and the entrepreneurs, which is a source of fluctuation in the system. By abolishing interest and bringing the capitalists and the entrepreneurs together on the basis of profit-sharing, Islam ends this duality and harmonises the interests of the two classes.

The above point is made by almost every writer on the subject. Mawdūdī points out that this removes the premium set on capital and shifts the emphasis on to the entrepreneur whose activity becomes the only source of income besides labour. The hold of the "rentier class" on society is destroyed and dynamic entrepreneurs are given the upper hand (521).

Elaborating on the first reason for the abolition of interest stated above, Hameedullah notes that the principle of unilateral risk involved in the institution of interest is the basis of its prohibition in Islam (119: paragraph 372). Ganameh (392: 86) also regards it to be the chief economic reason for Islam's prohibition of interest along with two other reasons: that it violates justice and is contrary to the Islamic dictum: no reward without effort.

Siddiqi argues (221, I: 173-75) that the borrowed capital whose repayment to the lender is guaranteed takes no part in the enterprise in which it is invested and is, therefore, not entitled to any returns even when the enterprise does make a profit. This capital does not expose itself to the risks and uncertainties of the enterprise. These are borne by the collateral pledged by the borrower as security, and by the alternative source of finance to which the borrower must turn for repaying the loan, in case there are losses in the enterprise. He cites the famous tradition from the Prophet (al Kharāj bi'l ḍamān) "income devolves on liability" in this context.

B: Interest, Savings and Investment

This brings us to the impact of the abolition of interest on savings and investment and on the level of economic activity and allocation of resources in the economy.

Many writers have dispelled the doubt that abolition of interest will decrease the propensity to save. Quoting Keynes they argue that savings are a function of income and earning interest is only a minor motive of savings. In the absence of interest the possibility of earning profits on common stock or through *muḍārabah* contract will serve the same purpose. Moreover, the bulk of the savings in a developed economy arise from institutional sources. Siddiqi gives an analytical exposition of the subject (417: 180–190) which has been discussed earlier.

As regards investment, it is argued that "interest holds back investment in production" (A. Mannan[94] (132: 169). Mawdūdī (521 : 110; 51 : 270) and Dr. Qureshi (526: 218) point out that interest prevents the flow of capital towards projects with a low yield even though they are socially most useful. It is argued that in the absence of interest the margin of investment could be extended till the rate of return approaches zero. As regards the supply of savings making such an extension of investment possible, it is pointed out that investment creates its own savings by increasing incomes – a view which is hardly tenable unless qualified carefully.

Mahmud Ahmad points out (168: 36–37) that "the institution of interest provides banks with unproductive channels to employ their capital". This causes scarcity of capital available for productive enterprise which raises the rate of interest. In the absence of interest people's money will either be spent on consumption causing demand to rise or be invested in productive enterprise. Both ways there will be greater production and larger employment. Obviously the argument presumes taxation of hoarded money.

Mawdūdī has argued that the institution of interest discourages long-term investment, as the capitalist has a strong desire for liquidity. This is detrimental to the real interests of society (521: 105–106). Furthermore, long-term loans based on a fixed rate of interest introduce an element of rigidity in costs which investment on the basis of profit-sharing would not.

The discouragements to long-term investment are not, however, confined to the interest cost. The real discouragement comes from the fact that uncertainties surrounding the returns to investment increase with the length of the time period involved. It is reasonable to assume that capitalists or banks advancing long-term capital on the basis of profit-sharing will do so only when the expected rate of return on long-term investment is higher than that expected on short-term investment by a margin that compensates for the greater uncertainties involved. It is also doubtful if the "real" interests of the society always favour longer-term investment. The above argument, therefore, remains inconclusive.

Chawdhri (620) has tried to demonstrate how ensuring a zero rate of interest which is a condition for Golden age equilibrium (in which capital labour and output are all growing at a constant relative rate) guarantees the best solution of resource allocation. He analyses the role of actually realised rate of profit in this context. Siddiqi also argues that "it is not the rate of interest but the priorities of a modern state and the rates of profit in various sectors of the economy that are decisive so far as allocation of investible funds is concerned" (158: 112).

Tracing the consequences of interest in a recent paper, Siddiqi[95] notes that fixed interest charges curtail the freedom of the entrepreneur who wishes to go by social priorities. The society is therefore obliged to admit low yield high priority undertakings into the public sector.

C: Abolition of Interest and Demand for Consumption Loans

Hasanuzzaman (629: 147–164) examines the argument that abolition of interest will increase the demand for consumption loans, accelerating inflation and, in under-developed countries, worsening the balance of payments. He finds little functional relationship between demand for consumer credit and the rate of interest. It is "increase in income and not the rate of interest that governs the demand for loans" (629: 160). Hence "abolition of interest even in the developed countries would not cause any substantial change in the existing set up" (629: 160). As regards the under-developed countries, he concludes that "when the supply of consumer loans and of goods is limited, the increase in demand, if at all, will be ineffective and will not materially disturb the economy and finance of the country" (629: 162).

D: Interest on Internal and External Debt

The "tyranny of interest" reaches its peak in relation to the public debt whose servicing has become a great headache for the modern state. Mawdūdī (521), Qureshi (526: 189–201) and A. Mannan (132) decry interest on this basis. Abolition of interest and replacement of interest-bearing public debt by interest-free debt and funds obtained for the public sector projects on the basis of profit-sharing (Siddiqi: 417: 185–170) will relieve the state of this crippling burden.

Foreign debts based on interest have done irreparable harm to the poor nations of the world. Issa Abdouh (505) focuses attention on this role of interest and Mawdūdī (521: 113–114) describes interest as the greatest instrument of exploitation at the international level.

E. Interest and Trade Cycles

Interest is seen as the root cause of the instability characterising the modern economic system. Interest creates "liquidity preference" for speculative purposes and results in keeping a large part of the money supply in hoards waiting for the rate of interest to rise. It encourages speculation which is the cause of instability in the system (Mawdūdī, 521: 194, Mahmud Ahmad, 168: 13–14).

Several writers including Hameedullah (433), Mahmud Ahmad (168: 13–14, 45–50), Mawdūdī (521: 104), Muhammad Uzair (422) and A.

Mannan (132: 170) have emphasised a causal link between the institution of interest and the occurrence of crises in the economic system, postulating that abolition of interest will contribute decisively towards elimination of trade cycles. Hameedullah regards the institutions of interest as the villain of the piece; "just when the vital interests of the entrepreneur demand that they should have financial resources to cope with the situation, the interest of the lending class demands a payment of the loans and are against their renewal. . . . The institution of lending on interest causes the whole trouble. It makes the lowering of prices so harmful and withholding of supplies impossible" (433: 221). Analysing in detail the role of interest in the various phases of the trade cycle, Mahmud Ahmad concludes that "the abolition of interest can abolish the crises" (168: 49). Abdul Hameed Siddiqi (631) disagrees with this view. A change of the entire system, involving a change in the basic attitude of economic agents, specially in the "acquisitive mentality" is a pre-condition to the solution of this problem.

Siddiqi,[96] however, envisages that a reduction in the volume of credit instruments and public debt, consequent upon the abolition of interest, will have important implications for business cycles. Moreover, investment based on production possibilities directly assessed by businessmen and bankers, in a profit-sharing banking system, are not likely to overstep themselves to an extent that makes a crash in share prices inevitable at a later stage.

F: Prohibition of *Ribā Al-Faḍl*

The prohibition of *ribā al faḍl* (interest involved in barter) has been looked upon as a discouragement of barter and a step directed at monetisation of the economy (509: 9; 555). The primary aim of this injunction is, however, to eliminate the possibilities of exploitation and injustice similar to that which is the target or prohibition of interest on money loans. There is some controversy regarding the coverage of this prohibition, which is a juridical issue not concerning us in this paper.

G: Accounting Concept of Interest

Waqar Husaini (121: 191) pleads for using an accounting concept of interest in economic planning and for project evaluation. Awsaf Ali (114: 199, 264) also thinks that in an Islamic economy the accounting rate of interest must of necessity be used and it is only in the sense of abolishing interest as a source of private income that the Islamic economy can function as an interestless economy. It is not entirely clear, however, why an estimated average rate of profit should not be sufficient for this purpose.

Abdul Bāqi[97] also suggests that the Islamic Bank should fix an accounting rate of interest to serve as a guide in allocation of investible resources, especially as a criterion for giving priority to one project over others. But the underlying assumption that the use of such a rate is inevitable has not been fully justified by him nor the possible alternatives examined in detail. Why are the social priorities and the expected rates of profit not sufficient guides to allocation of resources and selection of projects? If the idea is that the Central Bank keep a certain rate of profit in view and reject such projects as fail to promise a return commensurate with that rate, why insist on calling it an accounting rate of interest?

Sabri F. Ulgener notes that interest serves as "the most dependable factor in evaluating and comparing different investments" (632: 11). Without raising or answering the point why the current "rate of profit-share" paid by *muḍārabah*-based interest-free banks should not form the basis of such an evaluation, supplemented by other estimates based on realised profits, he proceeds to declare that there is no escape from modern bank interest. Hence "the crux of the problem for under-developed countries is to differentiate between interest as a surplus and interest as a factor in computing the overall efficiency of their economies" (632: 14). He does not refer to the various techniques of "computing the overall efficiency" developed in the socialist countries, nor does he clarify how interest as a surplus can be denied to the capitalists while using interest as a factor in computation.

(viii) Nature of Islamic Economics

An important theoretical issue discussed by Islamic economists is the nature, scope and methodology of Islamic economics. They have tried to distinguish Islamic economics from economics as such and state its *raison d'etre*.

Bāqir al Sadr distinguishes between the science of economics which deals with production and the laws that govern it, and the art of economic policy which is concerned with distribution and social justice. The function of an economic system is to solve the economic problems in the context of the ideal state of justice (171: 343–347). Capitalism and Marxism are "schools of economics" advocating different economic systems. Islamic economics is akin to political economy, its function being "the discovery of laws and analysis of real life in the context of an Islamic society in which the Islamic way of life is fully established" (171: 291). Such a science can appear only after the real Islamic society has come to exist – a condition yet to be fulfilled. It is, however, possible "to start investigation on certain given assumptions and derive the economic tendencies and course of events from them" (171: 226–227).

Bāqir considers modern economics to be relevant for modern capitalist societies and not for all societies all the time. Examining its laws, he finds that the only ones having universal validity are the laws of returns (in the theory of production), based as they are on nature rather than on man. All "laws" relating to man are relative as human behaviour depends on human volition which is shaped by beliefs and ethical ends. The celebrated law of demand and supply is no exception (171: 226–227).

Siddiqi also thinks that "Islam's science of economics or the economic analysis relevant to an Islamic society . . . will come into being when we have a people whose behaviour is Islamic, an economy which is truly Islamic" (73: 32). But he proceeds to define Islamic economics "in the context of the endeavour of the present-day Islamic peoples to live according to Islamic injunctions and ideals. It requires a study of the contemporary economic behaviour and socio-economic institutions, comparing and contrasting them with what could be their Islamic alternatives, with a view to defining the changes required to effect a transition to modes of behaviour and institutional arrangements conforming to the Islamic norms" (73: 22). Accordingly, "the task of Islamic economics lies in building bridges between the is and the ought" (73: 33). Both Kahf (611) and Khurshid Ahmad (47) seem to have this role of Islamic economics in mind when they outline the task of Islamic economists today. Kahf wants Islamic economists "to visualise" an economic theory based on "free co-operation rather than on free competition" and to "reformulate" consumer's utility theory "in a way which makes it to cover morals and the consent of Allah". His Islamic economics will be a behavioural science which takes as given the framework provided by "all the religious, moral, social, political and legal rules which constitute the surroundings of the behaviour of any member in the Islamic society" (611: 5–6). For Khurshid Ahmad, "Islamic economics is borne of the challenge thrown to a Muslim economist by the incongruities, paradoxes and complex problems" he observes in the contemporary Muslim world. This calls for "a critical reappraisal of the contemporary economic situation of the Muslim world", "A study of economic teachings of Islam", "an appraisal of the different variants of modern economic theory and policy", and, finally, for a "reconstruction and reformulation of the theory and policy of Islamic economics so as to identify the objectives and the modes of operation of economic activity in an Islamic or Islamising society" (644: 1–3).

This stress on contemporaneity is quite recent in origin, the earlier emphasis being on model building. Shabbir Khan wanted us "to prepare a simple model based on certain simplified assumptions and then introduce the Islamic code of economic life into that model" (643), a suggestion appreciated by Faridi (637). Medhat Hassanain also emphasised the need for building the Islamic economic model (641). A similar view has been expressed by Fanjari (636) and Fareed Naggar.[98]

A. Mannan is closer to Bāqir when he defines Islamic economics as "a social science which studies the economic problems of a people imbued with the values of Islam" (132: 3). Of special interest is Professor Farooqi's stress on the need for "meta-economics" which could judge human processes according to moral norms – "the divine pattern relevant to man's economic life" (638). The idea has been further explicated in a later note (639).

In one of the earliest contributions to this discussion Abdul Hameed Siddiqi (71) finds that economics ignored free will and focused its attention on "the animal aspects" of human behaviour, seeking to discover "laws" which had the finality of the physical laws of nature, thus severing all relations between the principles of economics and morality. Economics of Islam rectifies this error. Taking human volition into account it seeks to guide man in the light of the Islamic injunctions and to orient man's economic attitudes towards the Islamic ends and ideals.

Bāqir's discussion of the process through which the economic philosophy and economic policies of Islam can be "discovered" is detailed and illuminating (171: 341–390). Siddiqi (647), A. M. Manzar (645), Fanjari (636), Khurshid Ahmad (644: 34) and Kahf (611) have indicated some of the areas for research in Islamic economics and the methods which should be adopted.

The methodology of Islamic Economics necessitates a fresh look at the role of values in economics. Sakr (646) finds recent thinking gravitating towards the view that all economic thinking is value loaded and it would be better for an economist to be aware of his value premises and state them clearly. Islam's contribution in this regard lies in providing a set of values which is, because of its divine origin, universal, permanent and immune from tampering by man. The subject has been taken up at a philosophical level by Faruqi.[99]

VI

ECONOMIC THOUGHT IN ISLAM

The advent of Islamic Economics directed the attention of scholars towards the economic thinking of the Muslim thinkers in the past, of which the works on history of economic thought had taken no notice at all, with the sole exception of a casual mention of Ibn Khaldun in Schumpeter's compendium.[100]

Besides the economic thinking of the early jurists and the great philosophers in the later Abbasid period, attention has been paid to such writers as Abū Yūsuf, Abū 'Ubaid, Yahyā Ibn Ādam, Qudāma bin Ja'far, Ibn al-Muqaffa', al-Jāḥiẓ, al-Māwardī, Ibn Ḥazm, Ibn Taimīyah, Ibn Qayyim, Shātibī, Dimashqī, Ibn Khaldūn, Ṭūsī, Ghazālī, al-Ḥarīrī, Aḥmad 'Alī al-Dalajī and Shāh Walīallāh al-Dehlavi.

A: Ibn Khaldūn (1332–1406)

Ibn Khaldūn has rightly been hailed as the greatest economist of Islam. Besides Ezzat's doctoral thesis (655) and Nasha't's work (659) we have contributions by Rosenthal (661), Spengler (664), Boulakia,[101] Ahmad Ali

(656), Ibn al Sabil (192), Abdul Qadir (651; 652), Rifa'ṭ (660), Somogyi (650), Ṭaḥāwī (77), T. B. Irving (657) and Abdu Saṭṭar (654).

Ibn Khaldūn has a wide range of discussions on economics including the subjects of value, division of labour, the price system, the law of supply and demand, consumption and production, money, capital formation, population growth, public finance, trade cycles, etc. He discusses the various stages through which societies pass in economic progress. We also get the basic idea embodied in the backward-sloping supply curve of labour (664: 303). Spengler (664: 293) compares and contrasts his cycle theory of civilisation with Hicks' theory of trade cycles and Abdus Saṭṭar ascribes to him the theory that economic development passes through stages (654). We get the macro-economic view that "income and expenditure balance each other in every city . . . and if both income and expenditure are large . . . the city grows". He also noticed, in the Keynesian sense, the importance of the demand side, particularly government expenditure, in avoiding business slumps and maintaining economic development (654: 161). T. B. Irving also notes that according to Ibn Khaldūn "taxes have a point of diminishing returns and pump priming is important to keep the business running smoothly" (657: 32).

Abdul Qadir (651: 438) notes that labour has the central place in Ibn Khaldūn's theory of value, and Abdus Saṭṭar ascribes a labour theory of value to him (654: 164). Somogyi (650) rightly points out that Ibn Khaldūn anticipated Adam Smith on several points, and Abdul Qadir regards him as a precursor of the mercantilists, because of his views on the importance of Gold and Silver (651: 439). He highlights Ibn Khaldūn's emphasis on economic factors in the interpretation of history and his effort to relate economic progress with political stability (651: 434, 441). Ibn al-Sabil regards Ibn Khaldūn a precursor of Proudhon, Marx and Engels on the basis of his views on poverty and its causes (192: 154).

Rifa'ṭ refers to Ibn Khaldūn's discussion on utility which anticipates later analysis (660: 26). To money, he ascribed the two roles of standard of exchange and store of value (654: 165).

Rifa'ṭ compares his theory of population with that of Malthus and finds a number of common points, though Ibn Khaldūn did not mention preventive checks (660: 26).

In his exhaustive discussion on Ibn Khaldūn, Ṭaḥāwī (77, I: 473–603) explains how population and economic progress are related to one another in his model. Ibn Khaldūn also warned against state intervention in the economy and thought that a free market ensured proper distribution (77, I: 633). Ṭaḥāwī summarises Ibn Khaldūn's views on determination of prices by the forces of supply and demand, money, its values and its functions and the principles of taxation and government expenditure.

Boulakia notes Ibn Khaldūn's emphasis on the importance of social organisation of production whose main factor is human labour. Then comes the role of international division of labour which is based more on the skill of the inhabitants of various regions than their natural resources.[102] "His theory constitutes the embryo of an international trade theory, with the analysis of terms of exchange between rich and poor countries, of the propensity to import and export, of the influence of economic structures on development and of the importance of intellectual capital in the process of growth".[103] After surveying the wide-ranging contributions of Ibn Khaldūn on money, prices, distribution, public finance, trade cycles and population, Boulakia concludes that "Ibn Khaldūn discovered a great number of fundamental economic notions a few centuries before their official birth. He discovered the virtue and the necessity of a division of labour before Smith and the principle of labour value before Ricardo. He elaborated a theory of population before Malthus and insisted on the role of the state in the economy before Keynes. But much more than that, Ibn Khaldūn used these concepts to build a coherent dynamic system in which the economic mechanism inexorably led economic activity to long-term fluctuations. . . . ."[104] Boulakia can, therefore, feel more than justified in affirming that "His name should figure among the fathers of economic science".[105]

B: Ibn Taimīya (1262–1328)

Ibn Taimīya's economic views have been discussed by Muhammad al-Mubārak (134), Sherwani (667), Ilyas Ahmad (665), Kahf (666) and Siddiqi (221, II: 189–203).

Kahf discusses his notion of "price of the equivalent" and the complementary concept of "fair profit". Ibn Taimīya wanted to investigate what the price would be if there were no imperfections in the market. He held that the price of labour was determined in the same way as the other prices (666). Siddiqi has discussed Ibn Taimīya's view on price control at some length (221, II: 189–203).

He justified state intervention in the market on account of monopoly, monopsony, hoarding and speculation. Mubārak (134) discusses his work on *Hisbah*. Maintenance of fair competition and honest dealings were to be ensured through enforcement of the Islamic code of conduct on producers, traders and the middle men. Mubārak has also highlighted Ibn Taimīya's views on other responsibilities of the state, including that of ensuring fulfilment of the basic needs of the people by organising production and distribution (134: 106–127).

Sherwani (667) focuses his attention of Ibn Taimīya's views on the concept of ownership in Islam, emphasising the right of the state to abridge or abrogate this right in certain circumstances.

Ṭahāwī (77, I: 455) regards Ibn Taimīya's emphasis on the state's responsibility to ensure the fulfilment of the basic needs of the people as his unique contribution.

C: Abū Yūsuf (731–798)

Abū Yūsuf's main subject was taxation and the economic responsibilities of the state. His contribution lies in demonstrating the superiority of proportional taxation over the system of fixed levy on land, both from the viewpoint of revenue and equity. In his discussion he also refers to the other canons of taxation: capacity to pay, a consideration for the convenience of assessees in fixing the time of collection and its mode, and centralisation of decision making in tax administration. Siddiqi (671: 83–84) discusses these points along with Abū Yūsuf's emphasis on public works especially irrigation facilities and highways. He also urges upon the ruler to take other measures to ensure the development of agriculture (671: 89).

Siddiqi notes that Abū Yūsuf's brief comments on the relation between the supply of goods and their prices do not go deep enough and his advice to the ruler against price control is not accompanied by a thorough discussion on the subject (671: 78–79).

D: Nasiruddīn Ṭūsī (1201–1274)

Ṭūsī's contribution has been discussed by Rifa't (679), A. Mannan (132: 8), Anzarul Haq (678) and Habibul Haq Nadwi (235). Ṭūsī discussed the revenue and expenditure of the household as well as those of the ruler. He emphasised saving and warned against extravagance and expenditure on unproductive assets such as jewellery and uncultivable land (679: 124). He accorded supreme importance to agriculture giving trade and other vocations a second place (235: 148). He also discussed exchange and division of labour. His brief work on Public Finance has been reviewed by Rifa't (679) wherein he disapproves of certain taxes which had no sanction in Islam.

Jalāl al Din al Dawwani (678) closely follows Ṭūsī in his discussion of the household and the public treasury.

E: Shāh Walīullāh (1702–1763)

A resume of Shāh Walīullāh's broad sweep on the subject has been given by Tufail Ahmad Qureshi.[106] He regarded economic well-being to be a prerequisite of a good life and proceeded to discuss needs, ownership, means of production, co-operation, distribution and consumption with remarkable insight. Discussing the evolution of society from the primitive stages to the affluent culture of his day he points out the decadence that sets in with the growth of conspicuous consumption. In his discussion on means of production he tends to place a number of natural resources in the public sector.[107] He condemned hoarding and profiteering on economic as well as social grounds.[108]

The economic philosophy of Shāh Walīullāh had been earlier interpreted by Ubaidullah Sindhi (688). Ibn al Sabil compares Walīullāh's analysis of the decline of the Mughals with Marx's critique of capitalism (192: 515). Walīullāh's *Ḥujjatullāh al Bālighah* offers a wealth of material on the subject that awaits the attention of economists.

F: Other Thinkers

Kifayatullah[109] has recently reported on a work by Imām Muḥammad Ibn Ḥasan al Shaibānī (750–804) entitled "The Earning", which discusses what is right and what is wrong in ways of earning and spending. He regarded agriculture as the noblest of all professions because it is the most useful for the entire society, a view which sharply distinguishes Imām Muḥammad from most of his contemporaries who preferred trade and commerce over agriculture.

Ṭaḥāwī (77, I: 151–154) takes some notice of those Islamic thinkers who paid special attention to eradication of poverty and to ensuring social justice. He mentions Abu Dharr Ghifārī (d. 654), Ibn Hazm (d. 1064) and Ahmad 'Alī al Dalajī (d. 1421). Ibrahim Labban (614) also discusses the views of Abu Dharr Ghifārī and Ibn Hazm.

It could not be possible for the present writer to consult the numerous works on Ghazālī, Fārābī, Ṭūsī, Ibn Qayyim, Shāh Walīullāh and others for brief references to their economic views. Nor could he do justice to the works on the few thinkers discussed in this section. Here is a field that awaits the attention of researchers in Islamic Economics. But the material listed in our own bibliography should be sufficient to refute the thesis recently propounded by Meyer (648) that the "Arabic, Turkish and Persian speaking East has experienced no continuity of economic ideas such as those which come from the Judeo-Christian West". The West experienced systematic economic thinking since the time of the Renaissance and Economics came into its own in the wake of the Industrial Revolution – a period of history in which the East was sliding down the scale of decadence. The ascendancy of the Islamic civilisation and its dominance of the world scene for a thousand years could not have been unaccompanied by economic ideas as such. From Abū Yūsuf in the second century to Ṭūsī and Walīullāh we get a continuity of serious discussion on taxation, Government expenditure, home economics, money and exchange, division of labour, monopoly, price control, etc. Unfortunately, no serious attention has been paid to this heritage by centres of academic research in Economics.

Epilogue

The variety of subjects discussed by Islamic economists and their distinctive approach to some of the economic problems is brought out in our survey of the literature presently available. The new approach has a clearly defined frame of reference and there are certain common premises shared by all writers on the subject. The issues raised and discussed by them are relevant to the human situation and have a direct bearing on contemporary life. These discussions have a special significance for the Muslim countries and communities, but their relevance for a comparative study of economic systems and philosophies is universal and general.

To the students of Islamic economics in particular and the Muslim students of economics in general the survey provides an opportunity of stock-taking and programming for further research. Both Islam and economics would be benefited if closer attention is paid to an approach that seeks to relink economics with moral values and to evolve a framework in which man's quest for justice achieves fulfilment while ensuring maximum efficiency and satisfying the will to economise.

Notes

1 Research Report 1: Contemporary Literature on Islamic Economics, 1978. 69p.

2 "Allah coineth a similitude: a township that dwelt secure and well content, its provisions coming to it in abundance . . . ." (XVI: 112.)
"So let them worship the Lord of this House, Who hath fed them against hunger; and hath made them safe from fear." (CVI: 3–4).

3 'Ali 'Abd al-Rasūl: "*Sulūk al Mustahlik wa'l munsh'ah fi'l 'itar al Islāmī*". Paper presented at the First International Conference on Islamic Economics, Makka, 1976. Mimeo 31p.

4 Morris Bernstein: *Comparative Economic Systems,* Richard & Irwin Inc. Homewood, Illinois, 1965, Preface.

5 Also his paper, "The Islamic Welfare State and its Role in the Economy", p. 17. Presented at the First International Conference on Islamic Economics, Makka, 1976. Mimeo 51p. Included in *Studies in Islamic Economics*, Leicester, The Islamic Foundation, 1981, pp. 143–169.

6 Manna' Qaṭṭān: *Mafhūm wa manhaj al-iqtiṣād al Islāmī*, pp.1–5. Paper presented at the First International Conference on Islamic Economics, Makka, 1976. Mimeo 11p. Included in *al-iqtiṣād al Islāmī*, Jeddah, al Markaz al 'Ālamī li Abḥāth al Iqtiṣād al Islāmī, 1980, pp. 132–154.

7 'Alī 'Abd al-Rasūl: *Salūk al mustahlik wa'l munsha'ah fi'l 'itar al Islāmī.* Paper presented at the First International Conference on Islamic Economics, Makka, 1976. Mimeo 31p.

8 Chapra, Muhammad Umar: "The Islamic Welfare State and its Role in the Economy", p.17. Paper presented at the First International Conference on Islamic Economics, Makka, 1976. Mimeo 51p. Included in *Studies in Islamic Economics*, op. cit. pp. 143–169.

9 Op. cit., p.18.

10 Shihab, Rafiullah, *Islāmī riyāsat kā māliyātī Nizām*, Islamabad: Islamic Research Institute, 1973, 157p.

11 Also the following papers presented at the First International Conference on Islamic Economics, Makka, 1976.
Hasanuzzaman, S. M.: "Zakāt and Fiscal Policy". Mimeo 52p.
al-Syed, 'Atif: "Fikrat al-'Adālah al ḍarībīyah fi'l Zakāt fī ṣadr al Islām." Mimeo 67p. Included in *al Iqtiṣād al Islāmī*, op.cit. pp. 272–326.
Salih Tug: "The Centralization of *Zakāh* and Individual Freedom". Mimeo 18p.
Faridi, F. R.: "*Zakāt* and Fiscal Policy". Mimeo 28p. Included in *Studies in Islamic Economics*, op.cit. pp. 119–130.
Qardāwī, Yusuf: "Athar al Zakāh fi 'ilāj al mūshkilāt al īqtisādīyah". Mimeo 44p. Included in *al Iqtiṣād al Islāmī*, op.cit. pp. 226–271.
Gorayah, Muhammad Yusuf: *Nizām-e-Zakāt aur jādid ma'āshī masā'īl,* Islamabad: Islamic Research Institute, 1972, p. 158.

12 Op.cit., pp. 12–13.
13 Al Fanjari, Muhammad Shauqi: "al Maḍhab al-iqtiṣādī fi'l Islām", p. 38. Paper presented at the First International Conference on Islamic Economics, Makka, 1976. Mimeo 74p. Included in *al Iqtiṣād al Islāmī*, op.cit. pp. 72–131.
14 Hasanuzzaman, S. M.: "Zakāt and Fiscal Policy", pp. 27–28. Paper presented at the First International Conference on Islamic Economics, Makka, 1976. Mimeo. Included in *al Iqtiṣād al Islāmī*, op.cit. pp. 327–352.
15 *ibid.* p. 205.
16 'Abd al-Salām, Muhammad Said: *Daur al fikr al mālī wa'l muhāsibī fī taṭbīq al-Zakāt*, p.21. Paper presented at the First International Conference on Islamic Economics, Makka, 1976. Mimeo 30p.
17 al-Sayyid, 'Ātif: *Fikr al-'Adālah al ḍarībīyah fi'l Zakāt fī ṣadr al-Islām*, pp. 5–17. Paper presented at the First International Conference on Islamic Economics, Makka, 1976. Mimeo 67p. Included in *al Iqtiṣād al Islāmī*, op.cit. pp. 272–326.
18 Kashif, Ahmad Sami Musa: Al Islām wa'l amn al-īqtiṣādī wa'l ījtimā'ī–ishārah khāṣṣah ilā al-ta' mīnāt al-ījtimā'īyah, pp. 12–22. Paper presented at the First International Conference on Islamic Economics, Makka, 1976. Mimeo 26p.
19 Zarqa, Mustafa Ahmad: "Niẓām al ta'min: mawqafahū fi'l maidān al-iqtiṣādī bi-wajhin 'ām wa-mawqif al Sharī'āh al Islāmīyah minhu". Makka, 1976. Mimeo 40p. Included in *al Iqtiṣād al Islāmī*, op.cit. pp. 373–414.
20 Shaheedi, Jafar: al-Ta'mīn: hukmuhū fi'l fiqh al Islāmī-wa-ārā' al-madhāhib al Islāmīyah fīh. Makka, 1976. Mimeo 14p.
Awad, Ali Jamaluddin: al-Ta'mīn fī 'itar al-Sharī'āh al Islāmīyah. Makka, 1976. Mimeo 39p.
21 Khan, Shaukat Ali: al-Ta'mīn wa badīluhū fī naẓar al-Islām. Makka, 1976. Mimeo 40p.
22 al Sayyad, Jalal Mustafa: al-Ta'mīn wa ba'ḍ al-shūbhāt, Makka, 1976. Mimeo 14p. Included in *al Iqtiṣād al Islāmī*, op.cit. pp. 520–532.
23 As in 21 above.
24 Abu Sunnah, Ahmad Fatimi: Al-Ta'mīn 'ind al-nawāzil wa'l ḥawa' ij. Makka, 1976. Mimeo 15p.
25 At Attār, 'Abd al Nasir Tawfīq: Hukm ash-Sharī'ah al Islāmīyah fi'l ta'min, Makka, 1976. Mimeo 42p.
All papers presented at the First International Conference on Islamic Economics, Makka, 1976.
26 Also Zarqā, Mustafa Ahmad, op.cit., p. 35.
27 First International Conference on Islamic Economics, Makka, 1976. General Recommendations, No.6.
28 Khafif, Sheikh Ali: al-Ta'mīn wa hukmuhū 'alā hadī al-Sharī'ah wa Uṣūlihā al-'āmmah, pp. 19–20. Paper presented at the First International Conference on Islamic Economics, Makka, 1976. Mimeo 64p.
Attar, Abd al Nasir Tawfiq, op.cit., pp. 20–22.
29 Awad, Ali Jamaluddin, op.cit., pp. 15, 17–18, 20.
al Sayyad, Mustafa Jalal, op.cit., pp. 11–12.
30 Fanjari, Muhammad Shauqi: Al-Ta'āwun lā al-istighlāl asās 'aqd al-ta'mīn al-Islāmī. Paper presented to the Council of *ulema* in Saudi Arabia, Makka, May, 1976. Mimeo 56p.
31 Also his paper at the First International Conference on Islamic Economics, Makka, 1976. "Interest-Free Banking", Mimeo 164p.
Ahmad, Shaikh Mahmud: "Man and Money". Mimeo 380p. (Under print.)
32 It implies "creating artificial carrying costs for money through the device of requiring legal tender currency to be periodically stamped at a prescribed cost in order to retain its quality as money" (Keynes, J. M.: *General Theory*, London, 1957, p. 234). Though Keynes thought the proposal "deserves consideration" he pointed out the difficulties involved (pp. 357–358).

33 The same proposal had been made earlier by Arthur Birnie in his thought provoking pamphlet: *The History and Ethics of Interest* (William Hodge & Co., London, 1952, 40p.). Birnie, however, notes that the proposal "excites so much misunderstanding and alarm". He, therefore, suggests "the issue of a currency of dated notes, which would be recalled at intervals and exchanged for a new dated currency" (p. 38).

34 al Jarhi, Mabid Ali Mohammad Mahmoud: *The Relative Efficiency of Interest-Free Monetary Economics: The Fiat Money Case.* Paper presented at the First International Conference on Islamic Economics, Makka, 1976. Mimeo 44p. Included in *Studies in Islamic Economics*, op.cit. pp. 85–118.

35 Al-Assāl, Ahmad Muhammad and Fathi Ahmad Abdul Karim: *al Niẓām al-iqtisādī fi'l Islām*, p.21. Paper presented at the First International Conference on Islamic Economics, Makka, 1976. Mimeo 111p. Published: al Qahira, Maktaba Wahbah, 3rd edition, 1980, 192p.

36 Muslehuddin, Muhammad: Interest-Free Banking and the Feasibility of Muḍārabah. Paper presented at the First International Conference on Islamic Economics, Makka, 1976. Mimeo 37p.

37 al Shawi, Muhammad Tawfiq: al Khaṣā'iṣ al-mumaiyyazah li'l bunk al-Islāmī li-tanmiyah min khilāl al-nuṣūṣ itti fāqīyah ta'sīsuhū wa malāmih al-niẓām al-maṣrafī wa'l iqtiṣād al-Islāmī. Mimeo 47p. Paper presented at the First International Conference on Islamic Economics, Makka, 1976.

38 Siddiqi, Muhammad Nejatullah: Banking in an Islamic Framework. Paper presented at the International Economic Conference: The Muslim World and the Future Economic Order, London, July, 1977. Mimeo 22p. Included in *Issues in Islamic Banking*, Leicester, The Islamic Foundation, 1983, pp. 51–65.

39 Op. cit. p. 10.

40 Siddiqi, Muhammad Nejatullah: "Interest-Free Banking–Problems and Prospects". Mimeo 15p. Paper presented at the University of Petroleum and Minerals, Dhahrān, 1976.

41 Op. cit. p. 34.

42 Abu Saud, Mahmud: "Interest-Free Banking". Mimeo 164p. Paper presented at the First International Conference on Islamic Economics, Makka, 1976. Included with some abridgement in *Studies in Islamic Economics*, op. cit. pp. 59–84.

43 *Ibid*, p. 114.

44 *Ibid*, p. 115.

45 *Ibid*, p. 116.

46 *Ibid*, p. 117

47 *Ibid*, p. 153.

48 *Ibid*, p. 112.

49 Hamud, Sami Hasan Ahmad: Tatwīr al-a'māl al maṣrafiyah bi mā yattafiqu wa'l Shar'īyah al-Islāmīyah. Dār al-ittihād al-'Arab li'l tibā'ah, 1976. 552p.

50 Siddiqi, Muhammad Nejatullah: *Banking in an Islamic Framework*. Paper presented at the International Economic Conference: The Muslim World and the Future Economic Order, London, July, 1977. Mimeo 22p. See also his Dhahrān paper cited above.

51 Abdur Rasul, Ali: *Bunūk bilā fawāi'd.* Paper presented at the First International Conference on Islamic Economics, Makka, 1976. Mimeo 31p.

52 *Ibid*, p. 2.

53 *Ibid*, pp. 9–11.

54 Uzair, Muhammad: *Some Conceptional and Practical Aspects of Interest-Free Banking*, p. 26. Paper presented at the First International Conference on Islamic Economics, Makka, 1976. Mimeo 34p. Included in *Studies in Islamic Economics*, op. cit. pp. 37–57.

55 *Ibid*, pp. 26–27.

56 *Ibid*, p. 25.

57 *Ibid*, p. 2.

58 Siddiqi, Muhammad Nejatullah: *Teaching of Economics at the University Level in Muslim Countries–Challenge of Alien Concepts and Formulation of Islamic Concepts*. Paper presented at the First World Conference on Muslim Education, Makka, 1977. Mimeo 17p. Included in *Social and Natural Sciences: The Islamic Perspective*, London, Hodder and Stoughton, 1981, pp. 71–86.
59 Shawi, Muhammad Tawfiq: al Khaṣā'is al mumaiyyazah li'l bunk al-Islāmī li'l tanmiyah min khilāl nuṣūṣ ittifāqīyah ta'sīsīhī wa malāmih al-niẓām al-maṣrafī wa'l iqtiṣād al-Islāmī. Paper presented at the First International Conference on Islamic Economics, Makka, 1976. Mimeo 47p.
60 *Ibid*, p. 31.
61 Islamic Development Bank: The First Annual Report 1395/96 H–1975/76 Jeddah, 36p.
62 Abdur Rasul, Ali: Sutūk al mustahlik wa'l munsha'āt fi'l 'iṭar al Islāmi. Paper presented at the First International Conference on Islamic Economics, Makka, 1976. Mimeo 31p.
63 Abdul Hadi, Hamdī Amin: Muqawwinat idārah al-tanmiyah fi'l fikr al Islāmī. Paper presented at the First International Conference on Islamic Economics, Makka, 1976. Mimeo 27p.
64 al Assal, Ahmad Muhammad and Fathi Ahmad Abdul Karim: al-Niẓām al iqtiṣādī fi'l Islām. Paper presented at the First International Conference on Islamic Economics, Makka, 1976. Mimeo 111p. See note 35 above.
65 Zubair, Muhammad Umar: "al iqtisād al Islāmī wa dauruh fi tanmiyat al mujtama," in *Nadwah al Shabāb al 'Ālamiyah li'l Da'wah al-Islāmīyah,* pp. 192–201. Riyadh, 1972, 344p.
66 Namiq, Salāh al Din: *Limādhā lā yakūn lanā mafhūm Islāmī akhlāqī jadid li tanmiyah al-iqtiṣādiyah.* Paper presented at the First International Conference on Islamic Economics, Makka, 1976. Mimeo 19p.
67 Khurshid Ahmad: *Economic Development in an Islamic Framework–Some Notes on the Outline of a Strategy*. Paper presented at the First International Conference on Islamic Economics, Makka, 1976. Mimeo 30p. Included in *Studies in Islamic Economics*, op. cit. pp. 171–188.
68 Siddiqi, Muhammad Nejatullah: *An Islamic Approach to Economic Development,* the Muslim Institute for Research and Planning, Slough, Berks, U.K. 1977, 8p.
69 Khurshid Ahmad, op. cit., pp. 23–26.
70 Shahin, Rahim Bakhsh: Iqbal kē ma-ashī nazariyāt. Lahore: All Pakistan Islamic Educational Congress, n.d. 118p.
71 Abu Saud, Mahmud: "Interest-Free Banking". Paper presented at the First International Conference on Islamic Economics, Makka, 1976. Mimeo 164p. See note 42 above.
72 Also, Shaikh Mahmud Ahmad: "Social Justice in Islam", pp. 1–31. Lahore: Institute of Islamic Culture, 1975, 120p. and "Man and Money", Mimeo 380p (under print) by the same author.
73 Uzair, Muhammad: "Some Conceptual and Practical Aspects of Interest-Free Banking". Paper presented at the First International Conference on Islamic Economics, Makka, 1976. Mimeo 36p. See note 54 above.
74 e.g. Siddiqi, Muhammad Nejatullah: "Teaching of Economics at the University Level in Muslim Countries: The Challenge of Alien Concepts and the Formulation of Islamic Concepts". Paper presented at the First World Conference on Muslim Education, Makka, 1977. Mimeo 17p. See note 58 above.
75 Abu Saud, Mahmud, op. cit., pp. 34–70.
76 *Ibid*, p. 35.
77 *Ibid*, p. 39.
78 *Ibid*, p. 41.
79 *Ibid*, p. 46.
80 *Ibid*, p. 50.

81 *Ibid*, p. 52.
82 *Ibid*, p. 52.
83 *Ibid*, pp. 53–54.
84 *Ibid*, p. 62.
85 See under V.
86 Zarqa, Muhammad Anas: "Social Welfare Function and Consumer Behaviour: An Islamic Formulation of Selected Issues". p. 30. Paper presented at the First International Conference on Islamic Economics, Makka, 1976. Mimeo 65p. Arabic version included in *al Iqtiṣād al Islāmī*, op. cit. pp. 155–197. Also see his paper 'Islamic Economics: An Approach to Human Welfare' in *Studies in Islamic Economics*, op. cit. pp. 3–18.
87 *Ibid*, p. 42
88 Uzair, Muhammad: "Some Conceptual and Practical Aspects of Interest-Free Banking", p. 12. See note 54 above.
89 *Ibid*.
90 *Ibid*.
91 Hasanuzzaman, S. M.: "Zakāt and Fiscal Policy", p. 37. Paper presented at the First International Conference on Islamic Economics, Makka, 1976. Mimeo 52p.
92 *Ibid*, p. 35.
93 So that the saved part of income earns additional income equal to the *Zakāt* payable on wealth plus new income, as $\frac{10}{100} \times 27.5 = 2.75 = \frac{(100 + 10)\,2.5}{100}$
94 He quotes Keynes: *General Theory*, p. 235. "It seems that the rate of interest on money plays a peculiar part in setting a limit to the level of employment, since it sets a standard to which marginal efficiency of a capital asset must attain if it is to be newly produced."
95 Siddiqi, Muhammad Nejatullah: "Banking in an Islamic Framework". Paper presented at the International Economic Conference: "The Muslim World and Future Economic Order, London, 1977. Mimeo 22p.
96 Siddiqi, Muhammad Nejatullah: "Banking in an Islamic Framework". Paper presented at the International Economic Conference: The Muslim World and the Future Economic Order, London, 1977. Mimeo 22p.
97 Abdul Bāqi, Mahmud Salāh: *al Iqtiṣād al Islāmī: farḍiyat al Zakāt wa ḥurmat al Ribā*. Paper presented at the First International Conference on Islamic Economics, Makka, 1976. Mimeo 10p.
98 el Naggar, Fareed: "The Methodology of Islamic Economics: A Systems Approach". Paper presented at the First International Conference on Islamic Economics, Makka, 1976. Mimeo 30p.
99 Faruqi, Ismail Ragi: "Islamicising the Social Sciences". Paper presented at the First World Conference on Muslim Education, Makka, 1977. Mimeo. Included in *Social and Natural Sciences: The Islamic Perspective*, op. cit. pp. 8–20.
100 Schumpeter, J. A.: History of Economic Analysis, Oxford University Press, London, 1959, p. 136 and p. 788.
101 Boulakai, Jean David C.: "Ibn Khaldūn: A Fourteenth Century Economist" – Journal of Political Economy 79 (5) September-October 1971: 1105–1118.
102 Boulakia, Jean David C.: op. cit. pp. 1107–1108.
103 *Ibid*, p. 1109.
104 *Ibid*, p. 1117.
105 *Ibid*, p. 1118.
106 Qureshi, Tufail Ahmad: "Shāh Walīullāh kī naẓar men musalmānon kē ma'āshī masā'il kā ḥal", *Fikr-o-Nazar* (Islamabad) 7 (3) September 69: 218–226; 7 (4) October 69: 304–310.
107 *Ibid*, pp. 223–225.
108 *Ibid*, pp. 309–310.
109 Kifayātullah: "Economic Thought in the Eighth Century: The Muslim Contribution", *Voice of Islam* (Karachi), March, 1976, pp. 301–304.

Appendix
CLASSIFIED BIBLIOGRAPHY
Contents

		Entry Numbers
1	ECONOMIC PHILOSOPHY OF ISLAM	1– 80
2	ECONOMIC SYSTEM OF ISLAM	81–498
i	Sources and Precedents	81–102
ii	General	103–166
iii	Comparative Studies	167–181
iv	Socialistic Trends	182–208
v	Ownership	209–223
vi	Land: Ownership and Tenure	224–242
vii	Sharecropping	243–244
viii	Partnership and Profit Sharing	245–250
ix	Consumption	251–252
x	Business and Trade	253–260
xi	*Ḥisbah*	261–273
xii	Co-operation	274–279
xiii	Hoarding	280–282
xiv	Public Finance: General	283–299
xv	Public Finance: *Zakāt*	300–321
xvi	Public Finance: *'Ushr, Kharāj*, etc.	322–329
xvii	Inheritance	330–333
xviii	Social Security	334–344
xix	Endowments	345–348
xx	Insurance	349–380
xxi	Banking without Interest	381–422
xxii	Foreign Trade	423
xxiii	Labour and Industrial Relations	424–445
xxiv	Family Planning	446–472
xxv	Economic Development	473–494
xxvi	Audit and Accounts	495–498
3	ISLAMIC CRITIQUE OF CONTEMPORARY ECONOMICS —Theories and Systems	499–609
i	Capitalism	499–500
ii	Interest	501–533
iii	Commercial Interest	534–553
iv	*Ribā'l-Faḍl*	554–555
v	Speculation and Stock Exchange	556–559
vi	Lottery	560–562
vii	Socialism and Communism	563–597
viii	Marxian Theories	598–599
ix	Socialism and Capitalism, etc.	600–610
4	ECONOMIC ANALYSIS IN AN ISLAMIC FRAMEWORK	611–646
i	General	611–614
ii	Consumption	615
iii	Production and Enterprise	616–619
iv	Profit-sharing	620
v	*Zakāt*	621–627
vi	Abolition of Interest	628–632
vii	Nature of Islamic Economics	633–647

5 HISTORY OF ECONOMIC THOUGHT IN ISLAM 648–691
i General 648–650
ii Ibn Khaldūn 651–664
iii Ibn Taymīyah 665–667
iv Abū Yūsuf 668–672
v Yaḥyā ibn Ādam 673–675
vi Abū Ja'far Dimashqī 676–677
vii Naṣīr al-Din Ṭūsī 678–679
viii Others 680–691

6 MISCELLANEOUS 692–698

7 BIBLIOGRAPHIES 699–700

1. ECONOMIC PHILOSOPHY OF ISLAM
[1–80]

1. ‘Abd al-Mujeeb — "Ma‘īshat-e-Islām: fikr-o-niẓām" (Islam's economy: philosophy and system), *Tarjumān al-Qur'ān* (Lahore) 74(2), 91–108; 74(3), 165–173. (U)

2. ‘Abd al-Rasūl, ‘Alī — *al-Mabādi'l-iqtiṣādīyah fi'l-Islām wa'l-binā' al-iqtiṣādī li'l-dawlat al-Islāmīyah* (Economic principles of Islam and the Economic structure of Islamic State). al-Qāhirah, Dār al-Fikr al-‘Arabī, 1968. 294p. (A)

3. Abū Aiman — "Ma‘ālim al-Ṭarīq: al-nāḥīyah al-iqtiṣādīyah" (Guideposts of the road: The Economic aspect), *al-Muslimūn* (Dimashq), 3(5), July 55: 20–25. (A)

4. Abu 'l-Makārim, Zaidān — *Binā al-iqtiṣād fi'l-Islām* (Structure of economy in Islam). al-Qāhirah, al-Dār al-‘Arabīyah, 1951. 210p. (A)

5. Abū Sa‘ūd, Maḥmūd — "The Economic Order within the General Conception of the Islamic Way of Life", *Islamic Review* (London) 55(2), Feb. 67: 24–26; 55(3), Mar. 67: 11–14.

6. ,, ,, ,, — *Khuṭūṭ ra'īsīyah fi'l-iqtiṣād al-Islāmī* (Salient Features of Islamic Economy). Beirut, Maṭba'ah Ma‘tūq Ikhwān, 1965. 96p. (A)

7. Abū Sulaimān, ‘Abdul Ḥamīd Aḥmad — *Naẓarīyat al-Islām al-iqtiṣādīyah: al-falsafah wa'l-wasā'il al-mu‘āṣirah* (Economic Theory of Islam: The Philosophy and Contemporary Means). al-Qāhirah, Dār Miṣr li'l-Ṭibā‘ah, 1960. 124p. (A)

8. ,, ,, ,, — "The Theory of the Economics of Islam: The Economics of Tawhīd and Brotherhood; Philosophy, Concept and Suggestions", in: *Contemporary Aspects of Economic and Social Thinking in Islam.* Gary, Indiana, M.S.A. of U.S. & Canada, 1973: 26–78.

9. Afzal-Ur-Rehman — Economic Doctrines of Islam. Lahore, Islamic Publications, 1974. 3v. v.I, 224p.; v.II, 275p. v.III, 273p.

10. Alavi, Q. Ahmadur Rahman — "An Introduction to the Economic Philosophy of Islam", *Islamic Literature* (Lahore) 2(4), Apr. 50: 25–34.

11. ‘Alī, Ibrāhīm Fu'ād Aḥmad — "Naḥwa iqtiṣād Islāmī mutaḥarrir" (Towards a free Islamic Economy), *al-Wa‘y al-Islāmī* (Kuwait) (109), Jan. 74: (114), June 74: 99–103. (A)

12. Ali, Syed Ahmad — *Economic Foundations of Islam—a Social and Economic Study.* Calcutta, Orient Longmans, 1961. 203p.

13. Amīnī, Muḥammad Taqī — *Tahdhīb kī jadīd tashkīl* (Reconstruction of Civilisation). Delhi, Nadwat al-Muṣannifīn, 1974. 339p. (U)

14.	al-'Araby, Muḥammad 'Abdullāh	"Economics in the Social Structure of Islam", *World Muslim League* (Singapore) 3(7), July–Aug. 66: 10–25.
15.	,, ,,	*al-Iqtiṣād al-Islāmī fī taṭbīqihi 'ala'l-mujtama' al-mu'āṣir* (Islamic Economics as applied to Contemporary Society). Kuwait, Maktabah al-Manār, n.d. (A)
16.	,, ,,	"Some Aspects of Islamic Economics", *Islamic Thought* (Aligarh) 6(2), Mar.–Apr. 57: 8–19.
17.	,, ,,	*Ta'ālīm al-Islām al-iqtiṣādīyah* (Economic Teachings of Islam). Kuwait, Maktabah al-Manār, n.d. (A)
18.	Ashraf, Muḥammad	"Ḥuḍūr Anwar Ṣallallāh 'alaihi wa ṣallam aur ma'āshī niẓām" (The Prophet of Allah, peace be upon him, and the Economic System), *Bayyināt* (Karachi) 16, (6), Aug. 70: 22–40. (U)
19.	Ashraf, Shaikh Muḥammad	"Islāmī ma'īshat" (Islamic Economy), *Salsabīl* (Karachi) 8, July 70: 19–23. 208p. (U)
20.	Bābullī, Maḥmūd Muḥammad	*Al-Iqtiṣād fī ḍau' al-sharī'at al-Islāmīyah* (Economics in the light of Islamic Law). Beirut, Dār al-Kitāb al-Lubnānī, 1975. (A)
21.	,, ,,	"Khaṣā'iṣ al-iqtiṣād al-Islāmī" (Characteristics of Islamic Economy), *Nadwat al-Muḥāḍarāt, Rābiṭat al-'Ālam al-Islāmī*, Makka, 1969: 79–102. (A)
22.	Dastgīr, Ghulām	*Islām kē ma'āshi taṣawwurāt* (Economic Concepts of Islam), Karachi, 'Abbāsī Kutub Khāna (U)
23.	al-Fanjarī, Muḥammad Shauqī	*al-Madkhal ila'l-iqtiṣād al-Islāmī* (Introduction to Islamic Economics). al-Qāhirah, Dār al-Nahḍat al-'Arabīyah, 1972. V.1 235p. (A)
24.	Farīdī, Fazlur Rahman	*Nature and Significance of Economic Activity in Islam*. Aligarh, Muslim University, Theological Society, n.d. 19p.
25.	al-Fāsī, 'Allāl	"Islām kā ma'āshī naẓarīyah" (Economic Theory of Islam), *Fikr-o-Naẓar* (Islamabad) 7(II), May 70: 814–30. (U)
26.	,, ,,	*al-Naqd al-Dhātī* (Self Criticism). Beirūt, Dār al-Kashshāf, 1966. 477p. (A)
27.	Fazlur Rahman	"Economic Principles of Islam", *Islamic Studies* (Islamabad), 8(1), Mar. 69: 1–8.
28.	Gīlānī, Sayyid Manāẓir Aḥsan	"Ahammīyat al-iqtiṣād fī ḍau' al-sunnah" (Importance of Economics in the light of Sunnah), *al-Ba'th al-Islāmī* (Lucknow) 10(4), Dec. 65: 55–61. (A)
29.	,, ,,	*Islāmī ma'āsniyāt* (Islamic Economics). Hyderabad, Idāra Ishā'at-e-Urdū, 1947. 453p. (U)
30.	Hameedullah, Muḥammad	"Review on J. Hans: *Homo Oeconomicus Islamicus* (Vienna, Austria, Joh, Sen. Klegnfurt, 1952, 144p.) with a map showing Foreign Investment in Muslim Petro Countries", *Islamic Quarterly* (London) 2(2), July 55: 142–146.
31.	Ḥamūda, 'Abd al-Wahhāb	"Siyāsat al-māl fi'l-Islām" (Financial Policy in Islam), *Liwā' al-Islām* 13(10), Dec. 59: 592–594. (A)
32.	Ḥasan, Ḥasan Ibrāhīm	*Islam: A Religious, Political, Social and Economic Study*. Beirut, Khayats, 1967.
33.	Ḥasan al-Bannā, Shaikh	*Mushkilātunā fī ḍau' al-niẓām al-Islāmī* (Our Pro-

blems in the light of Islamic System). al-Qāhirah, Dār al-Kitāb al-'Arabī, 1952. 96p. (A)

34. Huda, M. N. — "Islam and Economics", in: *Some Economic Aspects of Islam*, Karachi, Motamar Ālam-e-Islami, 1965: 15–26.

35. Ḥusainī, Aḥmad — *al-'Ilm wa'l-māl fi'l-Islām* (Knowledge and Wealth in Islam). al-Qahirah, Dār al-Taḥrīr li'l-Tibā'ah wa'l-Nashr, 1971. 126p. (A)

36. Ibrāhīm, 'Issa 'Abdou — "Ḥaula al-siyāsāt al-iqtiṣādīyah" (Regarding Economic Policies), *al-Muslimūn* (Dimashq), 3(1), Mar. 55: 52–55. (A)

37. Idrīs, Gaafar — "Economics Sans Man Sans Purpose: review Article on J. K. Galbraith's *Economics and the Public Purpose*", *Impact* (London) 4(12), 28 June, 11 July 74: 8.

38. Ja'farī, Ra'īs Aḥmad — *Islam aur 'adl-o-iḥsān* (Islam, Justice and Benevolence). Lahore, Idāra-e-Thaqāfat-e-Islāmiyah, 1960. 391p (U)

39. Jāmi'ah Fu'ād al-Awwal, Kullīyat al-Tijārah, Jam'īyat al-Dirāsāt al-Islāmīyah — al-Iqtiṣād fī ḍau' al-Islām (Economics in the light of Islam) al-Qāhirah, Dār al-Kitāb al-'Arabī, 1951. 114p. (A)

40. Kagaya, Kan — "Islam as a Modern Social Force", *Developing Economics*. (Tokyo) 4(1), March 66: 70–89.

41. Khān, Muḥammad 'Abdur Raḥmān — "Islāmī ma'āshiyāt" (Islamic Economics), *Burhān* (Delhi) 12(2), Feb. 44: 125–132. (U)

42. Khān, Muḥammad Murtaḍā — "Islām kī ma'āshī aqdār" (Economic Values of Islam), *Sayyārah* (Lahore) 16(xvi), 27–31. (U)

43. al-Khaṭīb, 'Abd al-Karīm — "Naḥwa iqtiṣād Islāmī mutaḥarrir" (Towards a Free Islamic Economy), *al-Wa'y al-Islāmī* (Kuwait) (113), May 74: 32–37. (A)

44. al-Khaṭīb, Muḥibb al-Din — "Daulah ta'āwunīyah wa ummah muta'āwanah" (Cooperative State and a Cooperating People), *al-Azhar* (Cairo) 29(4), Oct. 57: 289–294. (A)

45. ,, ,, ,, — "al-Māl fī niẓām al-Islām" (Wealth in Islamic System) *al-Azhar* (Cairo) 26 (17, 18), May 55: 945-953. (A)

46. al-Khaulī, Amīn — *Fī Amwālihim* (In their Wealth). Cairo. Dār al-Hana li'l Ṭibā'ah, 1963, 142p. (A)

47. Khurshīd Ahmad — *Islam and the Contemporary Economic Challenges*. Xerox Unpublished, 1973.

48. al-Labbān, Ibrāhīm — "Haqq al-fuqarā' fī Amwāl al-Aghniyā' " (Right of the Poor in the Wealth of the Rich). *Kitāb al-mu'tamar al-awwal li majma' al-buḥūth al-Islāmīyah*, Cairo, Mar. 64. (A)
Eng. Tr. "The Right of the Poor to the Wealth of the Rich", *al-Azhar* (Cairo) Mar. 64: 167–187.

49. Mawdūdī Sayyid Abul A'lā — "Economic and political teachings of the Quran" in Sharif, M. M. (ed.) *A History of Muslim Philosophy*, V. I. Wiesbaden, Otto Harrassowitz, 1963: 178–90.

50. ,, ,, ,, ,, — *The Economic Problem of Man and its Islamic Solution*. Lahore, Islamic Publications, 1975. 40p.

51. ,, ,, ,, ,, — "*Ma'āshiyāt-e-Islām* (Economics of Islam). Lahore, Islamic Publications, 1969. 436p. (U)

52.	Mawdūdī Sayyid Abul A'lā	"Principles and Objectives of Islam's Economic System", *Criterion* (Karachi), 4(2), Mar.–Apr. 69: 44–58.
53.	al-Miṣrī, 'Abd al-Samī'	*Naẓarīyat al-Islām al-iqtiṣādīyah* (Economic Theory of Islam). al-Qāhirah, Maktabah al-Anjalū al-Miṣrīyah, 1972. 246p. (A)
54.	Moulavi, C. N. Ahmad	*Principles and Practice of Islamic Economy* tr. from Malyalam by K. Hasan. Calicut (Kerala, India) Ansari Press, 1964. 200p.
55.	Muslehuddin, Muhammad	*Economics and Islam.* Lahore, Islamic Publications, 1974. 112p.
56.	Muzaffar Hussain	*Motivation for Economic Achievement in Islam.* Lahore, All Pakistan Educational Congress, 1974. 50p.
57.	Nadwī, 'Abd al-Bārī	*Tajdīd-e-ma'āshiyāt* (Reconstruction of Economics). Ṣidq-e-Jadīd Book Agency, 1955. 518p. (U)
58.	al-Najjār, Aḥmad	*al-Madkhal ila'l-naẓarīyat al-iqtiṣādīyah fi'l-minhāj al-Islāmī.* (Introduction to Economic Theory in the Framework of Islamic Methodology). Beirut, Dār al-Fikr, 1973. 315p. (A)
59.	,, ,,	*al-Naẓarīyat al-iqtiṣādīyah fi'l-Islām* (Economic Theory of Islam). al-Qāhirah, Dār al-Ṭaḥrīr li'l-Ṭibā'ah wa 'l-Nashr, 1973. 85p (A)
60.	Parwez, G. A.	*Quranic Economics.* Lahore, Quranic Research Centre, n.d. 24p.
61.	Qādrī, Sayyid Aḥmad	"Islāmī ma'āṣhiyāt kē chand rahnumā uṣūl" (Some guiding principles of Islamic Economics), *Zindagī* (Rāmpur) 41(2), Aug. 68: 31–40. (U)
62.	Quṭb, Sayyid	*al-'Adālat al-ijtimā'īyah fi'l-Islām* (Social Justice in Islam). 7th ed. 1967 294p. (A). (First published in 1948.) Urdu tr. by Siddiqi, Muhammad Nejatullāh: *Islam meṇ 'adl-e ijtimā'.* Lahore, Islamic Publications, 1969. 576p. English tr.: *Social Justice in Islam* by John D. Hardie, American Council of Learned Societies, New York, 1970, 298p.
63.	Quṭb, Muḥammad	*Shubhāt ḥaul al-Islām* (Islam: the Misunderstood Religion). Beirut, Dār al-Shurūq, 1973. 242p. (A) (First published in 1953.) English tr.: Islam: the Misunderstood Religion, Islamic Publications, Lahore, 1972. 199p.
64.	Rafī'uddīn	"'Usus al-iqtiṣād al-Islāmī' " (Fundamentals of Islamic Economics) *al-Ba'th al-Islāmī* (Lucknow) 8(1), Sept. 63: 32–40 (A)
65.	Ra'ūf al-Ḥasan, Shaikh	"Islām kē iqtiṣādī nazarīyāt" (Economic theories of Islam) *al-Balāgh* (Karachi) 3(10), Jan. 70: 15–23 (U)
66.	Riḍwī, Sayyid Zāhid Qaiṣar	"Islām meṇ daulat-o-iflās kā tawāzun" (Balancing between wealth and poverty in Islam), *Burhān* (Delhi) 12(2), Feb. 44: 133–150. (U)
67.	Shalbī, Aḥmad	*al-Ḥayāt al-ijtimā'īyah fi'l-tafkīr al-Islāmī* (Social life in Islamic Thought). al-Qāhirah, Maktabah al-Nahḍat al-Miṣrīyah, 1968. 392p. (A)
68.	,, ,,	*al-Siyāsah wa'l-iqtiṣād fi'l-tafkīr al- al-Islāmī* (Politics and Economics in Islamic Thought).

al-Qāhirah, Maktabah al-Nahḍat al-Miṣrīyah, 1964. (A)

69. al-Sharbāsī, Aḥmad — *al-Dīn wa'l-mujtama'* (Religion and Society) al-Qāhirah, al-Maṭba't al-'Arabīyah, 1970. 255p. (A)

70. al-Sibā'ī, Muṣṭafā — *Ishtirākīyat al-Islām* (Socialism of Islam) 2nd ed. Dimashq, Mu'assasa al-Maṭbu'āt al-'Arabīya, 1960. 423p. (A)

71. Ṣiddīqī, 'Abdul Ḥamīd — "Islām kā falsafa-e-ma'āshiyāt" (Economic Philosophy of Islam), *Chirāgh-e-Rāh* (Karachi), Sept. 51 : 17–36. (U)

72. Ṣiddīqī, Muḥammad Maẓharuddīn — *Islām kā ma'āshī naẓarīya* (Economic Theory of Īslam) 2nd ed. Lahore, Idāra-e-Thaqāfat-e-Islāmiyah, 1955. 92p. (U)

73. Ṣiddīqī, Muḥammad Nejatullāh — "Economics of Islam", *Islamic Thought* (Aligarh) 14(3), 71: 22–34.

74. Ṣiddīqī, Na'īm — "Chand ma'āshiyātī ḥaqīqateṇ" (Some Economic Truths) *Tarjumān al-Qur'ān* (Lahore) 33(6), May 50: 340–360. (U)

75. Ṣiddīqī, Ṣiddīq Jamāl — *Islām aur ma'īshat* (Islam and the Economy) Hyderabad (Dn), Nizam Silver Jubilee Press, nd. 64p. (U)

76. Syed, J. W. — "Islam and Material Progress", *Islamic Literature* (Lahore) 6(7), July 54 : 15–9.

77. al-Ṭaḥāwī, Ibrāhīm — *al-iqtiṣād al-Islāmī madhhaban wa niẓāman wa dirāsah muqāranah.* (Islamic Economics—a School of Thought and a System, a Comparative Study). al-Qāhirah, Majma' al-Buḥūth al-Islāmīyah, 1974. 2v. 616, 400p. (A)

78. Ṭāsīn, Muḥammad — "Islām kē ma'āshī maqāṣid (Economic Objectives of Islam), *Fikr-o-Naẓar* (Karachi) May 65 : 668–677. (U)

79. 'Uthmān, Shaikh Muḥammad — "Qur'ān kā ma'āshī rujḥān" (Economic attitude of Islām) *Fikr-o-Naẓar* (Islamabad) 3(9–10) Mar.–Apr. 66 : 647–660. (U)

80. 'Uthmānī, Muḥammad Fahīm — "Islāmī ma'āshiyāt : tana'uum wa 'aish koshī" (Islamic Economics : Affluent and Luxurious Living). *al-Ḥaqq* (Karachi), 5, Aug. 70 : 39–48. (U)

2. ECONOMIC SYSTEM OF ISLAM [81–498]

i. Sources and Precedents : 81–102

81. 'Abd al-Bārī — " 'Ahd-e-Hishām kā ma'āshī jāi'zah" (Economic Survey of the reign of Hishām) *Ma'ārif* (Azamgarh) 110(4), Oct. 72 : 267–281. (U)

82. al-Afghānī, Sa'īd — *Aswāq al-'Arab fi'l-jāhilīyah wa'l-Islām* (The Arab Markets during Jāhiliyyah and Islam). Dimashq, Dār al-Fikr, 1960. 528p. (A)

83. Amīnī, Muḥammad Taqī — "Ḥaḍrat 'Umar kī ma'āshī iṣlāḥāt" (Economic Reforms of 'Umar) *al-Furqān* (Lucknow) 38 (9, 10) Dec. 70 : 15–26. (U)

84. ,, ,, ,, — "Khilāfat-e-Fārūqī meṇ arāḍi kī tanẓīm-o-tansīq" (Land Organisation during the Caliphate of

'Umar), *Ma'ārif* (Azamgarh), 91(6) June 63: 405–409. (U)

85. Ḍanāwī, Muḥammad 'Alī — *'Umar bin 'Abd al-'Azīz fi'l-ḥukm wa'l-iqtiṣād wa'l-qaḍā'* ('Umar bin 'Abd al-'Azīz: Governance, Economics and Justice) Beirut, al-Dār al-'Arabīyah, 1966. (A)

86. Fāriq, Khurshīd Aḥmad — " 'Ahd-e-Fārūqī kā iqtiṣādī jā'izah" (Economic Survey of the Era of 'Umar) *Burhān* (Delhi) 64(6), June 70: 81–98. (U)

87. ,, ,, ,, — " 'Ahd-e-Ṣiddīqī kā iqtiṣādī jā'izah" (Economic Survey of the Era of Abū Bakr), *Burhān* (Delhi) 64(3), Mar. 70: 167–180; 64(4), Apr. 70: 241–255; 64(5), May 70: 324–337. (U)

88. ,, ,, ,, — "Daur-e-Ḥaidarī kā iqtiṣādī jā'izah" (Economic Survey of the Era of 'Alī), *Burhān* (Delhi) 65(6), Dec. 70: 392–409. (U)

89. Fischel, W. — "The Bait Māl al-khāṣṣa: a contribution to the History of 'Abbasid Administration", 19th Cong. Int. degli. Or, 1935: 538–541.

90. Gibb, H. A. R. — "The Fiscal Rescript of 'Umar II", *Arabica* 2(1955), 1–16.

91. Goitein, S. D. — *A Mediterranean Society*, Vol. I *Economic Foundation—the Jewish Communities of the Arab World as portrayed in the documents of the Cairo Geniza.* Berkley, Calif., Univ. of Calfornia Press, 1967. 550p.

92. Ḥameedullah, Muḥammad — *Jāhilīyat-e-'Arab ke ma'āshī niẓām kā athar pehlī mamlakat-e-Islāmīya kē qiyām par* (Impact of the Economic System of Arab Jāhiliyah Period on the Establishment of the First Islamic State). Hyderabad (Dn.), Habib Co., 1362 A.H. 103p.(U)

93. Imamuddin, S. M. — "Bayt al-Māl and Banks in the Medieval Muslim World", *Islamic Culture*, 34(1), Jan. 60: 22–30.

94. Kister, M. J. — "The Market of the Prophet" *Journal of the Economic and Social History of the Orient* (Leiden) 8(3), Jan. 65: 272–276.

95. Ra'nā, 'Irfān Maḥmūd — *Economic System under Omar the Great.* Lahore, Muḥammad Ashraf, 1970. 152p.

96. al-Rayyis, Muḥammad Ḍiyā' al-Dīn — *al-Kharāj wal'l-nuẓum al-mālīyah fi'l-Islām ḥattā muntaṣif al-Qarn al-thālith al-hijrī* (Kharāj and the Financial Systems in Islam till the Middle of the Third Century Hijra) Ph.D. Thesis, Kulliyat al-Ādāb, Jāmi'ah al-Qāhirah, 1959.(A)

97. Ṣāliḥ, Muḥammad Amīn — *al-Nuẓum al-iqtiṣādīyah fī Miṣr wa'l-Shām fī ṣadr al-Islām* (Economic Systems in Egypt and Syria in the beginning of the Islamic Era). al-Qāhirah, Maktabah Sa'id Rifa't, 1971. 228p. (A)

98. al-Shāfi'ī, Aḥmad — *al-Niẓām al-iqtiṣādī fī 'ahd 'Umar bin al-Khaṭṭāb* (Economic System in the Era of 'Umar bin Khaṭṭāb) Ph.D. Thesis, Cairo University. (A)

99. Shalbī, Maḥmūd — *Ishtirākīyatu Muḥammad* (Socialism of Muḥammad) Cairo, Maktabat al-Qāhirah al-Ḥadīthah, 1962. (A)

100. ,, ,, — *Ishtirākīyatu 'Umar* (Socialism of 'Umar). Cairo,

Maktabat al-Qāhirah al-Ḥadīthah, 1965. (A)

101. Shalbī, Maḥmūd — Ishtirākīyatu 'Uthmān (Socialism of 'Uthmān). Cairo, Maktabat al-Qāhirah al-Ḥadīthah, 416p. (A)

102. Ṣiddīqī, Muḥammad Maẓharuddīn — "Haḍrat 'Umar kī Zar'ī iṣlāḥāt" (Agricultural Reforms of 'Umar) *Thaqāfat* (Lahore) 1(8), Aug. 55: 7–14. (U)

ii. General: 103–166

103. Abāẓah, Ibrāhīm Dasūqī — *al-Iqtiṣād al-Islāmī: muqawwimātuhū wa minhājuhū* (Islamic Economics: its Elements and Methodology). Cairo, Dār al-Sha'b, 1974. (A)

104. ,, ,, ,, — "al-Islām wa'l-binā' al-iqtiṣādī" (Islam and the Economic Structure) *al-Taḍāmun* (al-Rabāṭ) 1(3), Feb. 74: 166–173. (A)

105. Abū Sa'ūd, Maḥmūd — "Economic Policy in Islam", *Islamic Review* (London) 45(5), May 57: 7–15.

106. Abū Zahra, Muḥammad — *Tanẓim al-Islām li'l-mujtama'* (Islamic Organisation of Society). Cairo, Maktabah al-Anjalū al-Miṣrīyah. 208p. (A)

107. al-'Ādil, Fu'ād — *al-'Adālat al-ijtimā'īyah* (Social Justice). Beirut, Dār al-Kitāb al-'Arabī, 1969. (A)

108. Afghānī, Shams al-Ḥaqq — "Islām kā ma'āshī niẓām" (Economic System of Islam) *Fikr-o-Naẓar* (Islamabad) 2, 89–100; 3, 276–284. (U)

109. Aḥmad, Manẓūr al-Raḥmān — "Takwīn jadīd li'l-iqtiṣād al-Islāmī (Reconstruction of Islamic Economy). *al-Ba'th al-Islāmī* (Lucknow) 13(10), July 69: 51–55; 14(1), Aug. 69: 58–64; 14(2), Sept. 69: 67–74. (A)

110. Amīn al-Ḥaqq — "Ma'āshī buḥrān aur Islām (Economic Crisis and Islam) *al-Ḥaqq* (Pakistan) 5(10), July 70: 41–48. (U)

111. ,, ,, — "Maujūdah ma'āshī buḥrān aur Islām" (Contemporary Economic Crisis and Islam) *al-Ḥaqq* (Pakistan) 5, (9) June 70: 50–59. (U)

112. al-'Araby, Muḥammad 'Abdullāh — "Ṭuruq istithmār al-amwāl wa mauqif al-Islām minhā" (Islamic Viewpoint Regarding the Ways of Productive Employment of Property) *al-Azhar* (Cairo) al-Mu'tamar al-thānī li majma' al-buḥūth al-Islāmīyah, May 65: 124–136. (A)

113. al-'Ashmāwī, Yāqūt — *al-Khuṭūṭ al-Kubrā li'l-niẓām al-iqtiṣādī fi'l-Islām* (Prominent Features of Economic System in Islam) al-Qāhirah, al-Idārat al-'Āmmah li'l-Thaqāfat al-Islāmīyah bi'l-Jāmi' al-Azhar, 1959. 32p. (A)

114. Ausaf Ali — *Political Economy of the Islamic State*. Ph.D. Thesis, University of Southern California, 1970. 280p.

115. Chāprā, M. 'Umar — *The Economic System of Islam—a Discussion of its Goal and Nature*. London, Islamic Culture Centre, 1970. 54p.

116. Faiḍullāh, Muḥammad Fawzī — "Minhāj al-Islām fi'l-takāful al-ijtimā'ī" (Islamic Method of Collective Responsibility) *al-Wa'y al-Islāmī* (Kuwait) 115, July 74: 52–61. (A)

117. Ghaznavi, Syed Abu Bakr — *Circulation of Wealth in Islam*. Lahore, Islamic

Society, West Pakistan University of Engineering & Technology. n.d. 14p.

118. al-Ghazzālī, Muḥammad — *al-Islām wa'l-awḍā' al-iqtiṣādīyah* (Islam and the Economic Institutions). al-Qāhirah, Dār al-Kutub al-Ḥadīthah, 1961. (First published in 1947.) (A)

119. Hameedullah, Muhammad — "The Economic System of Islam" in: *Introduction to Islam*. I.I.F.S.O., 1970: 140–168.

120. Ḥifẓur Raḥmān, Muḥammad, Seohārwī — *Islām kā iqtiṣādī niẓām* (Economic System of Islam). 2nd ed. Delhi, Nadwat al-Muṣannifīn, 1942. 359p. (U)

121. Husaini, S. Waqar Ahmad — "Principles of Environmental Engineering Systems Planning in Islamic Culture, Law, Politics, Economics, Education, and Sociology of Science and Culture", *in* Programmes in Engineering, Economic Planning: Stanford University Report EEP–47, December 1971: 281p.

122. Ibn 'Āshūr, Muḥammad al-Ṭāhir — *Uṣūl al-niẓām al-ijtimā'ī fi'l-Islām* (Principles of Social System in Islam). Tunis, al-sharikat al-Qaumīyah li'l-Nashr, 1964. 236p. (A)

123. ,, ,, — "al-Iqtiṣād al-Islāmī" (Islamic Economics) *al- Fikr al-Islāmī* (Beirut) 1(8), June 70: 32–58. (A)

124. 'Izz al-Dīn, Mūsā — *al-Islām wa qaḍāyā al-Sā'ah* (Islam and the Issues of the Day). Beirut, Dār al-Undulus, 1966. (A)

125. Jamā'at-e-Islāmī Pakistan — *Manshūr barā'ē intikhābāt 1970* (Manifesto for 1970 Elections) Lahore, 20 December 1969, 40p. (U)

126. ,, ,, — *Maujūdah iqtiṣādī buḥrān aur Islāmī ḥikmat-e-ma'īshat* (Contemporary Economic Crisis and the Economic Policy of Islam). Comp. by Khurshīd Aḥmad and Na'īm Ṣiddīqī. Lahore, Shu'bah Nashr-o-Ishā'at, 1970. 271p. (U)

127. Kāndhlawī, Iḥtishām al-Ḥaqq — *Ādāb-e-ma'īshat* (Rules of Economic Life). Delhi, Kutub Khāna Anjuman Tarraqī-e-Urdū, 1954. (U)

128. al-Kattānī, Muḥammad al-Muntaṣir — *Mudhakkirāt fi'l-amwāl fi'l-Islām* (Discourses on Wealth in Islam). Dimashq, Kullīyat al-Sharī'ah bi-Jāmi'ah Dimashq. (A)

129. Khān, Ḥāmid 'Alī — *Kasb-e ma'āsh kā Islāmī naẓarīyah* (Islamic Theory of Earning). Delhi, Jamāl Press, 1968. 115p. (U)

130. al-Khaulī, al-Bahī — *al-Tharwah fī Ẓill al-Islām* (Wealth in Islam) al-Qāhirah, Maṭba'ah al-Istiqlāl al-Kubrā, 1971. 161–340p. (A)

131. Makhlūf, Ḥasnain — *Fatwā Shar'īyah fī Shu'ūn iqtiṣādīyah* (Religious Verdict on Economic Issues Relating to Islam). Cairo, Maṭba'ah Muṣṭafā al-Bābī al-Ḥalabī, 1948. 16p. (A)

132. Mannan, M. A. — *Islamic Economics—Theory and Practice*. Lahore, Muḥammad Ashraf, 1970. 386p.

133. Mawdūdī, Sayyid Abul A'lā — *Rasā'il wa masā'il* (Letters and Problems) Vol. I. Delhi, Markazī Maktabah Jamā'at-e-Islāmī Hind, 1960. 415p. (U)

134. al-Mubārak, Muḥammad — *Niẓām al-Islām-al-iqtiṣād, mabādī wa gawā'id 'āmma* (Islamic System: The Economy, Elements and General Principles) Beirut, Dār al-Fikr, 1972. 160p. (A)

135. Muḥammad Miyāṇ — *Daur-e ḥāḍir kē siyāsī aur iqtiṣādī masā'il aur*

Islāmī ta'līmāt-o-ishārāt (Economic and Political Problems of the Present Age and the Teachings of Islam). Delhi, Kitābistān, 1970. (U)

136. Mustafizul Hasan, Syed — "The Quranic Way Out of the Present Economic Tangle", *Islamic Thought* (Aligarh) 1(2), May–June 54: 17–19.

137. Mu'tamar al-Buḥūth al-Islāmīyah al-Sābī' (al-Qāhirah, Sept. 1972) — *Buḥūth iqtiṣādīyah wa tashrī'īyah* (Economic and Legal Discourses) al-Qāhirah, Majma' al-Buḥūth al-Islāmīyah, 1973. 410p. (A)

138. Nabhān, Muḥammad Fārūq — *al-īttijāh al-jamā'ī fi'l-tashrī' al-iqtiṣādi al-Islāmī* (Social trend in the Economic Legislation of Islam) Beirut, Dār al-Fikr, 1970. 528p. (A)

139. al-Nabhānī, Taqī al-Din — *al-Niẓām al-iqtiṣādī fi'l-Islām* (Economic System of Islam) 3rd ed. al-Quds, Ḥizb al-Taḥrīr, 1953. 266p. (A)

140. Nadhīr Aḥmad — "Uṣūl-e-taqsīm-e-daulat aur Islām" (Principles of Distribution of Wealth in Islam) *Ma'ārif* (Azamgarh) 14(2) Aug. 24: 130–132. (U)

141. Nadwī, Abu'l Ḥasan 'Alī — "Mu'āsāt ṭau'īyah au musāwāt jabrīyah" (Voluntary Mutual Assistance or Forced Equality) *al-Ba'th al-Islāmī* (Lucknow) 11(1), Sep. 66: 63–83. (A)

142. al-Nowaihī, Muḥammad — "Fundamentals of Economic Justice in Islam" in: *Contemporary Aspects of Economic and Social Thinking in Islam*, Gary, Indiana, M.S.A. of U.S. & Canada, 1973: 100–124.

143. Parwez, Ghulām Aḥmad — *Niẓām-e rubūbīyat* (System of Divine Sustenance). Karachi, Idāra-e Ṭulū'-e Islām. 1954. 296p. (U)

144. Qureshī, 'Abdul Majīd — *"Ma'āshiyāt kā bunyādī mutala'ah"* (Basic Study of Economics) *Zindagī* (Rampur) 14(4, 5), July–Aug. 55: 81–87.(U)

145. Rodinson, Maxime — *Islam and Capitalism*, tr. by Brian Pearce, Suffolk, Allen Lane, 1974. 308p. Arabic tr. Nuzbah al-Ḥakim: *al-Islām wa'l-ra'smālīyah*. Beirut, Dār al-Ṭalī'ah, 1968.

146. Sālim, Aḥmad Mūsā — *al-Islām wa qaḍāyāna'l-mu'āṣirah* (Islam and our Contemporary Problems). al-Qāhirah, Dār al-Hanā li'l-Ṭibā'ah, 1970. 293p. (A)

147. Shabāna, Zakī Maḥmūd — "Ma'ālim ra'īsīyah iqtiṣādīyah Islāmīyah li muwājaha al-mushkilāt al-iqtiṣādīyah al-ḥāḍirah" (Salient Economic Features of Islam for Meeting the Challenges of Present Economic Problems) *al-Muslimūn* (Dimashq) 3(2–6). (A)

148. Shafī', Muftī Muḥammad — "Distribution of Wealth in Islam", *Muslim News International* (Karachi) 7(8), Feb. 69: 5–10; 7(9), Mar. 69: 3–8.

149. ,, ,, ,, — "Taqsīm-e daulat kā Islāmī niẓām" (Islamic System of Distribution of Wealth) *al-Furqān* (Lucknow) 35(12), Apr. 68: 25–37 (U) Arabic tr. "Mauqif al-Islām min tauzī' al tharwah" in *al-Ba'th al Islāmī* (Lucknow) 13(1), Sep. 68: 57–65; 13(2), Oct. 68: 57–68.

150. Shākir, 'Abdul Mun'im Aḥmad — *Individual and Social Responsibility in Islamic Thought*. Ph.D. Thesis, 1966, New York University.

151.	Shaltūt, Maḥmūd	"Money and the Economic Independence in Islam", *al-Azhar* (Cairo) 33(3), Aug. 61 : 5–18. (A)
152.	Shamsul Hoda, Mīr	"Islamic Economy", *Islamic Literature* (Lahore) 5(5), May 53 : 17–25.
153.	al-Sharbāṣi, A.	*al-Islām wa'l-iqtiṣād* (Islam and the Economy). al-Qāhirah, Dār al-Qaumīyah li'l Ṭibā'ah wa'l-Nashr, 1965. 276p. (A)
154.	Sheikh, Nasir Ahmad	*Some Aspects of the Constitution and the Economics of Islam.* Woking, England, The Woking Mission & Literary Trust, 1967. 246p. (First Published in 1957.)
155.	Ṣiddīqī, Ḥaīdar Zamāṇ	*Islām kā ma'āshiyātī niẓām* (Economic System of Islam). Karachi, Feroz Sons. (U)
156.	Ṣiddīqī, Muḥammad Maẓharuddīn	"Islam and Economic Exploitation", *Islamic Literature* (Lahore) 14(6), June 68 : 25–40.
157.	,, ,,	"Islam kī ma'āshī Ta'līmāt aur hamāra Jadid Mu'āsharah" (Economic Teaching of Islam and the Modern Society) *Fikr-o-Nazr* (Rawalpindi) 4(5), Nov. 66 : 285–97. (U)
158.	Ṣiddīqī, Muḥammad Nejatūllah	*Some Aspects of the Islamic Economy.* Lahore, Islamic Publications, 1970; Delhi, Markazī Maktabah Islāmī, 1972. 137p.
159.	Ṣiddīqī, Na'īm	*Ma'āshī nāhamwāriyoṇ kā Islāmī ḥal* (Islamic Solution of Economic Inequities). Karachi, Maktabah Chirāgh-e-Rāh, 1958. (U)
160.	Wāfī, 'Alī 'Abd al-Wāḥid	*al-Musāwāt fi'l-Islām* (Equality in Islam). Cairo, Dār al-Ma'ārif, 1962, 112p. (A)
161.	Yamānī, Aḥmad Zakī	" 'Adālatuna'l-ijtimā'ī" (Our Social Justice) *al-Muslimoon* (Geneva) 9(9), July 65 : 12–24;.9(10), Nov. 65 : 55–62. (A)
162.	,, ,, ,,	"Social Justice in Islam", *World Muslim League* (Singapore) 3(4), Apr. 66 : 11–33.
163.	Yunus, H. Kahruddīn	"Economic System of Islam", *Islamic Thought* (Aligarh) 10(3 & 4), Jan. 65 : 33–60.
164.	Yusuf, S. M.	*Economic Justice in Islam.* Lahore, Muḥammad Ashraf, 1971. vii, 116p.
165.	Yūsufuddīn, Muḥammad	*Islām kē ma'āshī naẓariyē* (Economic Theories of Islam) 2nd ed. Hyderabad, Maṭba' Ibrāhīmīyah, 1950. 2v. 756p. (U)
166.	World Muslim Congress	*Some Economic Aspects of Islam.* Karachi, Umma Publishing House, n.d. 164p. Arabic tr. *Ba'ḍ al-nawāḥī al-iqtiṣādīyah fi'l-Islām.* Karachi, 1964.

iii. Comparative Studies: 167–181

167.	Abdur Rauf, M.	"Islam and Contemporary Economic Systems" in: *Contemporary Aspects of Economic and Social Thinking in Islam.* Gary, Indiana, M.S.A. of U.S. & Canada, 1973 : 79–84.
168.	Ahmad, Sheikh Mahmud	*Economics of Islam: A Comparative Study.* Lahore, Muhammad Ashraf, 1972. xv, 227p.
169.	al-'Araby, Muḥammad 'Abdullāh	"al-Iqtiṣād al-Islāmī wa'l-iqtiṣād al-mu'āṣir" (Islamic Economics and Contemporary Economics) *al-Azhar, Majma' al-Buḥūth al-Islāmīyah, al-Mu'tamar al-thālith,* 1966 : 209–313. (A)

170. al-'Awadī, Rif'at — *al-Iqtiṣād al-Islāmī wa'l-fikr al-mu'āṣir: naẓarīyat al-tauzī'*. Risālat al-Mājistir, Jāmi'at al-Qāhirah (Islamic Economics and Contemporary Thought: Theory of Distribution). Master's Thesis, Cairo University. (A)

171. Bāqir al-Ṣadr, Muḥammad — *Iqtiṣādunā* (Our Economics). Beirut, Dār al-Fikr, 1968. 2 V. 694p. (A) (First published in 1961.)

172. al-Būṭī, Muḥammad Sa'īd Ramaḍān — *al-Madhhab al-iqtiṣādī bain al-shuyū'īyah wa'l-Islām* (Economic Ideology in Communism and Islam). Dimashq, al-Maktabat al-Umawīyah, 1959. (A)

173. al-Ghazālī, Muḥammad — *al-Islām al-muftarā 'alaihi bain al-shuyūī'īyīn wa'l-r'asmālīyīn* (Islam the Misinterpreted Religion Contrasted with Communism and Capitalism). al-Qāhirah, Maktabah Wahbah, 1960. (A) (First Published 1950).

174. Ḥaqqī, Iḥsān — *al-Islām wa'l-Shuyū'īyah* (Islam and Communism). Jeddah, al-Dār al-Sa'ūdīyah, 1970. (A)

175. Imran, Muhammad — "Islamic Social Justice: the Alternative to the Curse of Capitalism and Socialism", *Criterion* (Karachi) 5(1), Jan.–Feb. 70: 21–31.

176. Khurshid Ahmad — "Limādhā Yufaḍḍal al-iqtiṣād al-Islāmī 'alā ghairihā?" (Why Islamic Economic System is Regarded Superior to Other Systems?) *al-Ba'th al-Islāmī* (Lucknow) 14(10), June 70: 71–75. (A)

177. Mawdūdī, Sayyid Abul A'lā — *Usus al-iqtiṣād bain al-Islām wa'l-nuẓum al-mu'āṣirah wa Mu'ḍalāt al-Iqtiṣād wa ḥalluhā fi'l-Islām* (Fundamentals of Economics in Islam and the Contemporary Systems and Economic Problems of Man and their Islamic Solutions). 2nd ed. Jeddah, Dār al-Sa'ūdīyah li'l-Nashr, 1967. 189p. (A) tr. Muḥammad 'Āṣim al-Ḥaddād.

178. al-Nabhān, Muḥammad Fārūq — "Makānat al-iqtiṣād al-Islāmī bain al-nuẓum al-iqtiṣādīyah al-mu'āṣirah" (The Place of Islamic Economy in the Contemporary Economic Systems) *al-Nadwah* (Makka) 26 Feb. 1967. (A)

179. al-Nimr, 'Abd al-Mun'im — "al-Islām wa'l-madhāhib al-iqtiṣādiyah al-ḥadīthah" (Islam and Modern Systems of Economics) *al-Ba'th al-Islāmī* (Lucknow) 2(8), May 57: 9–14. (A)

180. Qadri, Anwar Ahmad — "The Sharī'a and Other Economic Systems", *Criterion* (Karachi) 4(5), Sept.–Oct. 59: 39–53.

181. Ṣiddīqī, 'Abdul Ḥamid — *Insāniyat kī ta'mīr-e-nau aur Islām* (Reconstruction of Humanity and Islam) Ichra, Lahore, Markazī Maktabah Jamā'at-e-Islāmī (Pakistan), 1956. 304p. (U)

iv. Socialistic Trends: 182–208

182. Abu 'l-'Uyūn, Maḥmūd — "al-Ishtirākīyah fi'l-Islam" (Socialism in Islam) *al-Azhar* (Cairo) 23(2), Ṣafr 51: 89–95. (A)

183. Cragg, K. — "The Intellectual Impact of Communism Upon Contemporary Islam", *Middle East Journal* 8(2), 54: 127–138.

184. Farrāj, Aḥmad (ed.) — *al-Islām din al-Ishtirākīyah* (Islam—a Religion of

Socialism). al-Qāhirah, al-Dār al-Qaumīyah, 1961. (A)

185. Faudah, ‘Abd al-Raḥim — “al-Mujtama‘ al-ishtirākī fī ẓill al-Islām” (Socialistic Society under Islam) *al-Azhar* (Cairo) 37(8) Feb. 68 : 438–441 ; 37(9, 10), Mar.–Apr. 66 : 525–528. (A)

186. Gardner, G. H. and Hanna, S. A. — “Islamic Socialism”, *Muslim World* 56(2), Apr. 66 : 71–86.

187. Ḥafīẓ, ‘Abbās — *al-Shuyū‘īyah fi’l-Islām* (Communism in Islam). 3rd ed. al-Qāhirah, Maktabat al-‘Arab, 1955. (A)

188. Halpern, M. — “The Implications of Communism for Islam”, *Muslim World* 43(1), Jan. 53 : 28–41.

189. al-Ḥanbalī, Shākir — “al-Ishtirākīyat al-Islāmīyah” (Islamic Socialism) *al-Tamaddun al-Islāmī* (Dimashq) 13(4, 5), Rabī‘ II 1366 A. H. 55–57. (A)

190. Hanna, Sami A. — “al-Takāful al-ijtimā‘ī and Islamic Socialism”, *Muslim World* 59(3, 4), Jul.–Oct. ; 69 : 275–286.

191. Ḥijāzī, ‘Abd al-Badī‘ — *al-Musāwāt wa’l-ishtirākīyah fi’l-Islam* (Equality and Socialism in Islam). (A)

192. Ibn al-Sabīl, Waiṭlīf Khālid — “Islāmī ishtirākīyat kē chand pahlū” (Some Aspects of Islamic Communism) *Fikr-o-Naẓar* (Karachi) 7(7), Jan. 70 : 513–526. (U)

193. Inamul Haq — *Principles and Philosophy of Democratic Socialism in Islam*. Karachi, The Author, 1966.

194. al-Khaṭīb, Anwar — *al-Naz‘at al-ishtirākīyah fi’l-Islām* (Socialist Trend in Islam), Beirut, Dār al-‘Ilm li’l-Malāyīn. (A)

195. al-Khaulī, al-Bahī — *al-Ishtirākīyah fi’l-mujtama‘ al-Islāmī bain al-naẓarīyah wa’l-taṭbīq* (Socialism in Islamic Society: Theory and Application). al-Qāhirah, Maktabah Wahbah, 181p. (A)

196. Marek, J. — “Socialist Ideas in the Poetry of Muhammad Iqbāl”, *Studies in Islam* (Delhi) 5(1–3), 68 : 167–179.

197. al-Miḥṣār, Hāmid — *Li man al-māl ? ‘alā ḍau’ Ṣariḥ al-Kitāb wa Ṣaḥīḥ al-Sunnah* (To Whom Belongs the Wealth ? In the Light of Explicit Provisions of the Qur’ān and Authentic Sunnah), al-Fajālah, Maṭba‘ah al-Ḥaḍārah al-‘Arabīyah 1974. (A)

198. al-Munajjid, Ṣalāḥ al-Dīn — *Balshafat al-Islām* (Bolshevism of Islam). Beirut, Dār al-Kitāb al-Jadīd, 1966. 144p. (A)

199. Muslehuddin, Muhammad — “Islamī Socialism – What it Implies?” *Criterion* (Karachi) 7(9), Sep. 72 : 34–39 ; 7(10), Oct. 72 : 19–29.

200. Parwez, Ghulām Aḥmad — *Economics in the Social Structure of Islam*. Lahore, Quranic Research Centre, n.d. 12p.

201. ,, ,, ,, — “Rizq-e-Muḥammadī kī taqsīm” (Distribution of ‘Muhammadī’ Provisions) *Ṭulū‘-e-Islām* (Karachi) 23, June 70 : 18. (U)

202. Riḍwān, Aḥmad Muḥammad — *Ishtirākīyat al-Islām* (Socialism of Islam). al-Qāhirah, Dār al-Kitāb al-‘Arabī, 1950. 136p. (A)

203. Sarkar, Abdul Bari — *The Concept of Islamic Socialism*, Dacca, The Author, 1964.

204. Sharbāṣī, Sa‘īd al-Shirabīnī — *Mabādi’l-ishtirākīyah fi’l-Islām* (Socialist Elements in Islam). al-Qāhira Dār al-Qaumīyah, n.d. 86p. (A)

205. Sharqāwī, Maḥmūd — “Ṣūrah min ishtirākīyat al-Islām” (A form of

Islam's Socialism) *al-Azhar* (Cairo) 37(4), Oct. 65: 236–239. (A)

206. Ṣiddīqī, Muḥammad Maẓharuddin — "Socialistic Trends in Islam", *Islamic Literature* (Lahore) 4(10) Oct. 55: 5–18. (Also published in *Iqbal* (Lahore) 1(1), 52: 65–82).

207. Wāfī, 'Alī 'Abdul Wāḥid — "Islamic Socialism: The Best Guard Against Communism", *al-Azhar* (Cairo) 31(2), Aug. 59: 58–64; 31(3), Sep. 59: 91–93.

208. Yūsuf Ludhyānwī, Muḥammad — "Islāmī ishtirākīyat ba-silsila-e-Kitāb al-Amwāl" (Islamic Communism in connection with 'Kitāb al-Amwāl') *Bayyināt* (Karachi) 115, Jan. 70: 44–54; Feb. 70: 37–47. (U)

v. Ownership: 209–223

209. Abū-Sunnah, Aḥmad Fahmī — "Taḥdīd al-milkīyah fi'l-Islām" (Ceiling on Property in Islam) *al-Azhar* (Cairo) 24(3), Nov. 52: 300–363. (A)

210. 'Abdullah Knoun — "Private Property and its Limits in Islam" *Al-Azhar Academy of Islamic Research, First Conference*, Mar. 64.

211. al-'Araby, Muḥammad 'Abdullāh — "al-Milkīyat al-Khāṣṣah wa ḥudūduhā fi'l-Islām" (Private Property and its Limits in Islam) *Kitāb al-Mu'tamar al-Awwal li-majma' al-buḥūth al-Islāmīyah*, Cairo, 1964. (A)

212. al-'Araby, Muḥammad 'Abdullāh — "Private Property and its Limits in Islam" *al-Azhar Academy of Islamic Research, First Conference*, Mar. 64.

213. 'Arafah, Muḥammad — "Taḥdīd al-milkīyah fi'l-Islām", *al-Azhar* (Cairo) 24(2) Oct. 52: 141–145. (A)

214. 'Audah, 'Abd al-Qādir — *al-Māl wa'l-ḥukm fi'l-Islām* (Property and Government in Islam), 4th ed. Beirut, Manshūrāt al- 'Aṣr al-Ḥadīth, 1971. 116p. (A)

215. Ḥasan, 'Abd al-Ghaffār — "Infirādī milkīyat" (Individual Ownership) *Mīthāq* (Lahore) 17, May–June 70: 47–54. (U)

216. al-Ḥusainī, al-Sayyid Abu'l-Naṣr Aḥmad — *al-Milkīyah fi'l-Islām* (Property in Islam). al-Qāhirah, Dār al-Kutub al-Ḥadīthah, 1952. (A)

217. Ittiḥād Ṭullāb Handasat al-Qāhirah, al-Lajnat al-Thaqāfīyah, al-Jam'īyah al-Dīnīyah — *al-Māl wa'l-milkīyah fi'l-Islām* (Property and Ownership in Islam). al-Qāhirah, Maṭba'ah al-Jīlādī, 1972. (A)

218. Jamāl al-Dīn, Aḥmad — *Naz' al-Milkīyah fī aḥkām al-sharī'ah wa nuṣūṣ al-qānūn* (Confiscation of Property According to the *Sharī'ah* and Positive Law). Ṣaidā', al-Maktabat al-Miṣrīyah, 1966. (A)

219. al-Khafīf, Shaikh 'Alī — "al-Milkīyat al-fardīyah wa taḥdīduhā fi'l-Islām" (Individual Property and its Limits in Islam) *Mu'tamar 'Ulamā' al-Muslimīn al-Awwal, Kitāb al-Mu'tamar* (al-Qāhirah), Mar. 64: 128 ff (A) Eng. tr. "Individual Property and its Limits in Islam" *al-Azhar, Academy of Islamic Research, First Conference*, Mar. 64: 79–103.

220. Ṣiddīqī, Muḥammad Maẓharuddin — "Islām aur ijtimā'ī milkīyat" (Islam and Collective Ownership) *Thaqāfat* (Lahore) 3(5) Nov. 56: 46–51. (U)

221. Ṣiddīqī, Muḥammad Nejatullāh — *Islām kā naẓarīya-e-milkīyat* (Islam's Theory of Property). Lahore, Islamic Publications, 1968. 2 vols., 304. 299p. (U)

222. 'Uthmānī, Muḥammad Fahīm — "Infirādī milkīyat par Islām kī 'ā'id Karda ḥudūd wa quyūd" (Restrictions Placed by Islam on Individual Ownership) *al-Ḥaqq* 5 June 70: 23–33. (U)

223. 'Uthmānī, Muḥammad Muḥtaram Fahīm — "Islām Meṇ shakhṣī milkīyat "(Private Property in Islam), *al-Ḥaqq* 5, Apr. 70: 40–49. (U)

vi. Land: Ownership and Tenure: 224–242

224. Abd al-Kader, Ali — "Land Property and Land Tenure in Islam", *Islamic Quarterly* (London) 5(1, 2), Apr.–July 59: 4–11. (Also published in *Islamic Review* (London) 47(12), Dec. 59 (20–23)

225. Aḥmad, Shaikh Maḥmūd — *Mas'ala-e-Zamīn aur Islām* (The Problem of Land and Islam). Lahore, Institute of Islamic Culture, 1955. 234p. (U)

226. Amīnī, Muḥammad Taqī — *Islām kā zar'ī niẓām* (Agricultural System of Islam). Delhi, Nadwatul-Muṣannifīn, 1955. 303p. (U)

227. A'ẓamī, Nūr Muḥammad — "Ẓamīn aur us kē masā'il" (Land and its Problems) *al-Balāgh* (Karachi) 4(2–3): 46–53. (U)

228. Gabaliah, al-Syed — "The Significance of Some Aspects of Islamic Culture for Tenure Adjustment: a Comment", *Land Tenure*. Proceedings of the International Conference on Land Tenure and Related Problems in World Agriculture held at Madison, Wisconsin, 1956: 109–110.

229. Ḥāmid, Muḥammad — "Naẓarun fī istighlāl al-arḍ fi'l-Islām" (A Glance at Exploitation of Land in Islam) *al-Muslimoon* (Dimashq) 3(1), Mar. 55: 77–83; 3(2), Apr. 55: 54–59. (A)

230. al-Kattānī, Muḥammad Muntaṣir — "al-Arḍ: milkīyatuhā wa Kirā'uhā fi'l-Islām" (Land, its Ownership and Lease in Islam), *al-Muslimoon* (Dimashq) 6(1), Feb. 58: 33–41; 6(2), Mar. 58: 35–44; 6(3), May 58: 43–53; 6(4), Sep. 58: 24–30. (A)

231. al-Khaṭīb, Syed 'Abdul Ḥamīd — "Landed Property and Ownership of Land in Islam" in: *Some Economic Aspects of Islam*. Karachi, Motamar, al-Alam al-Islami, 1965: 109–119.

232. Mawdūdī, Sayyid Abul A'lā — *Mas'ala-e Milkīyat-e Zamīn* (The Problem of Land Ownership). Lahore, Maktabah Jamā'at-e Islāmī, 1950. 76p. (U) Arabic tr. *Mas'alat milkīyat al-arḍ fi'l-Islām*. Kuwait, Dār al-Qalam, 1969.

233. "Mauqif al-Ikhwān al-Muslimīn min taḥdīd al-milkīyah: ḥadīth ma' al-Murshid al-'Āmm" (Stand of al-Ikhwān al-Muslimūn on Ceiling on Property —Interview with Murshid al-'Āmm) *al-Akhbār* (Cairo) 2 Sept. 52: 6. (A)

234. Muḥammad Aḥmad — *Mas'ala-e-Zamīn* (The Problem of Land). Lahore, Idrāra-e Thaqāfat-e Islāmīyah. (U)

235. Nadwī, Syed Habeebul Haq — "al-Iqṭā': A Historical Survey of Land Tenure and Land Revenue Administration in some Muslim

Countries with Special Reference to Persia", *Contemporary Aspects of Economic and Social Thinking in Islam*. Gary, Indiana, M.S.A. of U.S. and Canada, 1973: 125–156.

236. Poliak, A. N. "Classification of Land in Islamic Law and its Technical Terms", *American Journal of Semetic Languages and Literatures* 57: 50–62.

237. Qureshi, Ishtiāq Ḥussain "Islām meṇ milkīyat-e-Zamīn kā mas'ala" (The Problem of Land Ownership in Islam) *Thaqāfat* (Lahore) 6(4), Apr. 58: 9–21. (U)

238. Rashad, Shah Muhammad "Land Ownership and Tenure in Islam", *Islamic Thought* (Aligarh) 6(2), 59: 29–34.

239. Ṣakr, Manṣūr Muḥammad "al-Islām wa Kirā' al-'ard". (Islam and the Rent of Land) *Liwā' al-Islām* (Cairo) 16(8), Aug. 62: 511–514. (A)

240. al-Sāyis, Shaikh Muḥammad Alī "Milkīyat al-afrād li'l-arḍ wa manāfi'uhā fi'l-Islām" (Individual Ownership of Land and its Benefits in Islam) in: *al-Azhar, al-Mu'tamar al-awwal li-majma' al-buḥūth al-Islāmīyah*, Cairo. 1964. (A) Eng. tr. "Ownership of Land and its Benefits in Islam" *Al-Azhar Academy of Islamic Research*, First Conference, Mar. 64: 127–151.

241. Shafī', Muftī Muḥammad *Islām kā niẓām-e arāḍī* (Land Tenure in Islam), Karachi, Idārah al-Ma'ārif, 1383 A.H. 288p. (U)

242. Yusuf, S. M. "Land, Agriculture and Rent in Islam", *Islamic Culture*, 31(1), Jan. 57: 27–39.

vii. Share Cropping: 243–244

243. Ḥasan, 'Abd al-Ghaffār "Muzāra'at par taḥqīqī naẓar" (A Critical Evaluation of Share Cropping), *Tarjumān al-Qur'ān* (Lahore) 33(1, 2, 3), Dec. 49–Jan. 50: 89–112. (U)

244. Ṣiddīqī, Ḥaidar Zamāṇ "Muzāra'at par taḥqīqī naẓar" (A Critical Evaluation of Share Cropping), *Tarjumān al-Qur'ān* (Lahore) 34(2, 4, 5) July–Aug.–Sep. 50: 121–168. (U)

viii. Partnerships and Profit-Sharing: 245–250

245. Gaiani, A. "The Juridical Nature of the Moslem Qirāḍ", *East & West* (Rome) (1953) 81–86.

246. al-Khafif, Shaikh 'Alī *al-Sharikāt fi'l-fiqh al-Islāmī: buḥūth muqārinah* (Partnerships in Islamic Law: Comparative Studies). al-Qāhirah, al-Jāmi'ah al-'Arabīyah, 1962. (A)

247. Khan, Muḥammad Akram "Types of Business Organisations in Islamic Economy", *Islamic Literature* (Lahore) 17(8), Aug. 71: 5–16.

248. al-Khayyāt, 'Abd al-'Aziz *al-Sharikāt fi'l-sharī'at al-Islāmīyah wa'l-qānūn al-waḍ'ī* (Partnerships in Islamic Law and Positive Law). 'Ammān, Wizārat al-Auqāf, 1971. 2v. 378, 342p. (A)

249. Ṣiddīqī, Muḥammad Nejātullāh *Shirkat aur muḍārabat kē Shar'ī uṣūl* (Islamic Legal Principles of Partnership and Profit Sharing). Lahore, Islamic Publications, 1969. 159p. (U) English tr. *Partnership and Profit-Sharing in Islamic Law*, Leicester, The Islamic Foundation, 1985, 111p.

250. Udovitch, Abraham L. *Partnership and Profit in Medieval Islam*. Princeton, N.J. Princeton Univ. Press, 1970. 282p.

ix. Consumption: 251–252

251. 'Abbāsī, Muḍṭar "Isrāf kā ma'āshī pahlū" (Economic Aspect of Extravagance), *al-Ḥaqq* (Pakistan) 5(1), Jan. 70: 41–50. (U)

252. Khurshīd Aḥmad "Islam and Simple Living", *Criterion* (Karachi) 5(4) July–Aug. 70: 5–12.

x. Business and Trade: 253–260

253. 'Alī Naqī *Tijārat aur Islām* (Trade and Islam). Lucknow, Imamia Mission, 1933. 73p. (U)

254. Hasanuzzaman, S. M. *Trade in Islam: Principles and Practices*. Karachi, Motamar al-Alam-al-Islami, n.d. 64p.

255. Ibrāhīm, Muḥammad "The Standard of Business Morality in Islam", *Islamic Literature* (Lahore) 23(5), May 71: 281–289.

256. Mūsā, Muḥammad Yūsuf *Fiqh al-Kitāb wa'l-sunnah: al-buyū' wa'l-mu'āmalāt al-mu'āṣirah* (Jurisprudence of the Qur'ān and Sunnah: Contemporary Trade and Transactions). Miṣr, Dār al-Kitāb al-'Arabī, 1373/1954. (A)

257. Nadwī, 'Abd al-Qayyūm *al-Tijārāt fi'l-Islām* (Trades in Islam). Lahore, Kutub Khana Punjab. 160p. (U)

258. De Somogyi, J. "Trade in Classical Arabic Literature", *Muslim World* 55(2), Apr. 65: 131–134.

259. ,, ,, "Trade in the Qur'ān and Ḥadīth", *Muslim World* 52(2), Apr. 62: 110–114.

260. Ṭihrānī *al-Bai' min Sharā'i' al-Islām* (Trade in Islamic Law). Tehran, 1320/1902. (A)

xi. Hisbah: 261–273

261. 'Abd al-Wahhāb, Ḥasan Ḥasanī "Aṣl al-Ḥisbah bi'l-Ifrīqīyā: taḥlīl Kītāb Aḥkām al-Sūq li Yaḥyā b. 'Umar." (Basis of *Ḥisbah* in Africa—an Analytical Study of Yaḥyā b. 'Umar's Book 'Rules of the Market'), *Hauliyāt al-Jāmi'ah, al-Jāmi'ah al-Tunisīyah*, 4. 67: 5–21. (A)

262. Fahmī, 'Alī Ḥasan "al-Ḥisbah fi'l-Islām Muqāranah ma' al-nuẓum al-mushābiha fi'l-tashrī' al waḍ'ī" (*Ḥisbah* in Islam: A Study in comparison with similar institutions in Positive Law) in: *Usbū' al-fiqh al-Islāmī*. Dimashq, 1961. (A)

263. Ḥusainī, Isḥāq Mūsā "al-Ḥisbah fi'l-Islām" (*Ḥisbah* in Islam) *al-Muslimūn* (Geneva) 9(2), Sept. 64: 17–26; 9(4), Jan. 65: 37–44. (A)

264. ,, ,, ,, "*Ḥisbah* in Islam" *al-Azhar, Academy of Islamic Research*, Cairo, First Conference. Mar. 64: 255–277.

265. al-Khafīf, Shaikh 'Alī "al-Ḥisbah" (*Ḥisbah*) in *Usbū' al-fiqh al-Islāmī*, Dimashq, 1961.

266. Latham, J. D. "Observations on the Text and Translation of Al-Jarsifi's Treatise on 'Ḥisba'," *Journal of Semetic Studies*, 5 (1960), 60: 124–143.

267. al-Sāmarrā'ī Ḥusām al-Dīn *Nihāyat al-rutbah fī ṭalab al-ḥisbah li Ibn Bassām al-Muḥtasib* (Highest Standards in Organising

Ḥisbah by Ibn Bassām al-Muḥtasib) 1968. (A)

268. al-Shaḥāwī, Ibrāhīm Dasūqī — *al-Ḥisbah fi'l-Islām* (*Ḥisbah* in Islam). al-Qāhirah Maktabah Dār al-'Urūbah, 1382–1962. (A)

269. ,, ,, — *al-Ḥisbah waẓīfah ijtimā'īyah* (*Ḥisbah* a Social Function). al-Qāhirah, Majma' al-Buḥūth al-Islāmīyah, 1973. 64p. (A)

270. al-Shūrijī, al-Bushrā — *al-Tas'īr fi'l-Islam* (Price Control in Islam). Kuwait. 155p. (A)

271. 'Urnūs, Maḥmūd — "Sharī'at al-Ḥisbah fi'l-Islam" (The Law relating to *Ḥisbah* in Islam) *Liwā' al-Islām* (Cairo) 8(2), June 54: 99–103. (A)

272. Wickers, G. M. — "Al-Jarsifi on the Hisba", *Islamic Quarterly* (London) 3(3), 1956–57: 176–187.

273. Ziadeh, Nicola — *al-Ḥisbah and al-muḥtasib in Islam: Old Texts Collected and Edited with an Introduction.* Beirut, Catholic Press, 1962.

xii. Co-operation: 274–279

274. Baryūn, Nūrī 'Abdussalām — *Mafhūm al-arbāḥ fi'l-iqtiṣād al-ta'āwunī ma' al-ishārah ila'l-fikr al-iqtiṣādī al-kilāsīkī* (Meaning of Profits in a Cooperative Economy with a Note on the Classical Economic Thought). Tripoli, Libya, Dār al-Fikr, 1969. (A)

275. Fahīm, Muḥammad — *Ṣuwar al-ta'āwun fi'l-Islām* (Forms of Cooperation in Islam) al-Qāhirah, Dār al-Kitāb al-'Arabī, 1968. 81p. (A)

276. Ḥimādah, 'Abd al-Mun'im — *al-Islām wa'l-ta'āwun* (Islam and Cooperation). al-Qāhirah, al-Majlis al-A'lā li-Shu'ūn al-Islāmīyah, 1968. 186p. (A)

277. ,, ,, ,, — "al-Sharikāt al-ta'āwunīyah" (Cooperative Partnerships) *Liwā' al-Islām* 19(11), 25 Oct. (A)

278. Ṣiddīqī, Na'īm — "Islāmī niẓām meṇ imdād-e bāhamī kē idārāt" (Cooperative Institutions in Islamic System) *Chirāgh-e Rāh* (Karachi) Jan. 51: 33–43. (U)

279. ,, ,, — "al-Ta'āwun fi'l-Islām" (Cooperation in Islam) *Liwā' al-Islām* 14(8), 22 Sep. 60: 507–516. (A)

xiii. Hoarding: 280–282

280. Abdul Majid — "Islam, Christianity and Monopoly", *Islamic Review* (London) Aug. 40: 287–290.

281. ,, ,, — "al-Iḥtikār wa'l-ribḥ al-fāḥish ḥarām ka'l-ribā" (Hoarding and Exhorbitant Profits are Prohibited like *Ribā*), *al-Azhar* (Cairo) 24(3), Nov. 52: 350–351 (A)

282. Madkūr, Muḥammad Salām — "al-Iḥtikār wa tas'īr al-sila' wa ḥukmuhā fi'l-fiqh al-Islāmī (Hoarding and Price Control and their Position in Islamic Law) *al-Wa'y al-Islāmī* (Kuwait) (116), Aug. 74: 33–39. (A)

xiv. Public Finance: General: 283–299

283. Abāẓah, Ibrāhīm Dasūqī — "al-Siyāsat al-mālīyah fi'l iqtiṣād al-Islāmī" (Financial Policy in Islamic Economy) *al-Manhal* (Jeddah) 34(10), Nov. 73: 712–717. (A)

284. Ahsan, M. Manazir — "Baytul māl and its Role in the Islamic Economy", *Criterion* (Karachi) 10(9), Sept. 75: 14–27.

285. Aghnides, Nicholas P. — *Mohammaden Theories of Finance*. Lahore, Premier, 1961. iv, 532p.

286. Bravmann, Meir M. — "The Surplus of Property—an early Arab Social Concept", *Der Islam* (Berlin) 38(62): 28–50.

287. Hameedullah, Muhammad — "Budgeting and Taxation in the time of Holy Prophet", *Journal of the Pakistan Historical Society* 8(pt. I), Jan. 55.

288. Ḥasan, 'Abd al Raḥmān — "al-Mawārid al-'āmma fi'l-Islām" (Public Revenue in Islam) *Kitāb al-Mu'tamar al-Awwal li Majma' al-Buḥūth al-Islāmīyah*, Cairo, Mar. 64. Eng. tr. "Financial Resources in Islam" *al-Azhar, Academy of Islamic Research*, First Conference March 1964.

289. Hasanuzzaman, S. M. — *Economic Functions of the Islamic State* (up to the end of the Umayyad period) Ph.D. Thesis, 1973. Edinburgh University. Published: Karachi, International Islamic Publishers, 408p.

290. 'Iwaḍ, Badawī 'Abd al-Laṭīf — *al-Mizānīyah al-ūlā fi'l-Islām* (The First Budget in Islam). Beirut, Jām'iah Beirūt al-'Arabīyah, 1973. 39p. (A)

291. ,, ,, ,, ,, — *al-Niẓām al-mālī al-Islāmī al-muqārin* (A Comparative Study of the Islamic Financial System). al-Qāhirah, al-Majlis al-A'lā li'l-shu'ūn al-Islāmīyah, 1972. 124p. (A)

292. al-Jamāl, Muḥammad 'Abd al-Mun'im — *Dirāsāt ḍarībīyah Islāmīyah mu'āṣirah* (Studies in Contemporary Islamic Taxation). al-Qāhirah, Ma'had al-Dirāsāt al-Islāmīyah. (A)

293. al-Jaraf, Muḥammad Kamāl — *al-Niẓām al-mālī al-Islāmī* (Islamic Financial System). al-Qāhirah, Maktabat al-Nahḍat al-Jadīdah, 1970. (A)

294. Khaṭīb, 'Abd al-Karīm — *al-Siyāsat al-mālīyah fi'l-Islām* (Financial Policy in Islam). al-Qāhirah, Dār al-Fikr al-'Arabī, 1961. (A)

295. Lokkegaard, Frede — *Islamic Taxation in the Classical Period with Special Reference to Circumstances in Iraq*. Copenhagen, Branner & Korch, 1950. 286p.

296. Marsī, Muḥammad Kāmil — *al-Amwāl* (Wealth). 2nd ed. al-Qāhirah, Maṭba'ah Fatḥ Allāh Ilyās, 1937. (A)

297. Nadwī, Muḥammad Isḥāq — "Mālīyat al-daulah fi'l-Islām" (State Finance in Islam), *al-Ba'th al-Islāmī* (Lucknow) 8(3), Nov. 63: 64–69. (A)

298. Ṣiddīqī, S. A. — *Public Finance in Islam*. Lahore, Sheikh Mohammad Ashraf, 1975, 252p. first published in 1948.

299. 'Uwaiḍah, Aḥmad Thābit — *al-Islām waḍa'a al-usus al-ḥadīthah li'l-ḍarībah* (Islam Formulated the Modern Canons of Taxation). al-Jāmi' al-Azhar, 1959. 10p. (A)

xv. Public Finance: Zakāt: 300–321

300. Abū Zahra, Shaikh Muḥammad — "al-Zakat" (*Zakāt*) *al-Azhar, al-Mu'tamar al-Thānī li-Majma' al-Buḥūth al-Islāmīyah*. Cairo, May 65: 137–201. (A)

301.	Ahmad, Shaykh (ed.)	*Some Socio-Economic Aspects of Zakāt*. Karachi, Pakistan Institute of Arts and Design. n.d.
302.	'Allām, Mahdī	"al-Ṣadaqah fi'l-Islām" (*Ṣadaqāt*) in Islam *al-Azhar* (Cairo) 37(1), May 65: 90–100. (A)
303.	Ataullah, Sheikh	*Revival of Zakāt*. Lahore, Rippon Printing Press, 1949. 110p.
304.	al-Bassām, 'Abdullāh bin 'Abd al-Raḥmān	"al-Zakāt fi'l-Islām (*Zakāt* in Islam) Nadwah *Muḥāḍarāṭ, Rābiṭat al- 'Ālam al-Islāmī* (Makka) 67: 198–212. (A)
305.	Faruki, Kamal A.	"Islam and Social Justice", *Criterion* (Karachi) 7(7), July–Aug. 72: 34–45.
306.	Ghulām, 'Alī, Malik	"Zakāt wa Ṣadaqāt kā niẓām" (The System of *Zakāt* and *Ṣadaqāt*) *Tarjumān al-Qur'ān* (Lahore) 60(2), May 63: 114–117. (U)
307.	Hussain, Mirza Moḥammad	"Zakāt—A Scheme of Social Insurance" in: *Islam and Socialism*. Lahore, 1947: 119–177.
308.	Ibrāhīm, Muḥammad Ismā'īl	*al-Zakāt* (*Zakāt*). al-Qāhirah, Dār al-Fikr al-'Arabī, 1959, 166p. (A)
309.	Iṣlāḥi, Amin Aḥsan	"Mas'ala-e-tamlīk aur Zakāt kē muta'alliq ba'ḍ dūsrē masā'il" (Transfer of Ownership and Some Other Problems Related to *Zakāt*) *Tarjumān al-Qur'ān* (Lahore) 44(6), Aug. 55: 395–410; 45(1), Sep. 55: 33–65. (U)
310.	Mawdūdī, Sayyid Abul A'lā	"Zakāt aur mas'ala-e tamlīk (*Zakāt* and Transfer of Ownership) *Tarjumān al-Qur'ān* (Lahore) 43(3), Nov. 54: 198–204. (U)
311.		"Naẓarāt fi'l-Zakāt min khilāl al-iṭār al-'āmm il'l-sharī'ah" (Observations on *Zakāt* in the Context of the General Framework of Islamic Law) *al-Fikr al-Islāmī* (Beirut) 1(3), Jan. 72: 84–88. (A)
312.	Niẓāmī, Khwāja Ḥasan	*Khudā'i income tax: aḥkām, masā'il aur maṣārif-e zakāt kā bayān*" (Divine Income Tax: A Statement of the Rules and Regulations relating to *Zakāt* and Heads of its Expenditure). Delhi, Dilli Printing Works, 1925. 80p. (U)
313.	al-Qarḍāwī, Yūsuf	*Fiqh al-Zakāt: dirāsah muqāranah li-aḥkāmihā wa falsafatihā fī ḍau' al-Qur'ān wa'l-sunnah* (Principles of *Zakāt*: A Comparative Study of its Philosophy and Laws in the Light of the Qur'ān and the *Sunnah*). Beirut, Dār al-Irshād, 1969. 2v. 1227p. (A)
314.	Rafiullah	"Niṣāb-e Zakāt par ēk taḥqīqī naẓar" (A Study of Exemption Limit in Relation to *Zakāt*) *Fikr-o-Naẓar* (Karachi) 3(5), Nov. 65: 349–362. (U)
315.	al-Sabsabī, 'Abd al-Qādir	"Ḥaula sharī'at al-*Ẓakāt*" (on Laws of *Zakāt*) *al-Muslimūn* (Dimashq) 6(8), June–July 59: 51–57; 6(9) Aug.–Oct. 59: 63–69. (A)
316.	Sakr, Muhammad Ahmad	*al-Zakāt wa muqāranatuhā bi'l-ḍarā'ib al-mu'āṣirah* (*Zakāt* and its Comparison with Contemporary Taxes). *Mimeo*, Baiḍā', Libya, 1972. 8p. (A)
317.	Shafī', Muftī Muḥammad	*Qur'ān meṇ niẓām-e Zakāt* (System of *Zakāt* in the Qur'ān). Karachi, Dār al-Ishā'at, 1963. 118p. (U)
318.	Shāh, Syed Ya'qūb	"Zakāt kē maṣārif" (Heads of *Zakāt* Expenditure) *Fikr-o-Naẓar* (Islamabad) 5(12), June 68: 917–927; 6(1), July 68: 46–55. (U)

319. Ṭasīn, Muḥammad — "*Ṣan'atī Sarmā'ē aur 'imārāt par Zakāt*" (*Zakāt* on Industrial Capital and Buildings) *Fikr-o-Naẓar* (Islamabad) 4(7): 435–448. (U)

320. Yūsuf, Mirzā Muḥammad — "Mas'ala-e tamlīk fi'l-Zakāt" (Transfer of Ownership and Giving Into Possession Regarding *Zakāt*) *Burhān* (Delhi) 37(9) Sept. 56: 150–161; 37(10) Oct. 56: 213–225; 37(11) Nov. 56: 273–291; 37(12) Dec. 56: 337–352; 38(1), Jan. 57: 24–38. (U)

321. de Zayas, Farishta G. — *The Law and Philosophy of Zakāt*. Damascus, al-Jadīdah Press, 1960. xxix, 420p.

xvi. Public Finance: 'Ushr, Kharāj, etc.: 322–329

322. Dennett, Danial C.Jr. — *Conversion and the Poll Tax in early Islam*. Cambridge, 1950. 13p. Urdu tr.: Mihr, Ghulām Rasūl, *Jizyah aur Islām*. Lahore, Ghulām Alī, 1962. 207p.

323. Khan, M. A. — "Jizyah and Kharaj (A Classification of the Meaning of the Terms as they were used in the 1st Century H.)" *Journal of Pakistan Historical Society* 4(76) (1956): 27–35.

324. Qādrī, Sayyid Aḥmad — " 'Ushr kē ēk Juz'iyē kī tauḍīḥ" (Classification of a Rule Relating to '*Ushr*). *Zindagī* (Rampur) 26(3), Mar. 66: 53–55. (U)

325. Qureshi, Aijaz Hasan — "A Critical Study of Wellhausen's Theory of Land and Poll Tax under Muslims" *Islamic Literature* (Lahore) 11(1, 2) Jan.–Feb. 59: 45–56.

326. ,, ,, ,, — "Assessment and Collection of Kharaj (Land Tax) under 'Umar I, the Second Caliph in Islam", *Journal of Punjab University Historical Society* 13(61): 83–92; *Voice of Islam* (Karachi) 10(11) Nov. 62: 531–541.

327. ,, ,, ,, — "The Terms *Kharāj* and *Jizya* and their implications", *Journal of Punjab Historical Society* 12 (June 1961): 27–38.

328. Tritton, A. S. — "Notes on the Muslim System of Pensions", *Bulletin of the School of Oriental and African Studies* 16(1), 54: 170–172.

329. De Zayas, Farishta G. — "Tithe Lands, Kharāj Lands, and the Law of *Zakāt*", *Islamic Literature* (Lahore) 13(5), May 67: 5–9.

xvii. Inheritance: 330–333

330. 'Abd al-Razzāq, Muḥammad — "Islāmī qānūn-e Wirāthat kī Khuṣūṣīyāt" (Characteristics of Islamic Law of Inheritance), *Ma'ārif* (Azamgarh) 34(1), July 34: 30–36. (U)

331. Abū Zahra, Muḥammad — *Aḥkām al-tarikāt wa'l-mawārīth* (Laws of Inheritance and Legacies). Cairo. Dār al-Fikr al-'Arabī, n.d. 344p. (A)

332. Mūsā, Muḥammad Yūsuf — *al-Tarikah wa'l-mirāth fi'l-Islām, ma' madkhal fi'l-mirāth 'inda'l-'Arab wa'l-Rūmān, baḥth muqārin* (Inheritance and Legacy in Islam, with an Introduction to Inheritance amongst Arabs and the Romans—A Comparative Study). al-Qāhirah, Ma'had al-Dirāsāt al-'Arabīyah al-'Āliah, 1960. 396. (A)

333. al-Ṣa'īdī, 'Abd al-Muta'āl — *al-Mīrāth fi'l-sharī'at al-Islāmīyah wa'l-sharāi' al-Samāwīyah wa'l-waḍ'īyah* (Inheritance in Islamic Law, Other Divine Laws and the Positive Laws). al-Qāhirah, Maktabat al-Ādāb. 183p. (A)

xviii. Social Security: 334–344

334. Abū Zahra, Muḥammad — *al-Takāful al-ijtimā'ī fi'l-Qur'ān* (Collective Responsibility in the Qur'ān). al-Dār al-Qaumīyah li'l-ṭibā'ah wa.'l-Nashr, 1964.

335. al-Fanjarī, Muḥammad Shauqī — "al-Islām wa mushkilat al-faqr" (Islam and the Problem of Poverty) *al-'Arabī* (Kuwait) (169), Dec. 72: 34–41. (A)

336. Ibrāhīm, Aḥmad Ibrāhīm — *Niẓām al-nafaqāt fi'l-sharī'ah al-Islāmīyah* (Rules Relating to Maintenance in Islamic Law). al-Qāhirah, Maṭba'ah Salafīyah, 1349 A.H. (A)

337. al-Labban, Ibrahim — "Islam and the Problem of Poverty", *Islamic Review* (London) 55(8), Aug. 67: 14–19.

338. al-Qarḍāwī, Yūsuf — *Mushkilat al-faqr wa kaifa 'ālajaha'l-Islām* (Problem of Poverty and how Islam has dealt with it). 'Ammān, Jordan, Maktabat al-aqṣā; Beirut, al-Dār al-'Arabīyah 1966. 168p. (A)

339. al-Ramadi, Gamal eldin — "Social Security in Islam", *al-Azhar* (Cairo) 36(10, Mar. 65: 9–12.

340. Rizq, 'Alī Shiḥateh — *Maṣra' al-faqr fi'l-Islām.* (Eradiction of Poverty in Islam), al-Qāhirah, Dār al-Ta'līf, 1951. 223p. (A)

341. al-Ṭanṭāwī, 'Alī — *Muḥāḍarah: Nafaqāt al-aqārib ka maṣdar li tamwīl mashrū'āt al-takāful al-ijtimā'ī. Halqat al-dirāsat al-ijtimā'īyah li'l duwal al-'arabiyah, al-mun'aqad fī Dimashq* āmm 1953. (Discourse: Maintenance of Near Relatives as a Source of Financing Schemes for Social Security.
Series of Social Studies of Arab Countries, conducted in Damascus in 1953. (A)

342. 'Ulwān, 'Abdullāh — *al-Takāful 'al-ijtimā'ī fi'l-Islām* (Collective Responsibility in Islam). Jeddah, al-Dār al Sa'ūdīyah. (A)

343. 'Uthmān, Muḥammad Fatḥī — *al-Islām Yuḥārib al-faqr* (Islam at War with Poverty). (A)

344. al-Zayyāt, A. Ḥasan — "How Islam Tackles Poverty", *Azhar* (Cairo) 31(7), Jan. 60: 153–157. (A)

xix. Endowments: 345–348

345. Cattan, H. — "The Law of Waqfs" in: *Law in The Middle East*, V.I. 1955: 203–222.

346. Schacht, J. — "Early Doctrines on Waqfs", *Mél Köprülü* 1953: 443–452.

347. Shaṭā, Muḥammad — "al-Waqf Wasīlah li-taḥqīq al-'adālah al-ijtimā'īyah fi'l-tashrī' al-Islāmī" (*Waqf* a Means of Ensuring Social Justice in Islamic Law) *Nadwat al-Muḥāḍarāt. Rābitāt al-'Ālam al-Islāmī*, Makka 1959: 29–37. (A)

348. Suhrawardi, A. al-Mamoon — "The *Wakf* of Moveables", *Journal Proceedings of the Asiatic Society of Bengal N.S.*, 7(1911): 323–340.

xx. Insurance: 349–380

349.	'Abdou, Muḥammad 'Issa	"al-Ta'mīn" (Insurance), *al-Balāgh* (Kuwait) 9 July 69:20; 20 Aug. 69. (A)
350.	,, ,, ,,	*al-Ta'mīn: al-aṣīl wa 'l-badīl* (Insurance: Original and Substitute). Beirut, Dār al-Buḥūth al-Islāmīyah, 1972. 48p. (A)
351.	al-Bahī, Muḥammad	*Niẓām al-Ta'mīn fī hadyi aḥkām al-Islām wa ḍarūrāt al-mujtama'* (Insurance according to Islamic Laws and the Needs of Society) 1965. (A)
352.	Dānish, Aḥmad	*Muḥāḍarah fi'l-ta'mīn* (A Lecture on Insurance). (A)
353.	,, ,,	"al-Ta'mīn wa hal huwa ḥill fī jamī' ṣuwarih?" (Insurance: Are All of its Forms Legal?). *al-Azhar* (Cairo) 26(5, 6), Nov. 54: 273–274. (A)
354.	al-Dasūqī, Muḥammad	"al-Ta'min bain al-naẓarīyah wa'l-taṭbiq" (Insurance in Theory and Practice) al-Wa'y al-Islāmī (Kuwait) (60), Feb. 70: 12–19. (A)
355.	al-Dasūqī, Muḥammad al-Syed	*al-Ta'min wa mauqif al-sharī'at al-Islāmīyah minhu* (Insurance and the Standpoint of Islamic Law) al-Qāhirah, al-Majlis al-A'lā li'l-Shu'ūn al-Islāmīyah, 1967. 198p. (A)
356.	al-Hindī, Abū Salmān	*Bīma-e-Zindagī Islāmī nuqṭa-e naẓar sē* (Life Insurance from Islamic Viewpoint). Karachi, Maktabah Sa'dīyah, n.d. (U)
357.	Ibrāhīm, Aḥmad Muḥammad	" 'Audah ilā'l-ta'mīn fi'l-sharī'ah wa'l-qānūn" (Insurance in Islamic Law and Secular Law) *al-Fikr al-Islāmī* (Beirut) 2(3), Mar. 71: 77–83; June 71: 67–71. (A)
358.	,, ,,	"al-Ta'mīn fi'l-sharī'ah wa'l-qānūn" (Insurance in Islamic Law and Secular Law), *al-Fikr al-Islāmī* (Beirut) 2(2), Feb. 70: 75–83. (A)
359.	'Īsā, 'Abd al-Raḥmān	*al-Mu'āmalāt al-ḥadīth wa aḥkāmuhā* (New Transactions and their Legal Position). 84p. (A)
360.	Jārullāh, Mūsā	"Islām aur bīma" (Islam and Insurance) *al-Raḥīm* (Karachi) Mar. 67 (U)
361.	al-Khafīf, Shaikh 'Alī	"al-Ta'min" (Insurance), *al-Azhar* (Cairo) 37(1), May 65: 79–89; 37(2, 3), Sep. 65: 156–160; 37(4), Oct. 65: 268–274; 37(5, 6), Nov. Dec. 65: 353–357; 37(7), Jan. 66: 416–420; 37(8), Feb. 66: 478–485; 37(9, 10) Mar. 66: 534–546; 38(1), Apr. 66: 110–115. (A)
362.	al-Khaṭīb, Muḥibb al-Dīn	"al-Ta'mīn" (Insurance), *al-Azhar* (Cairo) 26(3), Sep. 54: 130–133. (A)
363.	al-Khizām, Anṭoun Ḥabīb	*al-Ta'mīn* (Insurance), al-Qāhirah, 1950. 350p. (A)
364.	Kilingmulier, E.	"The Concept and Development of Insurance in Islamic Countries", *Islamic Culture* 43(1), Jan. 69: 27–37.
365.	al-Majlis al-A'lā li-Ri'āyat al-funūn wa'l-Ādāb wa'l-'ulūm al-ijtimā'īyah	*Usbū' al-fiqh al-Islāmī wa Mahrajān Ibn Taimīyah.* (Islamic Jurisprudence Week and Ibn Taimīyah Celebrations). Cairo, 1963. 925p. (A) Contributions: al-Zarqā', Muṣṭafā Aḥmad:

'Aqd al-ta'mīn wa mauqif al-sharī'at al-Islāmīyah minhu (Insurance Contract and the Stand Point of Islamic Law).
al-Qalqīlī, Muḥammad:
'Aqd al-ta'mīn (Insurance Contract).
al-Amīn, Muḥammad:
Ḥukm 'aqd al-ta'mīn fi'l-sharī'at al-Islāmīyah (Position of Insurance Contract in Islamic Law).
'Īsā, 'Abd al-Raḥmān:
'Aqd al-ta'mīn (Insurance Contract);
Ḥilmī, Bahjat Aḥmad: *Mazāyā niẓām al-ta'mīn* (Distinguishing Features of Insurance).
'Umaruddīn, Muḥammad:
'Aqd al-ta'mīn (Insurance Contract).

366. Majlis Taḥqīqāt-e Shar'īyah, Lucknow
Sawālnāma muta'alliqah insurance ma' jawābāt (Questionnaire Relating to Insurance with Replies) n.d. (U)

367. Malik, Muḥammad Rāmīz
"Ra'yun ākhar fi'l-ta'min" (Another Opinion on Insurance) *al-Fikr al-Islāmī* (Beirut) 2(10), Oct. 71: 25–37. (A)

368. Muḥammad, Sa'd Ṣādiq
"al-Ta'mīn fi'l-sharī'ah wa'l-qānūn" (Insurance in Islamic Law and Positive Law) *al-Wa'y al-Islāmī* (Kuwait) (61), Mar. 70: 51–59. (A)

369. Muṣleḥuddīn, Muḥammad
Insurance and Islamic Law. Lahore, Islamic Publications, 1969. 202p.

370. Nadwī, Muḥammad Isḥāq
"Mas'alat al-ta'mīn kamā yarahā Majlis al-Dirāsāt al-shar'īyah" (The issue of Insurance as Viewed by *Majlis Dirāsāt Sharī'yah, al-Ba'th al-Islāmī* (Lucknow) 10(7), Apr. 66: 61–65. (A)

371. al-Qarḍāwī, Yūsuf
"Naẓarat al-sharī'ah ila'l-ta'āwun wa'l-ta'mīn" (Cooperation and Insurance as Viewed by *Sharī'ah*) *al-Ba'th al-Islāmī* (Lucknow) 12(6), Mar. 68: 44–52. (A)

372. al-Rūḥanī, al-Sayyid Muḥammad Ṣādiq
al-Masā'il al-mustaḥdatha (The New Issues). Qum, 1384 A.H. (A)

373. al-Sanūsī, Aḥmad Ṭāhā
" 'Aqd al-tạm'īn fi'l-tashrī' al-Islāmī" (Insurance Contract in Islamic Legislation) *al-Azhar* (Cairo) 25(2), 232–236; 25(3), 303–307. (A)

374. Ṣiddīqī, Muḥammad Nejatullāh
Insurance Islāmī ma'īshat meṇ (Insurance in Islamic Economy). Delhi, Islam and the Modern Age Society, 1975. 95p. (U) English tr. *Insurance in an Islamic Economy*, Leicester, The Islamic Foundation, 1985, 74p. Arabic tr. *al Ta'mīn fi'l Iqtiṣād al Islāmī*, Jeddah, Markaz Abḥāth al Iqtiṣād al Islāmī, 1987, 105p.

375. Ṣiddīqī, Na'īm
Bīma-e Zindagī Islāmī nuqṭa-e nigāh sē (Life Insurance from Islamic Viewpoint). Lahore, Islamic Publications, 1960; Dehli, Markazī Maktabah Islāmī, 1974. 31p. (U)

376. ,, ,,
"al-Ṭa'mīn 'alā'l-Ḥayāt" (Life Insurance) Nadwah *Liwā' al-Islām* (Cairo) 8(11), 708–714. (A)

377. Tonkī, Muftī Walī Ḥasan
"Islām aur bīma" (Islam and Insurance) *Bayyināt* (Karachi) 5(5), Mar. 65: 18–40; 6(1), Apr. 65: 17–33. (U)

378. 'Uthmān, Muḥammad Fatḥī
al-Fikr al-Islāmī wa'l-taṭawwur (Islamic Thought, and Change) 2nd ed. Kuwait, al-Dār al-Kuwaitīyah, 1969. 559p. (A)

379. Wahbah, Taufiq 'Alī
"al-Ta'mīn fi'l-sharī'ah wa'l-qānūn" (Insurance in

		Islamic Law and Positive Law), *al-Wa'y al-Islāmī* (Kuwait) (53), July 69: 16–21. (A)
380.	al-Zarqā', Muṣtafā Aḥmad	*'Aqd al-ta'mīn (al-sūkarah) wa mauqif al-sharī'at al-Islāmīyah minhu* (Insurance Contract and the Standpoint of Islamic Law). Dimashq, Maṭba'ah Jāmi'ah Dimashq, 1962. 112p. (A)

xxi. Banking without Interest: 381–422

381.	Abāẓah, Ibrāhīm Dasūqī	"Ḥaula msharū' al-bunūk al-Islāmīyah" (On the Project of Islamic Banks) *al-Manhal* (Jeddah) 33(7), Aug.–Sept. 72: 730–737. (A)
382.	'Abdou, Muḥammad 'Issa	*Bunūk bilā fawā'id* (Banks Without Interest). al-Qāhirah, Dār al-Fikr, 1970. (A)
383.	Ahmad, Sheikh Mahmud	"Banking in Islam", *Muslim News International* 8(1), June 69: 5–11.
384.	al-'Araby, Muḥammad 'Abdullāh	"Contemporary Bank Transactions and Islam's Views Thereon" *Islamic Thought* (Aligarh) 11(3, 4), July 67: 10–43.
385.	,, ,,	"al-Mu'āmalāt al-Maṣrifīyah al-mu'āṣirah wa ra'y al-Islām fīh" (Contemporary Bank Transactions and Islam's Views Thereon), *al-Azhar. al-Mu'tamar al-thānī li-Majma' al-Buḥūth al-Islāmīyah.* May. 65: 79–122. (A)
386.		*Bank Dubai al-Islāmī* (Dubai Islamic Bank). Dubai, Matba'ah Dubai, 1975. 40p. (A)
387.	Bāqir al-Ṣadr	*al-Bank al-lā rabawī fi'l-Islām* (Interest Free Bank in Islam). Beirut, Dar al Kitāb al Lubnānī, Second edition, 1973, 283p. (A) (Urdu tr. 'Ali Jawādī, *Islamic Bank*. Bombay, Jamali Publications, 1974. 208p.
388.	Baryūn, Nūrī 'Abdussalām	*Kaifa Yakūn al-niẓām al-Maṣrifī fi'l-iqtiṣād al-Islāmī* (The Shape of the Banking System in Islamic Economy). Tripoli, Libya, Dār Maktabat al-Fikr, 1972. (A)
389.	Conference of Islamic Finance Ministers, Jeddah, Aug. 1974.	*Islamic Development Bank. Articles Establishing the IDB.*
390.		*The Egyptian Study on the Establishment of the Islamic Banking System* (Economics and Islamic Doctrine), Cairo, 1972.
391.	al-Gammāl, Gharīb	*al-Maṣārif wa'l-a'māl al-maṣrifīyah fi'l-sharī'at al-Islāmīyah wa'l-qānūn* (Banks and Banking Transactions in Islamic Law and Positive Law). al-Qāhirah, Dār al-Ittiḥād al-'Arabī li'l-Ṭibā'ah, 1972. 477p. (A)
392.	Ghanameh, Abdul Hadi	"The Interestless Economy" in: *Contemporary Aspects of Economic and Social Thinking in Islam.* Gary, Indiana, M.S.A. of U.S. and Canada, 1973: 85–99.
393.	Hammeedullah, Muḥammad	"Anjumanhā-e qarḍa-e bē sūd" (Interest Free Loan Societies), *Ma'ārif* (Azamgarh) 53(3) Mar. 44: 211–216. (U)
394.	,, ,,	"Bunūk al qarḍ bidūn rībā" (Interest Free Lending Banks) *al-Muslimoon* (Dimashq) 8(3), Dec. 62: 16–21. (A)

395. Hammeedullah, Muḥammad — "A Suggestion for an Interest Free Islamic Monetary Fund", *Islamic Review* (London) 43(6), June 55: 11–12.

396. al-Hamsharī, Muṣṭafā 'Abdullāh — *al-A'māl al-maṣrifīyah wa'l-Islām* (Banking Operations and Islam). Beirut, al Maktab al Islāmī, 1983, 363p.

397. Huda, M. N. — "Economics Accepting Islam", *World Muslim League* (Singapore) 1(3), Jan. 64: 10–17.

398. ,, ,, — "Hal Yumkin 'an ta'mala al-bunūk bighair fā'idah" (Is it possible for Banks to function without Interest?) *al-Muslimūn* (Dimashq) 3(4), June 55: 36–40. (A)

399. Irshad, Shaikh Ahmad — *Interest Free Banking*. Karachi, Orient Press of Pakistan, n.d. 100p.

400. ,, ,, ,, — *Bilā sūd bank kārī* (Banking Without Interest). Karachi, Maktabah Tahrīk Musāwāt, n.d. 152p. (U)

401. al-'Itr, Nūr al-Dīn — al-Mu'āmalāt al-maṣrifīyah wa ḥukmuhā fi'l-Islām (Banking Transactions and their Legal Position in Islam). (A)

402. Jamjūm, Aḥmad Ṣalāḥ — *al-Bank al-Islāmī* (Islamic Bank). Jeddah, Maṭābi' Dār al-Iṣfahānī wa Shurakā'hū. 33p. (A)

403. Khan, Muhammad Akram — "Interest Free Banking: Some Further Questions", *Islamic Education* (Lahore) 5(2), Mar.–June 72: 29–47.

404. ,, ,, ,, — "Islāmī ma'īshat meṇ bank aur bachateṇ" (Banks and Savings in Islamic Economy), *Chirāgh-e-Rāh* (Karachi) May–June 65: 68–83. (U)

405. al-Lajnah al-Tahḍīrīah li Mashrū' Bait al-Tamwīl al-Kuwaitī — *Mashrū' al-niẓām al-asāsī li-bait al-tamwīl al-Kuwaitī*. Kuwait, n.d. 21p. (A)

406. Mannan, M. A. — "Consumption Loan in Islam", *Islamic Review* (London) 58(3), Mar. 70: 19–22.

407. ,, ,, — "Islam and Trends in Modern Banking—Theory and Practice of Interest Free Banking", *Islamic Review* (London) 56(11, 12) Nov.–Dec. 68: 5–10; 57(1), Jan. 69: 28–33.

408. ,, ,, — "A Muslim World Bank; Urgent Need", *Criterion* (Karachi) 6(1) Jan.–Feb. 71: 15–20.

409. Muslehuddin, Muhammad — *Banking and Islamic Law*. Karachi, Islamic Research Academy, 1974. 153p.

410. ,, ,, — *Commonwealth of Muslim Countries and the Muslim World Bank*.

411. al-Najjār, Aḥmad Muḥammad 'Abd al-'Azīz — Bunūk bilā fawā'id ka-istirātijīyah li'l-tanmīyah al-iqtiṣādīyah wa'l-ijtimā'īyah fi'l-duwal al-Islāmīyah. (Banks Without Interest as a Strategy for Economic and Social Development of Muslim Countries) Jeddah, Jāmi'at al-Malik 'Abd al-'Azīz, 1972. 104p. (A)

412. Ready, R. K. — "The Egyptian Municipal Savings Bank Project", *International Development Review* 9, June 67: 2–5.

413. Sakr, Muhammad Ahmad — *Tanẓīm al-maṣārif fī ḍau' al-Islām* (Organisation of Banks in the Light of Islam. Baiḍā', Libya, 1972. 20p. mimeo. (A)

414. Sattar, S. A. — "Interest Free Banking", *Criterion* (Karachi) 9(6), June 74: 15–26.

415. Shalbī, Aḥmad — "al-Bank al-Islāmī" (Islamic Bank) *al-Wa'y al-Islāmī* (Kuwait) 5(56) Oct. 69: 19–25. (A)

416. Siddīqī, Muhammad Nejatullah — "A Model of Interest Free Banking", *Criterion* (Karachi) 6(4), July–Aug. 61: 19–33; *Journal of Islamic Studies* (Cairo) 2(3), Oct. 69: 1–22.

417. ,, ,, — *Ghair sūdī bank kārī* (Banking Without Interest). Lahore, Islamic Publications, 1969. 224p.; Delhi, Markazī Maktabah Jamā'at-e-Islāmī Hind, 1969. 235p. (U) English tr. *Banking Without Interest*. Lahore Islamic Publications, 1973. 207p. Leicester, The Islamic Foundation, 1983, 192p. Persian tr. *Bankdārī Bidūn Bahra*, Tehran, Sarosh Press, 1982, 176p. Arabic tr. *al Niẓām al Maṣrafī al la Rabwī*, Jeddah, King Abdulaziz University, 1985, 136p.

418. ,, ,, — "Islāmī ma'īshat kē ba'ḍ pahlū" (Some Aspects of Islamic Economy), *Chirāgh-e-Rāh* (Karachi) Oct. 65: 19–28. (U)

419. Ṣiddīqī, Na'īm — "Islamī uṣūl par banking" (Banking according to Islamic principles), *Chirāgh-e-Rāh* (Karachi) 1(11), Nov. 48: 60–64; 1(12), Dec. 48: 24–28. (U)

420. 'Uzair, Muḥammad — " 'Awāmil al-najāḥ fi'l-maṣārif al-lārabawīyah" (Factors Contributing to the Success of Interest Free Banks) *al-Muslimoon* (Dimashq) 6(1), Feb. 58: 81–85; 6(4), Sep. 58: 84–88; 6(5), Oct. 58: 70–77. (A)

421. ,, ,, — "Interestless Banking: Will it be a Success?", *Voice of Islam* (Karachi): 853–859.

422. ,, ,, — *An Outline of Interestless Banking*. Karachi; Dacca, Raihan Publications, 1955. 21p.

xxii. Foreign Trade: 423

423. 'Uzair, Muḥammad — "Foreign Trade in an Interestless Economy", *Voice of Islam* (Karachi) 7(2–3), Nov.–Dec. 58: 90–104.

xxiii. Labour and Industrial Relations: 424–445

424. Abū Zahra, Muḥammad — "al Waẓīfah wa'l-muwaẓẓif fi'l-Islām" (Service and the (Public) Servant in Islam), *Liwā'al-Islām* (Cairo) 16(4), 5 May 62: 225–231; 16(5), June 62: 290–295. (A)

425. 'Ayyad, M. Gamāluddīn — *al-'Amal wa'l-'ummāl* (Labour and the Labourers). al-Qāhirah, sharikat al-Ittiḥād wa'l-Ṭibā'ah, 1967. 136p. (A)

426. ,, ,, — "Ḥuqūq al-'ummāl fi'l-Islām" (Rights of the Labourers in Islam), *al-Azhar* 37(4), Oct. 65: 247–250; 37(5, 6) Nov.–Dec. 65: 312–328. (A)

427. ,, ,, — "al-Islām wa'l-'alāqāt al-insānīyah fī majāl al-'amal" (Islam and Human Relations in the Field of Labour), *al-Azhar* 37(7), Jan. 66: 410–412. (A)

428. ,, ,, — "The Merits of Labour in Islam", *al-Azhar* 38(1), Apr. 66: 7–10.

429. ,, ,, — "Wājibāt al-'ummāl fi'l-Islām (Duties of the Labourers in Islam), *al-Azhar* 37(8), Feb. 66: 469–471. (A)

430. al-Bakr, 'Abd al-Raḥmān — 'Alāqāt al-'amal fi'l-Islam (Labour Relations in Islam). al-Qāhirah, al-Mu'assasah al-Thaqāfīyah al-'Ummālīyah 1970. 151p. (A)

431. Faridi, Fazlur Rahman — "On Wages in an Islamic Economy", *Islamic*

Thought (Aligarh) 7(1), Apr.–June 60: 61–66.

432. Faridi, Fazlur Rahman — "The Problem of Industrial Peace", *Islamic Research Circle Bulletin* (Rampur) 5(1), Oct. 53: 5–18.

433. Hameedullah, M. — "Islam's Solution to the Basic Economic Problems —the Position of Labour", *Islamic Culture (Hyderabad)* 10(2), Apr. 36: 213–233.

434. Khan, Muhammad Akram — "The Theory of Employment in Islam", *Islamic Literature* (Lahore) 14(4), Apr. 68: 5–16.

435. Malik, Muhammad Shafi — "Wages in an Islamic Economy", *Islamic Thought* (Aligarh) 7(2), July–Sep. 60: 62–67.

436. Mawdūdī, Sayyid Abul A'lā — "Bērozgārī kā mas'alah ḥal karnē kē liyē sarmāya-dārī socialism aur Islām kā ṭarīq-e-kār" (The Methods of Capitalism, Socialism and Islam in Solving the Problem of Unemployment), *Zindagī* (Rampur), 41(2), Aug. 68: 41–42. (U)

437. ,, ,, — "Taqrīr—Labour Convention (Speech in Labour Convention) 12 May 1957", *Chirāgh-e-Rāh* (Karachi) Oct. 57: 44–48. (U)

438. Nadwī, Mujībullāh — "Islāmī qānūn-e ujrat kā ēk bāb" (A Chapter of the Islamic Law of Wages), *Ma'ārif* (Azamgarh) 77(6), June 56: 405–421. (U)

439. Qureshī, 'Abdul Majīd — *Miḥnat kē masā'il aur unkē ḥal* (Labour Problems and their Solutions). Ichra, Lahore, al-Ḥabīb Publications, n.d. 60p. (U)

440. ,, ,, ,, — "On 'Wages' in an Islamic Economy", *Islamic Thought* (Aligarh) 7(3), Oct.–Dec. 60: 40–45.

441. ,, ,, ,, — "Wages in an Islamic Economy", *Islamic Thought* (Aligarh) 6(2), Oct.–Dec. 59: 24–28.

442. Siddīqī, Muhammad Nejatullah — "Industrial Peace", *Islamic Thought* (Aligarh) 1(1) Mar.–Apr. 54: 17–18.

443. Udovitch, A. L. — "Labour Partnership in Early Islamic Law", *Journal of the Economic and Social History of the Orient* 10(1), 67: 64–80.

444. 'Uthmānī, Muḥammad Muḥtaram Fahīm — "Mazdūr Islāmī mu'āshrē meṇ" (The Labourer in Islamic Society), *al-Balāgh* (Karachi) 4(4) July 70: 51–59. (U)

445. Zain al-'Ābidīn, Wajīh — "al-Islām wa'l-'ummāl" (Islam and the Labourers) *al-Ba'th al-Islāmī* (Lucknow) 11(5), Feb. 67: 53–59. (A)

xxiv. Family Planning: 446–472

446. 'Abd al-'Azīz Bin Bāz — "Ḥaula taḥdīd al-nasl" (On Population Control) *Majallat al-Ḥajj* (Makka) 19(2) Dec. 64: 75. (A)

447. 'Abdullāh Knoun — "Qarār al-Rābiṭah bi-sha'n al-nasl" (Resolution of the *Rabitāh* on Population (control), *Akhbār al-'Ālam al-Islāmī* (Makka) (438), 28 July, 75: 7. (A)

448. Abū Zuhra, Muḥammad — "Tanẓīm al-nasl" (Population Planning) *Liwā' al-Islām* (Cairo) 16(11), Nov. 62: 676–680. (A)

449. ,, ,, ,, — "Tanẓīm al-usrah wa tanẓīm al-nasl" (Family Planning and Population Planning) *al-Azhar. al-Mu'tamar al-thānī li-Majma' al-Buḥūth al-Islāmīyah* (Cairo), May 65: 247–303. (A)

450. ‘Īsā, ‘Abd al-‘Azīz Muḥammad — *al-Islām wa tanẓīm al-usrah* (Islam and Family Planning), al-Qāhirah, Jihāz Tanẓīm al-Usrah, 1973. 23p. (A)

451. ,, ,, — *al-Islam wa tanẓīm al-usrah* (Islam and Family Planning) al-Qāhirah, Maṭba‘ah al-Abrām al-Tijārīyah, 1973. (A)

452. al-Ittiḥād al-‘Ālamī li-Tanẓīm al-Wālidīyah (International Planned Parenthood Federation). — *al-Islām wa tanẓīm al-usrah* (Islam and Family Planning). Beirut, 1973. 2v. 414, 596p. (A)

453. Khan, M. E. — "Is Islam against Family Planning?", *Islam and the Modern Age* (New Delhi) 6(2), May 75: 61–72.

454. Khurshīd Ahmad — "Taḥrik-e ḍabṭ-e Wilādat kā ‘Ilmī jā’izah" (Scientific Review of Birth Control Movement) in: Mawdūdī, Sayyid Abul A‘lā: *Islām aur ḍabṭ-e Wilādat*. Lahore, Islamic Publications, 1962: 163–204. (U)

455. al-Khaulī, al-Bahl — *al-Islām wa’l-mar’at al-mu‘āṣirah* (Islam and the Contemporary Woman). 3rd. ed. Kuwait, Dār al-Qalam. (A)

456. Madkūr, Muḥammad Salām — *Naẓarat al-Islām ilā tanẓīm al-nasl* (Islamic view point on family planning). al-Qāhirah, Dār al-Nahḍat al-‘Arabīyah, 1969. 98p. (A)

457. Mawdūdī, Sayyid Abul A‘lā — "Ḍabṭ-e Wilādat aur Waṣīyat al-‘ainain kē shar‘ī ḥaithīyat." (Position of Birth Control and Donation of Eyes in Islamic Law), *Tarjumān al-Qur’ān* (Lahore) 57(4), Jan. 62: 251–252. (U)

458. ,, ,, ,, — *Islām aur ḍabṭ-e Wilādat* (Islam and Birth Control), Lahore, Islamic Publications, 1962. 204p. (U)
First published in 1943.
English tr. *Birth Control, Its Social, Political, Economic, Moral and Religious Aspects* by Khurshid Ahmad and M. I. Faruqi. Lahore, 1968. 182p.

459. "Nadwat Liwā’ al-Islām: baḥth taḥdīd al-nasl", (Liwā’ al-Islām Conference: Discussion on Population Control), *Liwā’ al-Islām* (Cairo) 7(2), June 53: 117. (A)

460. al-Nadwī, Khaṭīb Aḥmad — "Taḥdīd al-nasl fī ḍau’ al-Kitāb wa’l-sunnah" (Population Control in the Light of the Qur’ān and the Sunnah), *al-Ba‘th al-Islāmī* (Lucknow) 14(1), Aug. 69: 64–69. (A).

461. Population Council. New York — *Muslim Attitudes Towards Family Planning*, New York, The Council, Aug. 1967.

462. al-Qūbanī, Muḥammad ‘Abd al-Salām — "Taḥdīd al-nasl" (Population Control) *al-Azhar* 29(6) Dec. 57: 550–552. (A)

463. Rābiṭat al-‘Ālam al-Islāmī. al-Majlis al-Ta’sīsī. — Taḥdīd al-nasl ibādah li’l-‘ālam al-Islāmī" (Population Control is Destruction of the Muslim World), *al-Mujtama‘* (Kuwait) (247) 29 Apr. 75: 31. (A)

464. Rafiullah — "Birth Control in the Light of Islamic Jurisprudence", *World Muslim League* (Singapore) 3(7), July–Aug. 66: 26–31.

465. ,, — "Ḍabṭ-e Wilādat kī fiqhī ḥaithīyat (Status of Birth

		Control in Fiqh) *Fikr-o-Naẓar* (Karachi). Nov.–Dec. 64: 332–334. (U)
466.	Sambhalī, 'Atīqur Raḥmān	"Nas bandī barā'ē Khāndānī manṣūba bandī" (Sterilization as means of Family Planning), *al-Furqān* (Lucknow) 35(10, 11, 12), Jan., Feb., Mar, 68: 73–88; 36(1), Apr. 68: 39–54. (U)
467.	,, ,, ,,	"Taḥdīd al-nasl min wijhat naẓar al-Islām" (Population Control from Islamic View Point), *al-Ba'th al-Islāmī* (Lucknow) 12(8), May 68: 58–66; 12(9), June 68: 66–72. (A)
468.	al-Sharbāsī, al-Shaikh Aḥmad	*al-Dīn wa tanẓīm al-Usrah* (Religion and Family Planning). al-Qāhirah, Matābi' al-Sha'b, 1384/1968. (A)
469.	al-Shūrī, Ibrāhīm	"al-Nasl bain al-taḥdīd wa'l-tanẓīm" (Population, its Control and Planning) *Akhbār al-'Ālam al-Islāmī* (Makka) (435) 7 July 75: 11. (A)
470.	Siddīque, Kaukab	"Population Explosion and Mankind's Future: a Scientific Reply" *Criterion* (Karachi) 3(2), Mar.–Apr. 68: 55–64. (Review of 'Nigel Colder: *The Environment Game*', London, Secker & Warburg, 1957. 240p.).
471.	Zerruq, A. R. M.	"Islam and Family Planning", *Islamic Literature* (Lahore) 10(8–9), Aug.–Sep. 58: 71–74.
472.	Zohurul Hoque	"Religion of Islam and Family Planning", *Islamic Review* (London) 58(1), Jan. 70: 6–11.

xxv. Economic Development 473–494

473.	Abaẓah, Ibrahīm Dasūqī	"al-Islām wa'l-tanmīyat al-iqtiṣādīyah" (Islam and Economic Development) *al-Manhal* (Jeddah) 33(11), Dec. 72–Jan. 73: 1123–1132. (A)
474.	Alexander, A. P.	"Industrial Entrepreneurship in Turkey, its origin and Growth", *Economic Development and Cultural Change* 8, 1960: 349–365.
475.	Austruy, Jaques	*al-Islām wa'l-tanmīyat al-iqtiṣādīyah* (Islam and Economic Development) tr. from French by Nabīl Ṣubḥī al-Ṭawīl. Dimashq, Dār al-Fikr, 1960. 118p. (A)
476.	Berger, Morroe	*The Arab World Today*. London, Weidenfeld & Nicholson, 1962. 480p.
477.	al-Fanjarī, Muḥammad Shauqī	"al-Iqtiṣād al-Islāmī wa'l-daur alladhī yumkin 'an yal'abah" (Islamic Economics and the Role it can Play) *al-Wa'y al-Islāmī* (Kuwait) (112), Apr. 74: 35–42. (A)
478.	,, ,,	"al-Islām wa'l-mushkilat al-iqtiṣādīyah (Islam and the Economic Problem) *al-Wa'y al-Islāmī* (Kuwait) (95), Dec. 72: 23–33. (A)
479.	Faridi, Fazlur Rahman	"Economic Development and Islamic Values", *Islamic Thought* (Aligarh) 10(1, 2) Apr. 64: 9–53.
480.	Haffar, Ahmed R.	"Economic Development in Western Scholarship", *Islam and the Modern Age* (New Delhi) 6(2), May 75: 5–22; 6(3), Aug. 75: 5–29.
481.	Issawi, Charles	*Egypt at Mid-century; An Economic Survey*. London, O.U.P., 1954. xiv, 289p.
482.	,, ,,	"The Entrepreneur Class" in Fisher, S. N. (ed.):

Social Forces in the Middle East, Ithaca, N.Y., Cornell U.P., 1955: 116–136.

483. Khan, Muhammad Akram — "Concept of Development in Islam", *Criterion* (Karachi) 4(4), July–Aug. 69: 7–16.

484. Mālik ben Nabī — *al-Muslim fī 'ālam al-iqtiṣād* (The Muslim in the Economic World). Beirut, Dār al-shurūq, 1972. 132p. (A)

485. ,, ,, ,, — *Shurūṭ al-nahḍah* (Conditions of Progress) tr. from French by 'Abd al-Ṣabūr Shāhīn wa 'Umar Kāmil Masqāwī, 1960. (A)

486. Manzar, Abdul Moiz — "On Economic Development and Islamic Values", *Islamic Thought* (Aligarh) 10(3, 4), Jan. 65: 66–70.

487. al-Mashriqī, Muḥammad Muḥyuddīn — "Ẓāhirat al-takhalluf al-iqtiṣādī fi'l-duwal al-Islāmīyah al-nāmīyah" (The Phenomenon of Economic Backwardness in the Developing Islamic Countries), *al-Baḥth al-'Ilmī* (Rabāt) 3(17), Jan.–May 71: 44–133. (A)

488. Meyer, A. J. — "Entrepreneurship and Economic Development in the Middle East", *Public Opinion Quarterly*, 22 (1958): 391–396.

489. ,, ,, — "Entrepreneurship, the Missing Link in the Arab States", *Middle East Economic Papers* (Beirut) 54: 121–132.

490. ,, ,, — *Middle Eastern Capitalism*. Cambridge, Mass., Harvard U.P. 1959. 161p.

491. al-Najjār, Aḥmad Muḥammad 'Abd al-'Azīz — "al-Tarbīyat al-Islāmīyah wa mushkilātūna'l-iqtiṣādīyah" (Islamic Education and our Economic Problems), *al-Wa'y al-Islāmī* (Kuwait) (50) 18 Apr. 69: 41–46. (A)

492. Quraishi, Marghoob A. — "Investment and Economic Development in Muslim Countries", *Association of Muslim Social Scientists, Proceedings, Third Seminar*, Gary, Indiana, U.S.A. May 74: 1–8.

493. Sayigh, Y. A. — *Entrepreneurs of Lebanon: the Role of the Business Leader in a Developing Economy*. Cambridge, Mass., Harvard U.P., 1962. 181p.

494. Siddīqī, Kalim — "Islamic Development Plan", *al-Islam* (Singapore) 5(1), Jan.–Mar. 74: 24–30. (Also printed separately: Karachi, Umma Publishing House, 1970).

xxvi. Audit and Accounts: 495–498

495. Quraishi, Marghoob Ahmad — *Annual Zakāt Payment Form*. Palo Alto, California. Al Manar Press, 1970. 19p.

496. Shiḥātah, Shauqī Ismā'īl — *al-Mabādi'l-Islāmīyah fī naẓarīyāt al-ṭaqwīm fi'l-muḥāsabah* (Islamic principles in the theory of value Assessment in Accounting), Ph.D. Thesis, Kullīyat-al-Tijārah, Jāmi'at al-Qāhirah, 1960. (A)

497. ,, ,, ,, — *Muḥāsabah Zakāt al-māl 'ilman wa 'amalan*. (A Scientific and Practical Accounting of *Zakāt* on Property). Cairo, Maktabah al-Anjalū al-Miṣrīyah, 1970. (A)

498. ,, ,, ,, — *Niẓām al-muḥāsabah li-ḍarībat al-Zakāt wa'l-dafātir al-musta'malah fī bait al-māl* (System of Accounting for *Zakāt* tax and the Registers used in *bait-al*

māl). M.A. Dissertation. Kullīyat al-Tijārah Jāmi'at al-Fu'ād al-Awwal. 1951. (A)

3. ISLAMIC CRITIQUE OF CONTEMPORARY ECONOMIC THEORIES AND SYSTEMS [499–609]

i. Capitalism: 499–500

499. Parwez, Ghulām Aḥmad — *Khudā aur sarmāyadār* (God and the Capitalist). Lahore, Idāra-e-Ṭulū'-e Islām, 1967. (U)

500. Quṭb, Sayyid — *Ma'rikat al-Islām wa'l-ra's mālīyah* (Confrontation of Islam and Capitalism). 3rd ed. al-Qāhirah, 1966. 122p. (A)

ii. Interest: 501–533

501. Abbasi, Masud Ahmad — "Interest—An Economic Study on the Three Economic Systems", *Islamic Review* (London) 57(3–4), Mar.–Apr. 69: 28–32.

502. 'Abd al-Bāsiṭ, Badr al-Mutawallī — "al-Ribā dā' al-basharīyah al-Wabīl" (*Ribā*, the Disastrous affliction of Mankind) *al-Azhar* 22(9), Ramaḍān 1370: 797–800. (A)

503. 'Abdou, Muḥammad 'Īssa — *al-Fā'idah 'alā ra's al-māl ṣūrah min ṣuwar al-ribā* (Interest on Capital is a Form of *Ribā*). Beirut, Dār al-Fatḥ, 1970. (A)

504. ,, ,, ,, — *Limādhā ḥarrama Allāh al-ribā* (Why Allah has Prohibited *Ribā*?). Kuwait, Maktabah al-Manār, n.d. 33p. (A)

505. ,, ,, ,, — *al-Ribā wa dauruhū fī istighlāl mawārid al-shu'ūb* (*Ribā* and its Role in the Exploitation of the Incomes of Nations). Kuwait, Dār al-Buḥūth al-'Ilmīyah, 1969. 86p. (A)

506. ,, ,, ,, — *Waḍ' al-ribā fī binā' al-iqtiṣādī* (Position of *Ribā* in the Economic Structure), Kuwait, Dār al Buḥūth al-'Ilmīyah, 1973. 190p. (A)

507. Abū Sa'ūd, Muḥammad — "Islamic View of *Ribā*", *Islamic Review* (London) 45(2), Feb. 57: 9–16.

508. Abū Shaḥbah, Muḥammad — *Naẓarat al-Islām ilā'l-ribā* (Islam's Viewpoint of *Ribā*). al-Qāhirah, Majma' al-Buḥūth al-Islāmīyah, 1971. (A)

509. Abū Zahra, Muḥammad — *Buḥūth fi'l-ribā* (Discourses on *Ribā*). Kuwait, Dār al-Buḥūth al-'Ilmīyah, 1970. 94p. (A)

510. ,, ,, ,, — "al-Ribā (tafsīr al-Qur'ān)" (*Ribā*, exegesis of the Qur'ān), *Liwā al-Islām* (Cairo) 8(3), July 54: 137–145. (A)

511. Ahmad, Sheikh Mahmud — "Interest and Unemployment" *Islamic Studies* (Islamabad) 8(1), Mar. 69: 9–46.

512. ,, ,, ,, — "Sūd kā mas'alah" (The Problem of Interest) *Thaqāfat* (Lahore) 2(2), Feb. 56: 33–43. (U)

513. Darāz, Muḥammad 'Abdullāh — *al-Ribā fī naẓar al-qānūn al-Islāmī* (*Ribā* according to Islamic Law) Kuwait, Maktabat al-Manār. n.d. (A) Also in *al-Azhar* 23(1), 51: 11–17; 23(2), Ṣafar 1371: 105–112; 23(3) Rabī' I, 1371: 193–195. (A)

514. Farid, Q. M. — "Is Interest Obsolete?", *Voice of Islam* (Karachi) 8(10), Jul. 64: 495–502.

515. al-Ghawālī, Ḥāmid — "al-Ribā bain al-ṭibb wa'l-Islām" (*Ribā* according to the Science of Medicine and Islam), *Liwā' al-Islām* (Cairo) 13(4), June 59: 246–248. (A)

516. Ghulām, 'Alī, Malik — "Jawāz-e sūd kē ḥaq meṇ ēk riwāyat sē ghalāṭ istidalāl." (Wrong Argument in Favour of Permissibility of interest derived from a tradition), *Tarjumān al-Qur'ān* (Lahore) 60(5), Aug. 63: 306–309. (U)

517. Ḥāmid, Muḥammad — "Ḥaula mushkilat al-ribā" (On the Problem of Interest) *al-Muslimūn* (Dimashq) 6(4) Sep. 58: 75–81. (A)

518. Hussain, S. Mushtaq — "Interest on Money and Islam—A Suggested Analysis", Report of *First Regional Conference of the M.S.A. of U.S. & Canada*. Stanford University, California, June 10–12, 1966: 9–14.

519. Irshad, Sheikh Ahmad — "Islamic Economy and the Elimination of Interest", *Voice of Islam* (Karachi) 12(2), Nov. 63: 78–85.

520. Kharūfah, 'Alā al-Dīn — "al-Ribā wa'l fā'idah" (*Ribā* and Interest), *Majma' al-'Ilmī al-Irāqī* 10(1), 63: 353–354. (A)

521. Mawdūdī, Sayyid Abul A'lā — *Sūd* (Interest). Lahore, Islamic Publications, 1961, 410p. (U)
Arabic tr. *al-Ribā*, Dimashq, Dār al-Fikr.

522. Muslim, A. G. — "The Early Development of the Islamic Concept of *Ribā*", *Current British Research in Middle Eastern and Islamic Studies*, University of Durham, Centre for Middle Eastern and Islamic Studies, 1971.

523. Nadwī, 'Abd al-Salām — "Taḥrīm-ē sūd" (Prohibition of Interest) *Ma'ārif* (Azamgarh) 14(1), July 24: 9–31; 14(2) Aug. 24: 93–128; 14(3), Sep. 24: 170–184. (U)

524. Nadwī, Muḥammad Na'īm — "Tāḥrīm-e- sūd 'ilm wa 'aql kī raushnī meṇ", (Prohibition of Interest in the Light of Science and Reason). *Zindagī* (Rampur) 38(1, 2) Jan. Feb. 67: 25–35. (U)

525. Qādrī Sayyid Mu'īnuddīn — "Sarmāyakārī kī ma'āshī ḥaqīqat aur Islāmī nuqṭaenaẓar sē us kē mu'āwaḍē kī wajh-e jawāz" (The Economic Nature of Investment and the Basis of Permission of its Reward from Islamic Viewpoint), *Burhān* (Delhi) 55(3), Sep. 65: 159–176; 55(4), Oct. 65: 221–229. (U)

526. Qureshi, Anwar Iqbal — *Islam and the Theory of Interest* with an Introduction by Syed Sulaiman Nadvi. Lahore, Muhammad Ashraf, xxiv, 223p. Arabic tr. *al-Islām wa'l ribā* by Fārūq Ḥilmī. al-Qāhirah, Maktabah, Miṣr, 158p.

527. Quṭb, Sayyid — *Tafsīr āyāt al-ribā* (Exegesis of the Verses (of the Qur'ān) related to *Ribā*). Kuwait, Dār al-Buḥūth al-'Ilmīyah, n.d. 66p. (A)

528. — "*al-Ribā*" (Interest), *Liwā' al-Islām* (Cairo) 8(10), Feb. 55: 648–657. (A)

529. — *al-Ribā fi'l-Islām wa fi'l-naẓarīyāt al-iqtiṣādīyah al-ḥadīthah* (*Ribā* in Islam and in recent Economic Theories). Kuwait, al-Dār al-Kuwaitīyah li'l-ṭibā'ah wa'l-Nashr, n.d. 72p. (A)

530. Riḍā, Muḥammad Rashīd — *al-Ribā wa 'l-mu'āmalāt fīl-Islām* (*Ribā* and Transactions in Islam). al-Qāhirah, Maktabat al-Qāhirah, 1960. (A)

531. Shafī', Muftī Muḥammad — *Mas'ala-e-sūd* (The Problem of Interest). Karachi, Idārat al-Ma'ārif, 3rd edition, 1390 A.H., 148p. (U)

532. Ṣiddīqī, Muḥammad Maẓharuddīn — "Sūd kā mas'alah" (The Problem of Interest), *Thaqāfat* (Lahore) 4(5), May 57: 54–62. (U)

533. Zakī al-Dīn, Ibrāhīm — *Nazriat al ribā al Muharram fi'l Sharī'at al Islāmiyah* (The Theory of the Prohibited interest in Islamic law). Al Qāhira, al Majlis al a'la li ri'ayat al funūn wa'l ādāb wa'l 'ulūm al ijtimā'īyah, 1964, 276p.

iii. Commercial Interest: 534–553

534. 'Abbāsī, Manẓūr Aḥsan — "Qurūḍ wa ribā" (Loans and Interest), *Thaqāfat* (Lahore) 8(8), Aug. 60: 43–62. (U)

535. Anwārullāh, Muḥammad — *Mas'alat al-Ribā* (The Problem of Interest). Hyderabad (Dn.), Majlis Ishā'at al-'Ulūm, n.d. 27p. (U)

536. Ḍanāwī, Muḥammad 'Alī — "Hal bai' al-taqsīṭ Jā'iz?" (Is Instalment Purchase Legal?), *al-Ba'th al-Islāmī* (Lucknow) 11(5), Feb. 67: 60–65. (A)

537. Fazlur Rahman — "Riba and Interest", *Islamic Studies* (Karachi) 3(1), Mar. 64: 1–43.

538. Fazlur Rahman (Gunnauri) — "Mabḥath taḥlīlī ḥaula al-ribā al-tijārī" (An Analytical Study of Commercial Interest), *al-Ba'th al-Islāmī* (Lucknow) 12(7), Apr. 68: 48–57; 12(8), May 68: 67–71. (A)

539. „ „ „ — "A Study of Commercial Interest in Islam", *Islamic Thought* (Aligarh) 5(4 & 5) July–Oct. 58: 24–46.

540. „ „ „ — *Tijāratī sūd tārīkhī aur fiqhī nuqṭa-e naẓar sē* (Commercial Interest from the Stand Point of History and Islamic Law). Aligarh Muslim University, 1967. xv, 176p. (U)

541. Ḥasan, Abū 'Usāmah — "Faẓlur Raḥmānī taḥqīq-e ribā kī ḥaqīqat" (An Evaluation of Fazlur Rahman's Study on *Ribā*), *Bayyināt* (Karachi) 3(2) Jan. 64: 105–123; 3(3) Feb. 64: 177–189; 3(4) March 64: 231–251; 3(5) April 54: 311–317. (U)

542. 'Imādī, Tamannā — "Ribā aur bai'" (*Ribā* and Trade), *Fikr-o Naẓar* (Karachi) 2(7), Jan 65: 429–434. (U)

543. Ismā'īl, Ch. Muḥammad — "Mas'ala-e sūd (The Problem of Interest), Thaqāfat (Lahore) 9(1, 4, 6): 37–47, 35–50, 53–61, 40–50. (U)

544. Ja'far Shāh, Muḥammad, Phulwārwī — *Commercial Interest kī fiqhī ḥaythīyat* (Commercial Interest in Islamic Law). Lahore, Idāra-e Thaqāfat-e Islāmiyah, 1959. 234p. (U)

545. Khan, Mir Sa'ādat Ali — "The Mohammadan Laws Against Usury and how they are Evaded", *Comparative Legislation* 11 (1920): 233–244.

546. al-Nabhān, Muḥammad Fārūq — *al-Qurūḍ al-intājīyah wa mauqif al-Islām minhā* (Islam's Stand on Production Loans), M.A. Dissertation. Unpublished. Cairo University.

547. Nadwī, Muḥammad Na'īm — "Bank kā sūd" (Bank Interest), *Zindagī* (Rampur) 40(3), Mar. 68: 22–37. (U)

548.	Nadwī, Muḥammad Na'īm	"Mahājanī aur tijāratī sūd" (Money Lenders Interest and Commercial Interest), *Zindagī* (Rampur) 40(2–3). (U)
549.	Nāṣif, Hafnī Beck	"Bank aur sūd" (Banks and Interest), *Thaqāfat* (Lahore) 9(2), Mar. 61 : 57–64. (U)
550.	Shāh, Syed Ya'qūb	*Chand ma'āshī masā'il aur Islām* (Some Economic Problems and Islam). Lahore, Idāra-e Thaqāfat-e Islāmīyah, 1967. 259p. (U)
551.	,, ,, ,,	"Islam and Productive Credit", *Islamic Review* (London) 47(3) Mar. 59: 34–37.
552.	Shāmī, Amīr Ḥamza	"Commercial Interest aur Islām" (Commercial Interest and Islam) *Tarjumān al-Qur'ān* (Lahore), 57(1), Oct. 61 : 32–46. (U)
553.	Suhail, Iqbāl Aḥmad	*Ḥaqīqat al-ribā* (Nature of *Ribā*), Badāyūn, Niẓāmī Press, 1936, 14, 178p. (U)

iv. Ribā'l-Faḍl: 554–555

554.	'Awaḍ, Aḥmad Ṣafī al-Dīn	"Taṣawwur jadīd li ribā'l-faḍl" (A New Conception of *ribā'l-faḍl*), *al-Wa'y al-Islāmī* (Kuwait) (111), Mar. 74: 57–69. (A)
555.	al-'Itr, Nur al-Dīn	" 'Illat ribā'l-faḍl" (Legal Basis of (Prohibiting) *Ribā'l-faḍl*) *al-Wa'y al-Islāmī* (Kuwait) (116), Aug. 74: 51–53. (A)

v. Speculation and Stock Exchange: 556–559

556.	Amīnī, Muḥammad Taqī	*Maqālāt-e-Amīnī* (Essays of Amini), Aligarh Muslim University Press, 1970. 268p. (U)
557.	Hārūn, Abdussalām Muḥammad	*al-Maisir wa'l-azlām* (Games of Chance and Raffles), al-Qāhirah, Dār al-Fikr al-'Arabī, 1953. 106p. (A)
558.	Khan, Muḥammad Akram	"International Monetary Crisis: Causes and Cure", *Criterion* (Karachi) 62(2), Mar. Apr. 71 : 5–19.
559.	,, ,, ,,	"Stock Exchanges: Function and Need to Reform", *Criterion* (Karachi) 7(1), Jan. 72: 28–38.

vi. Lottery: 560–562

560.	Pīrzāda, Shams	*Lottery*. Delhi, Markazī Maktabah Jamā'at-e-Islāmī Hind 1971, 23p. (U)
561.	Syed 'Alī	"Lottery" *Zindagī* (Rampur) 44(4), Apr. 70: 47–50. (U)
562.	Ṣiddīqī, Na'īm	"Qur'ah aur lottery" (*Qur'ah* and lottery), *Tarjumān al-Qur'an* (Lahore) 41(3), Dec. 53: 205–206. (U)

vii. Socialism and Communism: 563–597

563.	'Abd al-Bārī, Muḥammad	"Islam and Socialism", *Islamic Literature* (Lahore) 3(8), Aug. 51 : 21–27.
564.	Abdul Hakim, Khalifa	*Islam and Communism*. Lahore, Institute of Islamic Culture, 1953. 262p.
565.	Abū Zahra, Muḥammad	"al-Shuyū'īyah wa'l-Islām" (Communism and Islam), *Liwā' al-Islām* (Cairo) 13(9), 2 Nov. 59: 535–538; 13(10), Dec. 59: 599–604; 13(11), Jan. 60: 663–668; 13(12), Feb. 60: 727–733. (A)

566. Akbar Murādpūrī, Muḥammad — *Conflict between Socialism and Islam*, Lahore, Muhammad Ashraf, 1970. 125p.

567. al-'Aqqād, 'Abbās Maḥmūd — "A Doctrine in Bankruptcy (Communist Materialism Incapable of Survival)", *al-Azhar* 31(1), June 59: 26–30.

568. al-'Aqqād, 'Abbās Maḥmūd — *al-Shuyū'īyah wa'l-insānīyah* (Communism and Humanity). Cairo, 1956, 335p. (A)

569. al-'Aqqād, 'Abbās Maḥmūd; 'Aṭṭār, Aḥmad 'Abd al-Ghafūr — *al-Shuyū'īyah wa'l-Islām* (Communism and Islam). 2nd ed. Beirut, 1072. 213p. (A)

570. al-Badrī, 'Abd al-'Azīz — *Ḥukm al-Islām fi'l-Ishtirākīyah* (Islam's Verdict on Socialism). al-Madīnat al-Munawwarah, al-Maktabat al-'Ilmīyah, 1969. 172p. (A)

571. al-Bahī, Muḥammad — "Communism and Religion", *al-Azhar* 31(3), Sep. 59: 76–90.

572. al-Bannā, Muḥammad Kāmil — "al-Shuyū'īyah (Communism), *Liwā' al-Islām* (Cairo) 13(10), Dec. 59: 605–608. (A)

573. al-Bārūdī, 'Alī — *Durūs fi'l-ishtirākīyat al-'Arabīyah* (Discourses on Arab Socialism). Alexandria, Maktabat al-Ma'ārif, 1967. 262p. (A)

574. Bashīr al-'Auf — *Ishtirākīyatuhum wa Islāmunā* (Their Socialism and Our Islam). Beirut, Mu'assasat al-Intāj al-Ṭibā'ī, 1966. 158p. (A)

575. Dawālībī, Ma'rūf — *Naẓaratun Islāmiyah fi'l-Ishtirākiyat al-thauriyah* (An Islamic Review of Revolutionary Socialism). Beirut, Dār al-Kitāb al-Jadīd, 1965. 144p. (A)

576. Enayat, Hamid — "Islam and Socialism in Egypt", *Middle Eastern Studies* 4(2), Jan. 68: 141–172.

577. al-Ghazālī, Muḥammad — *al-Islām wa'l manāhij al ishtirākīyah* (Islam and the Socialistic Methods). Cairo, 1951. 120p. (A)

578. Ghulām Rasūl, Sayyid — "Islām aur socialism kā bunyādi farq" (Basic Difference between Islam and Socialism), *Fārān* (Karachi) 22(1), Apr. 70: 11–12. (U)

579. Ḥussain, Mirzā Muḥammad — *Islam and Socialism: A Critical Study of Capitalism, Socialism, Fascism and Nazism as contrasted with the Quranic Concept of a New World Order*. Lahore, Muhammad Ashraf, 1947. xii, 446p.

580. ,, ,, — *Islam versus Socialism*. Lahore, Muhammad Ashraf, 1970. 170p. (First Published in 1947.)

581. — "al-Ishtirākīyah" (Socialism), *Liwā' al-Islām* (Cairo) 14(7), 23 Aug. 60: 443–453. (A)

582. Kerr, M. H. — "Islam and Arab Socialism", *Muslim World* 56(4) Oct. 66: 276–281.

583. Khan, Muḥammad Ihsanullah — "Communism and Islam Contrasted", *Islamic Literature* (Lahore) 3(4), Apr. 51: 11–21.

584. Khurshīd Aḥmad (ed.) — "*Chirāgh-e Rāh*". Socialism Number (Karachi) Dec. 1967. 525p. (U)

585. ,, ,, — *Socialism Yā Islām* (Socialism or Islam). Karachi, Maktabah Chirāgh-e-Rāh, 1969, 320p. (U)

586. Lewis, Bernard — "Communism and Islam", *International Affairs* (London) 30(1), 54: 1–12.

587. Mubārak, Muḥammad — "Ishtirakīyāt aur Islām" (Communism and Islam), *Bayyināt* (Karachi), 15(1) Jan. 70: 24–33. (U)

588. al-Munajjid, Ṣalāḥ al-Dīn — *al-Taḍlīl al-ishtirākī* (The Socialist Misguidance).

		Beirut, Dār al-Kitāb al-Jadīd, 1966. 144p. (A)
589.	Nadwī, Mas'ūd 'Ālam	*Ishtirākīyat aur Islām* (Communism and Islam) Karachi, Maktabah Chirāgh-e-Rāh, 1949. 80p. (U)
590.	al-Nawawī, Maḥmūd; Khafājī, 'Abd al-Mun'im	*Bain al-shuyū'īyah wa'l-Islām* (Between Communism and Islam). al-Qāhirah, Dār al-'Ahd al-Jadīd, 1959. 102p. (A)
591.	Sa'īd, 'Abd al-Mughnī	*al-Islām wa'l-uṣūl al-fikrīyah li'l-ishtirākīyat al-'Arabīyah* (Islam and the Intellectual Bases of Arab Socialism). al-Qāhirah, Maktabat al-Anjalū Miṣrīyah, n.d. 109p. (A)
592.	Shaltūt, Maḥmūd	"Socialism and Islam" in Karpat, Kemal H. (ed) *Political and Social Thought in the Contemporary Middle East*. New York, Praeger, 1970: 126–132.
593.	Shamsī, Syed Mughni al-Dīn	"Taḥrīk-e-socialism par ēk tanqīdī naẓar" (A Critical Study of the Socialist Movement), *Burhān* (Delhi) 3(2), Aug. 39; 3(5), Nov. 39: 119–134. (U)
594.	Ṣiddīqī, 'Abd al-Ḥamīd	"Ishtirākīyat aur 'amal-e taṭhir" (Purges in Communism), *Zindagī* (Rampur) 45(6), Dec. 70: 15–24. (U)
595.	Ṣiddīqī, Muḥammad Maẓharuddīn	*Ishtirākīyat aur niẓām-e Islām* (Communism and the Islamic System). Lahore, Markazi Maktabah Jamā'at-e-Islāmī, 1949. (U) (Earlier Published under the Title: *Hegal, Marx aur niẓām-e-Islām* (Hegal, Marx and the Islamic System). Pathankot, Daftar Risālah Tarjumān al-Qur'ān, 1943. 240p.
596.	,, ,,	*Marxism or Islam*, Lahore, Orientalia, 1952. 168p.
597.	Zayid, Sa'īd	"al-Islām wa'l-ishtirākīyah" (Islam and Socialism), *al-Azhar* 22(7), Rajab 1370: 665–669; Ram. 1370: 826–828; 22(10) Shaw. 1370: 921–923; Muhar. 1371: 61–63. (A)

viii. Marxian Theories: 598–599

598.	Abāẓah, Ibrāhīm Dasūqī	"Naqd al-naẓarīyat al-mārxīyah" (Critique of Marxian Theory), *al-Baḥth al-'Ilmi* (Rabāṭ) 8(17), Jan.–May 71: 97–131. (A)
599.	'Abdullāh, Syed	"Karl Marx kē naẓarīyāt maghribī naqqādoṇ kī naẓar meṇ." (Western Critics on the Theories of Karl Marx), *Tarjumān al-Ḥadīth*, Jan. 70: 37–42. (U)

ix. Socialism and Capitalism, etc.: 600–610

600.	'Abdullāh, Amin 'Afīfī	"Islām aur daur-e jadīd kē iqtiṣādī madhāhib" (Islam and the Economic Ideologies of Modern Age), tr. by Ḍiyā' al-Dīn Iṣlāhī, *Ma'ārif* (Azamgarh) 88(3), Nov. 61: 391–396. (U)
601.	Darwish, Muṣṭafā	*al-Islām fī muwājahat al-ra'smālīyah wa'l ishtirākīyah* (Confrontation of Islam with Capitalism and Socialism). al-Qāhirah, al-Jāmi' al-Azhar, 1959. 20p. (A)
602.	Dawālībī, Ma'rūf	*al-Islām amām al-ra'smālīyah wa'l-Marksīyah* (Islam versus Capitalism and Marxism). Beirut, Dār al-Kitāb al-Jadīd. n.d. 22p. (A)
603.	Dawalībī, Ma'rūf	"Islam versus Capitalism and Marxism", *World Muslim League* (Singapore) 3(5), May 66: 14–24.

604.	Ismā'īl, Ibrāhīm Muḥammad	*Islam and Contemporary Economic Theories*, tr. from Arabic by Ismā'īl Kashmīrī. Cairo, Supreme Council for Islamic Affairs. n.d. 100p.
605.	al-Khaulī, al-Bahī	*al-Islām-lā shuyū'īyah wa lā ra'smālīyah* (Islam—neither Communism nor Socialism). (A)
606.	Mahmud Javed	"Capitalism and Socialism", *Criterion* (Karachi) 8(9), Sep. 73: 25–35; 9(4), Apr. 74: 14–31.
607.	Mawdūdī, Sayyid Abul A'lā	*Islam aur jadīd m'āshī naẓarīyāt* (Islam and Modern Economic Theories). Delhi, Markazi Maktabah Jamā'at-e-Islāmī (Hind) 1969. 136p. (U)
608.	,, ,, ,, ,,	"Mauqif al-Islām min al-shuyū'īyah wa'l-ra'smālīyah" (Islamic Stand *vis à vis* Capitalism and Communism), *al-Azhar* 24(4), Dec. 52: 458–460. (A)
609.	Shafī', Muftī Muḥammad	"Ishtirākīyat, qaumīyat aur sarmāyadārī" (Communism, Nationalism and Capitalism), *Zindagī* (Rampur) 44, May 70: 29–39. (U) (Also Published in *al-Balāgh* (Karachi) 3, Mar. 70: 15–22.
610.	Ṭamān, 'Alī Fahmī	*al-Fikrat al-Islāmīyah bain al-shuyū'īyah wa'l isti'mār* (Islamic Thought versus Communism and Imperialism). al-Qāhirah, al-Mu'allif, 1948. (A)

4. ECONOMIC ANALYSIS IN AN ISLAMIC FRAMEWORK [611–648]

i. General: 611–614

611.	Kahf, Monzer	*Challenges Confronting Islamic Economist*. Utah, U.S.A., Univ. of Utah, S.L.C., July 1972. 8p. mimeo.
612.	,, ,,	*A Contribution to the Study of the Economics of Islam*. Utah, U.S.A., Univ. of Utah, S.L.C., July 1973. 110p. mimeo. Published under the title *The Islamic Economy*, Indiana, The M.S.A., 1978, 110p.
613.	Khan, Muhammad Akram	*A Survey of Contemporary Economic Thought in Islam*, mimeo.
614.	Ṣiddīqī, Muhammad Nejatullah	*A Survey of Contemporary Literature on Islamic Economics*. Jeddah, First International Conference on Islamic Economics. 1975. 174p. mimeo. Published under the title *Muslim Economic Thinking*, Leicester, The Islamic Foundation, 1981, 130p.

ii. Consumption: 615

615.	Kahf, Monzer	"A Model of the Household Decisions in Islamic Economy" in: *Association of Muslim Social Scientists, Proceedings, Third National Seminar*. Gary, Indiana, May 1974: 19–28.

iii. Production and Enterprise: 616–619

616.	Hamid, Habeeb	"On Economic Enterprise in Islam", *Islamic Thought* (Aligarh) 5(3), May–June 55: 17–18.
617.	Mohiuddin, Ghulam	"On Market Mechanism under the Influence of Islamic Spirit", *Islamic Thought* (Aligarh) 5(1), Jan.–Feb. 58: 32.
618.	Ṣiddīqī, 'Abdul Hamid	"Economic Enterprise in Islam", *Islamic Thought* (Aligarh) 6(2) Mar.–Apr. 57: 27.

619. Ṣiddīqī, Muhammad Nejatullah — *Economic Enterprise in Islam*. Lahore, Islamic Publications, 1972. 179p.; Delhi, Markazī Maktabah-Islāmī, 1972. 179p.

iv. Profit-Sharing: 620

620. Chawdhari, A. B. M. Masudul Alam — "A Mathematical Formulation of 'Muḍārabah' the Profit Sharing in Islam", in: *Association of Muslim Social Scientists, Proceedings, Third National Seminar*. Gary, Indiana, May 1974: 19–28.

v. Zakat: 621–627

621. Ahmad, Afazuddin — "Economic Significance of *Zakāt*", *Islamic Literature* (Lahore), 4(8), Aug. 52: 5–11.

622. Hasanuzzaman, S. M. — "*Zakāt*, Taxes and Estate Duty", *Islamic Literature* (Lahore) 17(7), July 71: 407–411.

623. Izadi, Ali, M. — "The Role of az-Zakat (An Institutionalised Charity) in the Islamic System of Economics in Curing the Poverty Dilemma" in: *Association of Muslim Social Scientists, Proceedings, Third National Seminar*. Gary, Indiana, May 1974: 9–18.

624. Mahmoud, Mabid — "Frictions, Power Rationing and *al-Zakāt*" in: *Association of Muslim Social Scientists, Proceedings, Third National Seminar*. Gary, Indiana, May 1974: 29–43.

625. Mohammad bin Jamāl — "*Zakāt*—A Socio Economic Power for the Development and Progress of the Muslim Community', *World Muslim League* (Singapore) 1(6), May 64: 47–52.

626. — "Waẓīfat al-Zakāt fi'l-mujtama' (Function of *Zakāt* in Society), *Liwā' al-Islām* (Cairo) 15(8), Sep. 61: 463–469. (A)

627. De-Zayas, Farishta G. — "The functional role of *Zakāt* in the Islamic Social Economy", *Islamic Literature* (Lahore) 15(3), Mar. 69: 5–10.

vi. Abolition of Interest: 628–632

628. Ahmad, Mahmud — "Semantics of Theory of Interest", *Islamic Studies* (Rawalpindi) 6(2), June 67: 171–196.

629. Hasanuzzaman, S. M. — "Islām aur sharḥ-e sūd" (Islam and the Rate of Interest), *Burhān* (Delhi) 53(6), Dec. 64: 325–341. (U)

630. ,, ,, — "Islam *vis-à-vis* Interest Rate", *Islamic Culture* 40(1) Jan. 66: 1–12. Arabic tr. "Mauqif al-Islām min si'r al-fā'idah", *al-Muslimoon* (Dimashq) 9(6), Apr. 65: 36–53.

631. Siddiqi, Abdul Hamid — "Islāmī niẓām aur tijāratī chakkar" (Islamic System and Trade Cycles), *Tarjumān al-Qur'ān* (Lahore) 42(1). Apr. 54: 64–66 (U)

632. Ulgener, Sabri F. — "Monetary Conditions of Economic Growth and the Islamic Concept of Interest", *Islamic Review* (London) 55(2), Feb. 67: 11–14.

vii. Nature of Islamic Economics: 633–647

633. Alan, Hashmat — *Distribution Theory under Islamic Law*. Ph.D. Thesis, 1953, George Town University. 174p.

634. Chawdhri, A. B. M. Masudul Alam — "Foundations of Islamic Economics, Pt. I: General Methodology of Islamic Economics", *Criterion* (Karachi), 9(1) Jan. 74: 17–25.

635. Durrānī, Muḥammad Murtaḍa Aḥmad Kḥān — *Ma'āshī/yāt (Islāmi nuqṭa-e-naẓār se)*. (Economics from the Islamic point of view). Lahore, 1952. (U)

636. al-Fanjarī, Muḥammad Shauqī — "al-Iqtiṣād al-Islāmī—kaifa aghfal'l-Muslimūn tadrīsahū wa taṭbiqahū" (Islamic Economics: How Muslims have Neglected its Study and Application), *al-'Arabī* (Kuwait) (164), July 72: 64–67. (A)

637. Faridi, Fazlur Rahman — "Need for a Scientific Study of Islamic Economy", *Islamic Thought* (Aligarh) 2(5), Sep.–Oct. 55: 34–35.

638. al-Faruqi, Isma'il R. A. — "Foreword" in: *Contemporary Aspects of Economic and Social Thinking in Islam*. Gary, Indiana, M.S.A. of U.S. & Canada, 1973: 1–8.

639. ,, ,, ,, — "Introduction" in: *Association of Muslim Social Scientists, Proceedings, Third National Seminar*, Gary, Indiana, May 1974: V–IX.

640. Hamid, Habeeb — "On 'Problems of Islamic Research in Economics'," *Islamic Thought* 5(2) Mar.–April 58: 31–32; 5(3), May–June 58: 19–20.

641. Hassanein, Medhat — "Towards a Model of the Economy of Islam" in: *Contemporary Aspects of Economic and Social Thinking in Islam*. Gary, Indiana, M.S.A. of U.S. & Canada, 1973: 17–25.

642. Khan, Muhammad Akram — "Islamic Economics: An Outline Plan for Research" *Criterion* (Karachi) 10(4), Apr. 75: 27–35.

643. Khan, Muhammad Shabbir — "A Suggestion to the Students of Economics" *Islamic Thought* (Aligarh) 2(4), July–Aug. 55: 27.

644. Khurshid Ahmad — "Method of Approach to Economics", *Islamic Thought* (Aligarh) 2(2), Mar.–Apr. 55: 37.

645. Manzar, Abdul Moiz — "Economics Needs a Reconstruction", *Islamic Thought* (Aligarh) 2(2), Mar.–Apr. 55: 7–21.

646. Sakr, Muhammad Ahmad — al-Iqtiṣād al-Islāmī: mafāhīm wa murtakazāt (Islamic Economics: Its Foundations and Concept). Paper Presented at the First International Conference on Islamic Economics held at Makka on Feb. 21–26, 1976. *Mimeo*. 51p. Included in *al īqtiṣād al Islāmī*, Jeddah, al Markaz al 'Ālamī li Abḥāth al Iqtiṣād al Islāmī, 1980, 606p. pp. 25–71.

647. Siddiqi, Muhammad Nejatullah — "Problems of Islamic Research in Economics", *Islamic Thought* (Aligarh) 6(4, 5), Oct. Dec.– 57: 1–8.

5. HISTORY OF ECONOMIC THOUGHT IN ISLAM [648–691]

i. General: 648–649

648. Meyer, A. J. — "Economic Thought and its Application and Methodology in the Middle East", *Middle East Economic Papers* (Beirut) 56: 66–74.

649. Ṣāliḥ, Muḥammad Zakī — "al-Fikr al-iqtiṣādī al-'Arabī fi'l-qarn al-khāmis 'ashara" (Arab Economic Thought in the Fifteenth Century, *al-Qānūn wa'l-Iqtiṣād* (Cairo), Mar., Oct. 33.

650. De Somogyi, Joseph — "Economic Theory in the Classical Arabic Literature", *Studies in Islam* (Delhi) 2(1), Jan. 65: 1–6.

ii. Ibn Khaldūn: 651–664

651. 'Abd al-Qādir, Muḥammad — "Ibn Khaldūn kē ma'āshī khayālāt" (Economic Views of Ibn Khaldūn), *Ma'ārif* (Azamgarh) 50(6), Dec. 42: 433–441. (U)

652. ,, ,, ,, — *Ibn Khaldūn kē mu'ashartī, siyāsī, ma'āshi khayālāt* (Social, Political and Economic Ideas of Ibn Khaldūn) Hyderabad (Dn.), Idara Ishā'at Urdu, 1943, 32p. (U)

653. ,, ,, ,, — "The Social and Political Ideas of Ibn Khaldun", *Indian Journal of Political Science* (Delhi), 3(2), Oct.–Dec.41.

654. Abdus Sattar, M. — "Ibn Khaldun's Contribution to Economic Thought" in: *Contemporary Aspects of Economic and Social Thinking in Islam*. Gary, Indiana, M.S.A. of U.S. & Canada, 1973: 157–168.

655. el-Alfi, Ezzat S. — *Production, Distribution and Exchange in Khaldun's Writings*. Ph.D. Thesis, Univ. of Minnesota, 1968.

656. Ali, Syed Ahmad — "Economics of Ibn Khaldūn—A selection", *Africa Quarterly* (New Delhi) 10(3) Oct.–Dec. 70: 251–259.

657. Irving, T. B. — "Ibn Khaldūn on Agriculture", *Islamic Literature* (Lahore) 7(8), Aug. 55: 31–32.

658. Maharjān Ibn Khaldūn — "*A'māl Maharjān Ibn Khaldūn al-mun'aqid fi'l-Qāhirah min 2 ilā 6 yanāyir 1962*. (Proceedings of Ibn Khaldūn Celebrations held at Cairo from 2 to 6 January 1962). al-Qāhirah, al-Markaz al-Qaumī li'l-Buḥūth al-ijtimā'īyah wa'l-Jinā'īyah, 1962. (A)

659. Nash'at, Muḥammad 'Alī — *al-Fikr al-iqtiṣādī fī muqaddimat Ibn Khaldūn* (Economic Thought in the Prolegomena of Ibn Khaldūn). Ph.D. Thesis, Cairo University, Maṭba' Dār al-Kutub al-Miṣrīya, 1944. (A)

660. Rif'at, Sayyid Mubāriz al-Dīn — "Ma'āshīyāt par Ibn Khaldūn kē Khayālāt" (Ibn Khaldūn's Views on Economics), *Ma'ārif* (Azamgarh) 40(1) July 37: 16–28; 40(2), Aug. 37: 85–95. (U)

661. Rozenthal, Franz — *Ibn Khaldūn: The Muqaddimah, An Introduction to History*, V.I. London, Routledge & Kegan Paul, 1958. 481p. (Complete History is 3 Volumes.)

662. Sharif, M. Raihan — "Ibn Khaldūn, The Pioneer Economist", *Islamic Literature* (Lahore) 6(5), May 55: 33–40.

663. Sherwani, H. K. — "Ibn-e-Khaldūn and His Politico-Economic Thought" *Islamic Culture* 44(2), Apr. 70: 71–80.

664. Spengler, J. J. — "Economic Thought of Islam: Ibn Khaldūn", *Comparative Studies in Society and History* (The Hague), VI, 64: 268–306.

iii. Ibn Taimīyah: 665–667

665. Ahmad, Ilyas — "Ibn Taimiyah on Islamic Economics", *Voice of Islam* (Karachi) 9(11), Aug. 61 : 557–569.

666. Kahf, Monzer — *The Economic Views of Taqiuddin Taimeyah* (1263–1328): *The Great Radical Reformist of the Islamic Middle Ages*. 1973. 29p. *mimeo*.

667. Sherwani, H. K. — "Ibn-e-Taimiyah's Economic Thought", *Islamic Literature* (Lahore) 8(1), Jan. 56: 9–23.

iv. Abū Yūsuf: 668–672

668. Abū Yūsuf — *Kitāb al-Kharāj: Taxation in Islam*, tr. by Ben Shemesh. Leiden, Brill; London, Luzac, 1969, vii, 155p.

669. Ben Shemesh, A. — *Taxation in Islam* V.2: Qudāma B. Ja'far's Kitāb al-Kharāj, Part Seven, and Excerpts from Abū Yūsuf's Kitāb al-Kharāj. Leiden, Brill; London, Luzac, 1965. 146p.

670. Iṣlāḥī, Ḍiyā al-Dīn — "AbūYūsuf aur unkē fiqhī wa qānūnī Kārnāmē" (Abū Yūsuf and his Juridical and Legal Works), *Ma'ārif* (Azamgarh) 95(5), May 65: 361–384. (U)

671. Siddiqi, Muhammad Nejatullah — "Abū Yūsuf kā ma'āshī fikr" (Economic Thought of Abū Yūsuf), *Fikr-o-Naẓar* (Aligarh) 5(1), Jan. 64: 66–95. (U) Arabic Tr. 'al Fikr al Iqtiṣādī li Abī Yūsuf', Majallah Abḥāth al Iqtiṣād al Islāmī (Jeddah) II:2), Winter 85, pp.67–87.

672. Siddiqi, Muhammad Nejatullah — *Islām kā niẓāme maḥāṣil, tarjuma kitāb al-Kharāj: Qāḍī Abū Yūsuf* (Islam's Tax System, translation of Qāḍī Abū Yūsuf's Kitāb al-Kharāj). Lahore, Islamic Publications, 1966. 635p. (U)

v. Yahyā Ibn Ādam: 673–675

673. Ben Shemesh, A. — *Taxation in Islam*, V.I: *Yaḥyā Ben Ādam's Kitāb al-Kharāj*. Leiden, Brill, 1958. 172p.

674. Kister, M. J. — "The Social and Political Implications of Three Traditions in the *Kitāb al-Kharāj* of Yahya b. Adam", *Journal of Economic and Social History of the Orient* (Leiden) 3(3), Oct. 60: 326–334.

675. Nadwī, Mujībullāh — "Yaḥyā ibn Ādam aur unkī *kitāb al-Kharāj*" (Yaḥyā ibn Ādam and his *Kitāb al-Kharāj*), *Ma'ārif* (Azamgarh) 64(4), Oct. 49: 293–300; 64(5), Nov. 49: 367–375. (U)

vi. Abū Ja'far Dimashqī: 676–677

676. 'Āshūr, al-Sayyid Muḥammad — *Dirāsah fi'l-fikr al-iqtiṣādī al-'Arabī: Abu'l-Faḍl Ja'far bin 'Alī al-Dimashqī* (*Abu'l-iqtiṣād*) (A Study of Arab Economic Thought: Abū'l Faḍl Ja'far bin 'Alī al-Dimashqī—Father of Economics). al-Qāhirah, Dār al-Ittiḥād al-'Arabī li'l Ṭibā'ah, 1973. 69, 191p. (A)

677. al-Dimashqī, Abul Faḍl Ja'far bin 'Alī — *Kitāb al-ishārah ilā maḥāsin al-tijārah wa ma'rifat jaiyid al-a'rāḍ wa radīyihā wa ghushūsh al-mudallisīn fīhā* (A Guide Book on Virtues of Trade, and Distinction between Good and Bad Commodities and the Frauds Played by Adultrators). Cairo, Maṭba'at al-Mu'ayid, 1318 A.H. 76p. (A)

vii. Naṣīr al-Din Ṭūsī: 678–679

678. Anzarul Haque, Muhammad — *A Critical Study of Jalāl al-Dīn al-Dawwānī's Contribution to Social Philosophy*. Aligarh Muslim University, Ph.D. Thesis (Unpublished) 443p.

679. Rif'at, Sayyid Mubāriz al-Din — "Naṣīr al-Dīn Ṭūsī kā risāla-e mālīyāt" (Treatise on Economics by Naṣīr al-Dīn Ṭūsī), *Majallah 'Uthmānīyah* (Hyderabad) 7(2, 3): 1–14. (U)

viii. Others: 680–691

680. Abū 'Ubaid, al-Qāsim bin Sallām — *Kitāb al-amwāl* (Treatise on Wealth), Urdu tr. by A. R. Surti. Islamabad, Islamic Research Institute, 1968. 2v. (A), 543p, 408p.

681. Amedroz, H. F. — "The Ḥisba Jurisdiction in the Aḥkām Sultaniyyah of Mawardi", *Journal of the Royal Asiatic Society of Great Britain & Ireland* (London) 1916: 77–101; 287–314.

682. Ehrenkreutz, A. S. — "al-Būzanjānī (A.D. 939–997) *The Ma'āṣir*", *Journal of Economic and Social History of the Orient* (Leiden) 8(1), Aug. 65: 90–92.

683. Hanna, S. A. — "al-Afghānī; A Pioneer of Islamic Socialism", *Muslim World* 57(1), Jan. 67: 24–32.

684. al-Labbān, Ibrāhīm — *Ḥaqq al-fuqarā' fī amwāl al-Aaghniyā' 'ind Ibn Ḥazm*. (Right of the Poor to the Wealth of the Rich according to Ibn Hazm). (A)

685. Muḥsinī, Shams al-Raḥmān — *Shāh Walīullāh kē 'Umrānī naẓarīyē* (Sociological Theories of Shāh Walīullāh). Lahore, Sind Sagar Academy, 1946. 142p. (U)

686. Sharafuddīn, Abu 'l-Muḥsin Muḥammad — "Abū Ja'far al-Dāwūdī's Kitāb al-Amwāl" *Islamic Studies* (Rawalpindī) 4(4), Dec. 65: 441–448.

687. 'Ubaidullāh Sindhī — *Imām Walīullāh Dehlavī aur unkā falsafa-e-'Umrāniyāt wa ma'āshiyāt*. (Imām Walīullah of Delhi and His Sociological and Economic Philosophy), Tr. by Bashīr Aḥmad. Lahore, Kitab Manzil, 1953. (U)

688. ,, ,, — *Shāh Walīullāh aur unkā falsafah ya'nī Imām Walīullāh kī ḥikmat kā ijmālī ta'āruf* (Shāh Walīullāh and his Philosophy, i.e., A Brief Introduction to the Wisdom of Imām Walīullāh). Lahore, Sind Sagar Academy, 1944. 240p. (U)

689. Yādullāhī, Shihābuddīn — *Abū Dharr Ghifārī kā madhhab* (Viewpoint of Abū Dharr). Shahdadpur (Sind), Bazm-e-Adab, 1374/1954. (U)

690. al-Yāfī, 'Abd al-Karīm — "al-Nasl wa qaḍīyah taḥdīd 'ind al-Ghazālī, *Mahrajān al-Ghazzalī, Dimashq*, Mar. 61. (Population and its Control according to al-Ghazzālī—al-Ghazzālī Celebrations, Damascus, Mar. 61). al-Qāhirah (al-Majlis al-A'lā li-Ri'āyat Funūn wa'l-Ādāb wa'l-'Ulūm al-Ijtimā'īyah: 415–429. (A)

691. De Zayas, Farishta G. — "Considerations on al-Ghazzālī's Pragmatical and Mystical Approach to Zakāt" *Mahrajān al-Ghazzālī*, Dimashq—Mar. 61. al-Qāhriah, al-Majlis al-A'lā li-Ri'āyat al-Funūn wa'l-Ādāb wa'l-'Ulūm al-Ijtimā'īyah: 271–275.

6. MISCELLANEOUS [692–698]

692. Akbarābādī, Sa'īd Aḥmad — *Islām meṇ Ghulāmī kī ḥaqīqat* (*al-Riqq fi'l-Islām*), (Nature of Slavery in Islam). Delhi, Nadwatul Muṣannifin, 1357 A.H. 272p. (U)

693. Ghoraba, Hammoudah — "Islam and Slavery". *Islamic Quarterly* (London) 2(3) Oct. 55: 153–159.

694. a-Hadāwī, Muṣṭafā — *al-Riqq fi'l-ta'rikh wa fi'l-Islām* (Slavery in History and in Islam). al-Qāhirah, al-Sharikat al-'Arabīyah al-Sa'ūdīyah al-Muttaḥidah, 1963. (A)

695. Hasan, Riaz — "The Nature of Islamic Urbanization—A Historical Perspective", *Islamic Culture* (Hydrabad) 43(3), July 69: 233–237.

696. Iṣlāḥī, 'Abdul 'Aẓīm — "Qurbānī ma'āshi nuqṭa-e naẓar sē" (Immolation from Economic Viewpoint), Ta'mīr-e Ḥayāt (Lucknow) 12(4), 25 Dec. 74: 6, 13. (U)

697. Nadwī, Sayyid Sulaimān — "Qurbānī kā iqtiṣādī pahlū" (Economic Aspects of Immolation), *Ma'ārif* (Azamgarh) 39(2), Mar. 37: 170–176. (U)

698. al-Najjār, Aḥmad 'Abd al-'Azīz — *al-Mujtama' al-'Arabī fī marhalat al- taghyīr* (The Arab Society in Transition Phase). Beirut, Dār al-Fikr, 1970. (A)

7. BIBLIOGRAPHIES [699–700]

699. 'Aṭiyyah, Jamāl al-Dīn — "Dalīl al-bāḥith fi'l-iqtiṣād al-Islāmī" (A Guide to Researcher in Islamic Economics) *al-Muslim al-Mu'āṣir* (Beirut) Nov. 74: 142–151.

700. Khan, Muḥammad Akram — *Annotated Bibliography of Contemporary Economic Thought in Islam and Glossary of Economic Terms in Islam. Islamic Education* (Lahore). All Pakistan Education Congress, July–Aug., 1973.

INDEX

Bold figures relate to books. Numbers refer to lists, not pages.

Abāẓah, Ibrāhīm Dasūqi—(A) 598, 473, 381, 283, 104, **103**
'Abbāsī, Manẓūr Aḥsan—(U) 534
'Abbāsī, Mas'ūd Ahmad—501
'Abbāsī, Muḍṭar—(U) 251
'Abd al-'Azīz Bin Bāz—(A) 446
'Abd al-Bārī—(U) 81
Abd al-Bari, Muhammad—563
'Abd al-Bāsiṭ, Badr al Mutawallī—(A) 502
Abd al-Kader, Alı—224
'Abd al-Mujeeb—(U) 1
'Abd al-Qādir, Muḥammad—653; (U) 651, **652**
'Abd al-Rasūl, 'Alī—(A) 2
'Abd al-Razzāq, Muḥammad—(U) 330
'Abdou, Muḥammad 'Īssa (Also see: Ibrāhīm 'Issa 'Abdou).—(A) **504**, **505**, 349, **382**, **350**, **503**, 506
Abdul Hakim, Khalifa—**564**
Abdul Majid—280
'Abd al-Wahhāb, Ḥasan Ḥasanī—(A) 261
'Abdullāh, Amīn, 'Afīfī—(U) 600
Abdullah, Knoun—210 (A) 447
'Abdullāh, Syed—(U) 599
Abdur Rauf, M—167
Abdus Sattar, M.—654
Abū Aiman—(A) 3
Abu 'l-Makārim, Zaydān—(A) **4**
Abu 'l-'Uyūn, Maḥmūd—(A) 182
Abū Sa'ūd, Maḥmūd—507, 105, 5; (A) **6**
Abū Shahbah, Muḥammad—(A) 508
Abū Sulaimān, 'Abdul Ḥamīd—8, (A) **7**
Abū Sunnah, Aḥmad Fahmī—(A) 209
Abū 'Ubaid, al-Qāsim bin Sallām—(A) **660**
Abu Yūsuf—**668**
Abū Zahrā, Muḥammad—(A) **331**, **106**, **334**, 510, 565, 424, 448, 300, 449, **509**
al-'Ādil, Fu'ād—(A) **107**
al-Afghānī, Sa'īd—(A) 82
Afghāni, Shamsul Ḥaq—(U) 108
Afzalur Rahman—**9**
Aghnides, Nicholas P.—**285**
Ahmad, Afazuddin—621
Ahmad, Ilyas—665
Ahmad, Mahmud—628
Aḥmad, Manẓūr al-Raḥmān—(A) 109
Ahmad, Shaykh—**301**
Ahmad, Sheikh Mahmud—511, 383, **186**; (U) **225**, 512
Ahsan, M. Manazir—284
Akbar Muradpuri, Muhammad—**566**
Akbarābādī, Sa'īd Aḥmad—(U) **692**
Alan, Heshmat—**633**
'Alvi, Q. Ahmadur Rahman—10
Alexander, A. P.—474
el-Alfi, Ezzat S.—**655**
'Alī, Ibrāhīm Fu'ād Aḥmad—(A) 11
'Ali Naqī—(U) **253**
Ali, Syed Ahmad—**12**, 656
'Allām, Mahdī—(A) 302
Amedroz, H. F.—681
Amīn al-Ḥaqq—(U) 111, 110
Amīnī, Muḥammad Taqi—(U) **226**, 84, 83, **556**, **13**
Anwar Ullah, Muhammad—(U) 535
Anzarul Haque, Muhammad—678
al-'Aqqād, 'Abbās Maḥmūd—567; (A) 568
al-'Aqqād, 'Abbās Maḥmūd; 'Attar Aḥmad 'Abd al-Ghafūr—(A) **569**
al 'Araby, Muḥammad 'Abdullāh—16, 212, 14, 384, (A) **17**, **15**, 211, 112, 385, 169
'Arafah, Muḥammad—(A) 213
al-'Ashmāwī Yāqūt—(A) **113**
Ashraf, Muhammad—(U) 19, 18
'Āshūr, al-Sayyid Muḥammad—(A) **676**
Ataullah, Sheikh—**303**
'Atiyyah, Jamāl al-Din—(A) 699
'Audah, 'Abd al-Qādir—(A) 214
Ausaf Ali—114
Austruy, Jaques—(A) **475**
'Awad, Ahmad Ṣafi al Dīn—(A) 554
al 'Awaḍī, Rif'at—(A) 170
'Ayyad, M. Gamaluddīn—428; (A) 426, 427, 429, **425**
A'Zamī, Nūr Muḥammad—(U) 227
Bābullī, Maḥmūd—(A) 21, **20**
al-Badri, 'Abd al-'Azīz—(A) 570
al-Bahī, Muḥammad—571; (A) 351
al-Bakr, 'Abd al-Raḥman—(A) **430**
al-Bannā, Muḥammad, Kāmil—(A) 572
Bāqir al-Sadr—(A) **387**, **171**
al-Barūdi, 'Alī—(A) 573
Baryūn, Nūrī 'Abdussalām—(A) **274**, **388**
Bashīr al-'Awf—(A) **574**
al-Bassām, 'Abdullāh bin 'Abd al-Raḥmān —(A) 304
Ben Shemesh, A.—**673**, **669**
Berger, Morroe—**476**
Bravmann, Meir M.—286
al-Būṭī, Muḥammad Sa'īd Ramaḍān—(A) **172**

Cattan, H.—345
Chapra, M. Umar—**115**
Chowdhri, A. B. M. Masudul Alam—634, 620
Conference of Islamic Finance Ministers —**389**
Cragg, K.—183

Ḍanāwī, Muḥammad 'Alī—(A) **85**, 536
Dānish, Aḥmad—(A) 352, 353
Darāz, Muḥammad 'Abdullāh—(A) **513**
Darwish, Muṣṭafa—(A) **601**
Dastgir, Ghulam—(U) **22**
al-Dasūqi, Muḥammad—(A) **355**, 354
Dawālībī, Ma'rūf—603; (A) **602**, **575**
Dennett, Daniel C., Jr.—**322**
al-Dimashqī, Abu'l Faḍl Ja'far bin 'Alī—(A) **677**
Durrānī, Muḥammad Murtaḍā Aḥmad Khān—(U) 635

Ehrenkreutz, A. S.—682
Enayat, Hamid—576

Fahīm, Muḥammad—(A) **275**
Fahmī, 'Ali ḥasan—(A) **262**
Faiḍullah, Muḥammad Fawzī—(A) 116
al-Fanjari, Muḥammad Shauqī—(A) **23**, 636, 335, 478, 477
Farid, Q. M.—514
Faridi, Fazlur Rahman—**24**, 432, 637, 431, 479
Fāriq, Khurshid Aḥmad—(U) 87, 86, 88
al-Faruqi, Isma'il R. A.—638, 639
Farrāj, Ahmad, ed.—(A) **184**
Faruki, Kemal A.—305
al-Fāsī 'Allāl—(A) 26; (U) 25
Faudah, 'Abd al-Raḥīm—(A) 182
Fazlur Rahman—537, 27
Fazlur Rahman (Gunnauri)—539; (A) 538; (U) **540**
Fischel, W.—89

Gaballah, al-Syed—228
Gaiani, A.—245
al-Gammāl, Gharīb—(A) **391**
Gardner, G. H.; Hanna, S. A.—186
Ghanameh, Abdul Hadi—392
al-Ghawālī, Hamid—(A) 515
Ghaznavi, Syed Abu Bakr—117
al-Ghazzālī, Muḥammad—(A) **577**, **173**, **118**
Ghoraba, Hammouda—693
Ghulām 'Alī, Malik—(U) 306, 516
Ghulām Rasūl, Sayyid—(U) 578
Gibb, H. A. R.—90
Gīlanī, Sayyid Manāẓir Aḥsan—(A) 28; (U) **29**
Goitein, S. D.—91

al-Hadāwi, Muṣṭafā—(A) **694**
Haffar, Ahmad R.—480
Ḥafīẓ, 'Abbās—(A) 187
Halpern, M.—188
Hameedullah, (Dr.) Muhammad—433, 287, 395, 30, 119; (A) 394; (U) 393, **92**
Hamid, Habeeb—616, 640
Ḥāmid, Muḥammad—(A) 229, 517
Ḥammūda, 'Abd al-Wahhāb—(A) 31
al-Hamshari, Muṣṭafā 'Abdullah—(A) **396**
al-Ḥanbali, Sḥākir—(A) 189
Hanna, Sami A.—683; (A) 190
Ḥaqqī, Iḥsān—(A) **174**
Hārūn, 'Abdussalām Muḥammad—(A) **557**
Ḥasan, 'Abd al-Ghaffār—(U) 243, 215
Ḥasan, 'Abd al-Raḥmān—(A) 288
Ḥasan, Abū Usāma—(U) 541
Ḥasan al-Bannā, Sheikh—(A) **33**
Ḥasan, Ḥasan Ibrāhīm—**32**
Hasan, Riaz—695
Hasanuzzaman, S. M.—**254**, 630, 622, **289**, (U) 629
Hassanein, Medhat—641
Ḥifzur Raḥmān, Muhammad Seohārwī—(U) **120**
Ḥijāzī, 'Abd al-Badi'—(A) **191**
Ḥimādah, 'Abd al-Mun'im—(A) **276**
al-Hindī, Abū Salmān—(U) **356**
Huda, M. N.—397, 34; (A) 398
Ḥusainī, Aḥmad—(A) **35**
Ḥusainī, Isḥāq Mūṣā—264; (A) 263
al-Ḥusainī, al-Sayyid Abu'l Naṣr Aḥmad —(A) **216**
Husaini, S. Waqar Ahmad—**121**
Hussain, Mirza Muhammad—307, **579**, 580
Hussain, S. Mushtaq—518

Ibn 'Āshūr, Muḥammad al-Tāhir—(A) **122**
Ibn al-Sabīl, Waitlīf Khālid—(U) 192
Ibrāhīm, Aḥmad Ibrahīm—(A) **336**
Ibrāhīm, Aḥmad Muḥammad—(A) 358, 357
Ibrahīm, 'Īssa 'Abdou (also see: 'Abdou, Muḥammad 'Īssa)—(A) 36
Ibrāhīm, Muḥammad—255
Ibrāhīm, Muḥammad Ismāī'l—(A) **308**
Idris, Gaafar—37
'Imādī, Tamannā—(U) 542
Imamuddin, S. M.—93
Imran, Muhammad—175

Inamul Haq—**193**
Irshad, Shaykh Ahmad—**399**, 519; (U) **400**
Irving, T. B.—657
'Īsa, 'Abd al-'Aziz Muḥammad—(A) **450**
'Īsa, 'Abd al-Rahmān—(A) 359
'Iṣlāhī, 'Abdul 'Azīm—(U) 696
Iṣlāhī, Amīn Aḥsan—(U) 309
Iṣlāhī, Ḍiyā al-Dīn—(U) 670
Iṣmā'īl, Ch. Muḥammad—(U) 543
Ismail, Ibrahim Muhammad—604
Issawi, Charles—**481**, 482
al-'Iṭr, Nūr al-Din—(A) **401**, 555
al-Ittiḥād al-'Alamī li-Tanẓīm al-Wālidiyah—(A) **452**
Ittiḥād Ṭullāb Handasah al-Qāhirah, al-Lajnat al-Thaqāfiyah, al-Jam'īyah al-Dīniyah—(A) **217**
'Iwaḍ, Badawī 'Abd al-Latīf—**291**, **290**
Izadi, 'Ali M.—623
'Izz al-Dīn, Mūsa—(A) 124

Ja'far, Shāh, Muḥammad Phulwārwī—(U) **544**
Ja'farī, Ra'īs Aḥmad—(U) **38**
Jamā'at-e-Islamī, Pakistan—(U) **125**, **126**
al-Jamāl, Muḥammad 'Abd al-Mun'im—(A) **292**
Jamāl al-Dīn, Aḥmad—(A) **218**
Jāmi'ah Fu'ād al-Awwal. Kulliyat al-Tijārah, Jam 'Īyaī 'al-Dirāsāt al-Islāmiyah—(A) **39**
Jamjūm, Aḥmad Ṣalāḥ—(A) 402
al-Jaraf, Muḥammad Kamāl—(A) **293**
Jārullāh, Mūsā—(U) **360**

Kagaya, Kan—40
Kahf, Monzer—**611**, **666**, **612**, 615
Kāṇḍhlawī, Ihtishām al-Ḥaqq—(U) **127**
al-Kattānī, Muḥammad al-Muntaṣir—(A) **128**, 230
Kerr, M. H.—582
al-Khafīf, 'Alī—(A) 265, **246**, 219, 361
Khān, Ḥāmid 'Alī—(U) **129**
Khan, Mir Sa'adat Ali—545
Khān, Muḥammad 'Abd al-Raḥmān—(U) 41
Khan, M. A.—323
Khan, Muhammad Akram—**613**, **700**, 434, 483, 558, 247, 559, 403, 642; (U) 404
Khan, M. E.—453
Khan, Muhammad Ihsanullah—583
Khān, Muḥammad Murtaḍā—(U) 42
Khan, Muhammad Shabbir—643
Khrūfa, 'Alā al-Dīn—(A) 520
Khaṭīb, 'Abdul Karīm—(A) **294**, 43
al-Khatīb, Anwar—(A) **194**
al-Khaṭīb, Muḥibb al-Dīn—(A) 362, 45, 44
al-Khaṭīb, S. A. Hamid—231
al-Khaulī, Amīn—(A) **46**
al-Khaulī, al-Bahī—(A) **195**, **455**, **605**, 130
al-Khayyāṭ, 'Abd al-'Azīz—(A) **248**
Khizām, Antoun Ḥabīb—(A) **363**
Khurshīd Ahmad—644, 454, 252, **47**; (A) 176; (U) **584**, **585**
Kister, M. J.—674, 94
Klingmuller, E.—364

al-Labbān, Ibrāhīm—337; (A) **684**, 48
al-Lajnah al-Taḥdīrīah li-Mashrū'bait al-Tamwīl al-Kuwaitī—(A) 405
Latham, J. D.—266
Lewis, Bernard—586
Lokkegaard, Frede—295

Madkūr, Muḥammad Salām—(A) **456**, 282
Mahmoud, Mabid—624
Mahmud, Javed—606
Mahrajān Ibn Khaldūn—(A) **658**
al-Majlis al-A'lā li-Ri'āyat al-Funūn wa'l-Ādāb wa'l-'Ulūm al-Ijtimā 'Īyah—(A) 365
Majlis Taḥqīqāt-e-Shar'īyah Lucknow—(U) 366
Makhlūf, Hasnain—(A) 131
Mālik Ben Nabī—(A) **485**, **484**
Malik, Muhammad Shafi—435
Malik, Muḥammad Rāmiz—(A) 367
Mannan, M. A.—407, **132**, 406, 408
Manzar, Abdul Moiz—645, 486
Marek, J.—196
Marsī Muḥammad Kāmil—(A) **296**
al-Mashriqī, Muḥammad Muḥyuddin—(A) 487
Mawdudī, Syed Abdul Ala—49, 52, **50**; (A) **177**; (U) **458**, **232**, 310, 437, **133**, **521**, 457, 436, **51**, **607**
Meyer, A. J.—489, 648, 488, **490**
al-Miḥṣār, Ḥāmid—(A) 197
al-Miṣrī, 'Abd al-Sami'—(A) 53
Mohammad Bin Jamil—625
Mohiuddin, Ghulam—617
Moulavi, C. N. Ahmad—**54**
al-Mubārak, Muḥammad—(A) **134**, (U) 587
Muḥammad Aḥmad—(U) **234**
Muḥammad Miyaṇ—(U) **135**
Muḥammad, Sa'd Ṣādiq—(A) 368
Muhsinī, Shams al-Raḥman—(U) **685**
al-Munajjid, Ṣalāḥ al-Dīn—(A) **198**, **588**

Mūsā, Muḥammad Yūsuf—(A) 256, 332
Muslehuddin, Muhammad—369, 199, **55**, **409**, **410**
Muslim, A. G.—522
Mustafizul Hasan, Syed—136
Mu'tamar al-Buhūth al-Islāmiyah al-Sābi' —(A) 137
Muzaffar Hussain—56

Nabhān, Muḥammad Fārūq—(A) **546**, 178, **138**
al-Nabhānī Taqī al-Dīn—(A) **139**
Nadhīr Ahmad—(U) 141
Nadwī. 'Abdul Bārī—(U) **57**
Nadwī, 'Abdul Qayyūm—(U) **257**
Nadwī, 'Abd al-Salām—(U) 523
Nadwī, 'Abul Ḥasan 'Alī—(A) 140
Nadwī, Khatīb Aḥmad—(A) 460
Nadwī, Mas'ūd 'Alam—(U) 589
Nadwī, Muḥammad Isḥāq—(A) 297, 370
Nadwī, Muḥammad Na'īm—(U) 524, 547, 548
Nadwī, Mujībullāh—(U) 438, 675
Nadwī, Sayyid Sulaimān—(U) 697
Nadwī, Syed Habeebul Haq—235
al, Najjār, Aḥmad Muḥammad 'Abd al-'Azīz—(A) 491, **698**, **411**, **59**, **58**
Nash'at, Muḥammad 'Alī—(A) **659**
Nasif, Hafnī Beck—(U) 549
al-Nawawī, Maḥmūd; Khafājī, 'Abd al-Mun'im—(A) **590**
al-Nimr, 'Abd al-Mun'im—(A) 179
Niẓāmī, Khwāja Ḥasan—(U) **312**
al Nowaihi, Muhammad—142

Parwez, Ghulam Ahmad—**60**, **200**; (U) **143**, **499**, **201**
Pīrzāda, Shams—(U) 560
Poliak, A. N.—236
Population Council, New York—**461**

Qadri, Anwar Ahmad—180
Qādrī, Sayyid Aḥmad—(U) 324, 61
Qādrī, Sayyid Mu'īn al-Dīn—(U) 525
Qarḍāwī, Yūsuf—(A) **313**, **338**, 371
al-Qūbānī, Muḥammad 'Abd al-Salām—(A) 462
Quraishi, Marghoob Ahmad—**495**, 492
Qureshi, 'Abdul Majeed—441, 440; (U) **439**, 144
Qureshi, Aijaz Hasan—325, 326, 327
Qureshi, Anwar Iqbal—**526**
Qureshi, Ishtiaq Hussain—(U) 237
Quṭb, Muḥammad—(A) 63
Quṭb, Sayyid—(A) **527**, **62**, **500**

Rabitat al-'Ālam al-Islāmī: al-Majlis al-Ta' Sīsī—(A) 463
Rafi'uddin—(A) 64
Rafiullah—464; (U) 314, 465
el-Ramadī, Gamāl el-Dīn—339
Ra'na, Irfan Mahmūd—**95**
Rashad, Shah Muhammad—238
Ra'uf al-Hasan, Sheikh—(U) 65
Ready, R. K.—412
Riḍā, Muḥammad Rashīd—(A) **530**
Riḍwān, Aḥmad Muḥammad—(A) **202**
Riḍwī, Sayyid Zāhid Qaiṣar—(U) 66
Rif'at, Sayyid Mubāriz al-Dīn—(U) 679, 660
al-Rīs, Muḥammad Ḍiyā' al-Dīn—(A) **96**
Rizq, 'Ali Shiḥatah—(A) **340**
Rodinson, Maxime—**145**
Rozenthal, Franẓ—**661**
al-Ruḥānī, al-Sayyid Muḥammad Ṣādiq—(A) **372**

al Sabsabī, 'Abd al-Qādir—(A) 315
Sa'īd, 'Abd al-Mughnī—(A) **591**
al-Sa'idī, 'Abd al-Muta'āl—(A) **333**
Sakr, Mansur Muhammad—(A) 239
Sakr, Muhammad Ahmad—(A) **316**, **413**, **646**
Ṣaliḥ, Muḥammad Amin—(A) **97**
Ṣalih, Muḥammad Zakī—(A) 649
Sālim, Aḥmad Mūsā—(A) **146**
al-Sāmarrā'ī, Husām al-Dīn—(A) **267**
Sambhalī, 'Atīq al-Raḥmān—(A) 466, 467
al-Sanūsi, Aḥmad Ṭāḥā—(A) 373
Sarkar, Abdul Bari—**203**
Sattar, S. A.—414
Sayigh, Y. A.—**493**
al Sayis, Muhammad Ali—(A) 240
Schacht, J.—346
Shabāna, Zakī Maḥmūd—(A) 147
al-Shafi'ī, Aḥmad—(A) 98
Shafī', Muhammad—148; (U) **531**, **241**, **317**, 149, 609
Shah, Syed Ya'qoob—551; (U) 550, 318
al Shaḥāwī, Ibrāhīm Dasūqī—(A) **268**, **269**
Shākir, 'Abdul Mun'im Aḥmad—**150**
Shalbī, Aḥmad—(A) **68**, **67**, 415
Shalbī, Mahmūd—(A) **101**, **99**, **100**
Shalṭūt, Maḥmūd—151, 592
Ṣhami, Amir Hamza—552
Shamsī, Sayyid Mughnī al-Dīn. (U) 593
Shamsul Huda, Mir—152
al-Sharbāsī, Aḥmad—(A) **153**, **468**, **69**
Sharbāsī, Sa'īd al Shirbīnī—(A) **204**
Sharfuddin, Abul Muhsin Muhammad—686
Sharif, M. Raihan—662

al-Sharqāwī, Maḥmūd—(A) 205
Shaṭa, Muḥammad Aḥmad—(A) 347
Sheikh, Nasir Ahmad—**154**
Sherwani, H. K.—667, 663
Shiḥaṭah, Shauqī Ismā'īl—(A) **498**, **496**, **497**
al-Shūrī, Ibrāhīm—(A) 469
al-Shūrījī, Al-Bushra—(A) **270**
al-Sibā 'ī, Muṣṭafā—(A) **70**
Siddiqi, Abd al-Hamid—618; (U) 71, 631, **181**, 594
Ṣiddīqī, Ḥaidar Zamān—(U) 155, 244
Siddiqi, Kalim—494
Siddiqi, Muhammad Mazharuddin—**596**, 206, 156; (U) **595**, **72**, 102, 220, 157, 532
Siddiqi, Muhammad Nejatullah—442, 416, **158**, 73, **619**, **614**; (U) 671, 418, **672**, **221**, **249**, **417**, **374**
Ṣiddīqī, Na'īm—(U) 419, 74, 278, 562, **159**, **375**
Siddiqi, S. A.—**298**
Ṣiddīqī, Ṣiddīq Jamāl—(U) **75**
Siddique, Kaukab—470
de-Somogyi, Joseph—259, 650, 258
Spengler, J. J.—664
Suhail, Iqbāl Aḥmad—(U) **553**
Suharwardi, A. al-Mamoon—348
Syed 'Alī—(U) 561
Syed, J. W.—76

al Ṭaḥāwī, Ibrāhīm—(A) **77**
Ṭamān, 'Alī Fahmī—(A) **610**
al-Ṭanṭāwī, 'Alī—(A) **341**
Ṭasīn, Muḥammad—(U) 319, 78
Ṭihrānī—(A) 260
Tonki, Muftī Walī Ḥasan—(U) 377
Tritton, A. S.—328

'Ubaidullāh Sindhī—(U) **688**, **687**
Udovitch, A. L.—443, **250**
Ulgener, Sabri F.—632
'Ulwān, 'Abdullāh—(A) **342**
'Urnūs, Maḥmūd—(A) 271
'Uthmān, Muḥammad Fatḥī—(A) **343**, **378**
'Uthmān, Shaikh Muḥammad—(U) 79
'Uthmānī, Muḥammad Fahīm—(U) 222, 80
'Uthmānī, Muḥammad Muḥtaram Fahīm—(U) 233, **444**
'Uwaiḍa, Aḥmad Thābit—(A) 299
Uzair, Muhammad—**422**, 421, 423; (A) 420

Wāfī, 'Alī 'Abdul Wāḥid—207; (A) 160
Wahbāh, Taufīq 'Alī—(A) 379
Wickens, G. M.—272
World Muslim Congress—166

Yadullāhī, Shihabuddīn—(U) **689**
Yafī, 'Abd al-Karīm—(A) 690
Yamānī, Aḥmad Zakī—162, (A) 161
Yunus, H. Kahruddin—163
Yūsuf Ludhiyanvī, Muḥammad—(A) 208
Yūsuf, Mirza Muḥammad—(U) 320
Yusuf, S. M.—242, **164**
Yūsufuddīn, Muḥammad—(U) **165**

Zaed, Sa'īd—(A) 597
Zain al-'Ābidīn, Wajīh—(A) 445
Zakī al-Dīn, Ibrāhīm—(A) **533**
al Zarqā Muṣṭafā Aḥmad—(A) **380**
de Zayas, Farishta G.—**321**, 691, 329, 627
el-Zayyāt, A. Hasan—344
Zerruq, A. R. M.—471
Ziadeh, Nicola—**273**
Zohurul Hoque—472
Anonymous—**390**; (A) 233, 281, 608, 459, 528, 376, 529, 581, 279, 626, 277, 123, 311, **451**, 386